BUSINESS RECODED

BUSINESS RECODED

HAVE THE COURAGE TO CREATE A BETTER FUTURE FOR YOURSELF AND YOUR BUSINESS

Peter Fisk

WILEY

This edition first published in 2021
© 2021 by Peter Fisk

Registered office
John Wiley & Sons Ltd, The Atrium, Southern Gate, Chichester, West Sussex, PO19 8SQ,
United Kingdom

For details of our global editorial offices, for customer services and for information about how
to apply for permission to reuse the copyright material in this book please see our website at
www.wiley.com.

Wiley publishes in a variety of print and electronic formats and by print-on-demand. Some
material included with standard print versions of this book may not be included in e-books or
in print-on-demand. If this book refers to media such as a CD or DVD that is not included in
the version you purchased, you may download this material at http://booksupport.wiley.com.
For more information about Wiley products, visit www.wiley.com.

Library of Congress Cataloging-in-Publication Data

ISBN 9781119679868 (hardback) ISBN 9781119680000 (ePUB)
ISBN 9781119680024 (Adobe PDF)

10 9 8 7 6 5 4 3 2 1

Cover Design: Wiley
Cover Image: © tuulijumala / Shutterstock

Set in 12/18pt Minion Pro by SPi Global, Chennai, India

Printed by CPI Group (UK) Ltd, Croydon CR0 4YY

In memory of my father.

My dad always encouraged me to look for better. He grew up in a small coal-mining village in northern England, and never forgot his origins. As a teacher, he saw talent in everyone, whatever their background or ambition. As a headteacher, he was proud of his students and colleagues, and loved taking part in school plays and events. As leader of the nation's headteachers he worked tirelessly to create a better education for everyone.

I remember him as we travelled around Europe on family holidays, camping in apple orchards and playing endless games of boules. I remember him on cold winter evenings, standing with a stopwatch, as I sprinted around the local running track. I remember him raving about Tom Peters' book "In Search of Excellence", my introduction to business (an anecdote which I recently shared with Tom). I remember him at home with mum, and a glass of wine in his hand, as a great father and grandfather.

My dad was my inspiration to do more than I could ever imagine. To stay strong when things felt tough. And to make the most of everything in life. In a way, he was also my inspiration for this book. Not just to accept the codes of life, but to seek better ones. Not just to explore my world, but to challenge it. Not just to define new ideas, but to bring them to life through personal experiences and interesting stories that can inspire others.

To create a better future. I hope we can.

CONTENTS

INTRODUCTION
Recode

BUSINESS NEEDS A NEW CODE FOR SUCCESS.

Change is dramatic, pervasive and relentless. The challenges are numerous. The opportunities are greater. Incredible technologies and geopolitical shifts, demanding customers and disruptive entrepreneurs, environmental crisis and social distrust, unexpected shocks and stagnating growth.

The old codes that got us here are insufficient, or obsolete.

Business Recoded is for business leaders who seek to thrive in today's world, and to create the best companies of tomorrow.

It describes how to lead a better future, to reimagine your business, to reinvent markets, to reenergise your people, to redefine success. It brings together fresh insights and ideas from the leaders of many of the world's most innovative companies right now – Alibaba to BlackRock, Corning and Danone, Ecoalf to Fujifilm, Glossier and Haier, and many more.

And it's about you, developing your own codes for personal and business progress. And having the courage to step up – to be more, to achieve more, to be extraordinary.

WHY DO WE NEED TO RECODE?

We live in a time of great promise but also great uncertainty.

Markets are more crowded, competition is intense, customer aspirations are constantly fuelled by new innovations and dreams. Technology disrupts every industry, from banking to construction, entertainment to healthcare. It drives new possibilities and solutions, but also speed and complexity, uncertainty and fear.

As digital and physical worlds fuse to augment how we live and work, artificial intelligence (AI) and robotics enhance but also challenge our capabilities, whilst ubiquitous supercomputing, genetic editing and self-driving cars take us further.

Technologies with the power to help us leap forwards in unimaginable ways. To transform business, to solve our big problems, to drive radical innovation, to accelerate growth and achieve progress socially and environmentally too.

We are likely to see more change in the next 10 years than the last 250 years.

- **Markets accelerate** – 4 times faster than 20 years ago, based on the accelerating speed of innovation and diminishing life-cycles of products.
- **People are more capable** – 825 times more connected than 20 years ago, with access to education, unlimited knowledge, tools to create anything.
- **Consumer attitudes change** – 78% of young people choose brands that do good, they reject corporate jobs, and see the world through the lens of a gamer.

However, change goes far beyond the technology.

Markets will transform, converge and evolve faster. From old town Ann Arbor to the rejuvenated Bilbao, today's megacities like Chennai and the future Saudi tech city of Neom, economic power will continue to shift. China has risen to the top of the new global business order, whilst India and eventually Africa will follow.

Industrialisation challenges the natural equilibrium of our planet's resources. Today's climate crisis is the result of our progress, and our problem to solve. Globalisation challenges our old notions of nationhood and locality. Migration changes where we call home. Religious values compete with social values, economic priorities conflict with social priorities. Living standards improve but inequality grows.

Our current economic system is stretched to its limit. Global shocks, such as the pandemic of 2020, expose its fragility. We open our eyes to realise that we weren't prepared for different futures, and that our drive for efficiency has left us unable to cope. Such crises will become more frequent, as change and disruption accelerate.

However, these shocks are more likely to accelerate change in business, rather than stifle it, to wake us up to the real impacts of our changing world – to the urgency of action, to the need to think and act more dramatically.

THE FUTURE ISN'T LIKE IT USED TO BE

Business is not fit for the future. Most organisations were designed for stable and predictable worlds, where the future evolved as planned, markets were definitive, and choices were clear.

Dynamic markets are, by definition, uncertain. Whilst economic cycles have typically followed a pattern of peaks and troughs every 10–15 years, these will likely become more frequent. Change is fast and exponential, turbulent and unpredictable, complex and ambiguous, demanding new interpretation and imagination.

Yet too many business leaders hope that the strategies that made them successful in the past will continue to work in the future. They seek to keep stretching the old models in the hope that they will continue to see them through. Old business plans are tweaked each year, infrastructures are tested to breaking point, and people are asked to work harder.

In a world of dramatic, unpredictable change, this is not enough to survive, let alone thrive.

- **Growth is harder.** Global GDP growth has declined by more than a third in the past decade. As the west stagnates, Asia grows, albeit more slowly.
- **Companies struggle.** Their average lifespan has fallen from 75 years in 1950 to 15 years today; 52% of the Fortune 500 in 2000 were gone by 2020.
- **Leaders are under pressure.** Only 44% of today's business leaders have held their position for more than 5 years, compared to 77% half a century ago.

Profit is no longer enough; people expect business to achieve more. Business cannot exist in isolation from the world around it, pursuing customers without care for the consequence. The old single-minded obsession with profits is too limiting. Business depends more than ever on its resources – people and partners, local communities, natural environments – and will need to find a better way to embrace them.

Technology is no longer enough; innovation needs to be more human. Technology will automate and interpret reality, but it won't empathise and imagine new futures. Ubiquitous technology-driven innovation quickly becomes commoditised, available from anywhere in the world, so we need to add value in new ways. The future is human, creative, and intuitive. People will matter more to business, not less.

Sustaining the environment is not enough. Two hundred years of industrialisation has stripped the planet of its ability to renew itself, and ultimately to sustain life. Business therefore needs to give back more than it takes. As inequality and distrust have grown in every society, traditional jobs are threatened by automation and stagnation, meaning that social issues will matter even more, both globally and locally.

THE NEW DNA OF BUSINESS

As business leaders, our opportunity is to create a better business, one that is fit for the future, that can act in more innovative and responsible ways.

How can we harness the potential of this relentless and disruptive change, harness the talents of people and the possibilities of technology? How can business, with all its power and resources, be a platform for change, and a force for good?

We need to find new codes to succeed. We need to find new ways to work, to recognise business as a system that is virtuous, where less can be more, and growth can go beyond the old limits. This demands that we make new connections:

- **Future + Today** ... to achieve more progress
- **Purpose + Profits** ... to engage all stakeholders
- **Technology + Humanity** ... to drive more ingenuity
- **Innovation + Sustainability** ... to deliver positive impact

We need to create a new framework for business, a better business – to reimagine why and redesign how we work, to reinvent what and refocus where we do business.

Imagine a future business that looks forwards not back, that rises up to shape the future on its own terms, making sense of change to find new possibilities, inspiring people with vision and optimism. Imagine a future that inspires progress, seeks new sources of growth, embraces networks and partners to go further, and enables people to achieve more.

Imagine too, a future business that creates new opportunity spaces, by connecting novel ideas and untapped needs, creatively responding to new customer agendas. Imagine a future business that disrupts the disruptors, where large companies have the vision and courage to reimagine themselves and compete as equals to fast and entrepreneurial start-ups.

Imagine a future business that embraces humanity, searches for better ideas, that fuses technology and people in more enlightened ways, to solve the big problems of society, and improve everyone's lives. Imagine a future business that works collectively, self-organises to thrive without hierarchy, connects with partners in rich ecosystems, designs jobs around people, to do inspiring work.

Imagine also, a future business which is continually transforming, that thrives by learning better and faster, develops a rich portfolio of business ideas and innovations to sustain growth and progress. Imagine a future business that creates positive impact for the world, benefits all stakeholders with a circular model of value creation, that addresses negatives, and creates a net positive impact for society.

Creating a better business is an opportunity for every person who works inside or alongside it. It is not just a noble calling, to do something better for the world, but also a practical calling, a way to overcome the many limits of today, and attain future success for you and your business.

You could call it the dawn of a new capitalism.

THE NEW DNA OF BUSINESS

How do we create a better business, and a better future?

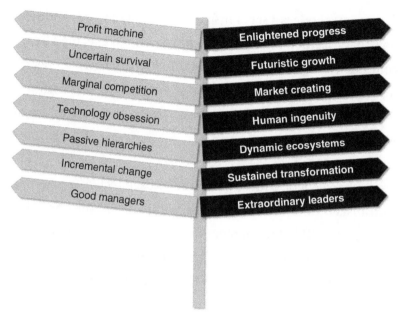

FIGURE 0.1 The seven business shifts to a better future.

Creating this better future requires change in how we think and behave, the way in which we design, manage and lead our organisations. The mindset shifts are profound, requiring leaders to let go of old beliefs, to embrace new paradigms and possibilities.

There are 7 shifts collectively required to create a better business future.

Underpinning these shifts are specific actions required for leaders. These are the 49 codes for you to apply in the right way for your organisation.

Coding is most often associated with technology.

A computer code is a set of instructions built of words and symbols that together form a program that is then executed by the computer. Codes become standardised as a language, mechanised as a system, and enable huge amounts of processing in fractions of a second. The revolutionary consequences are all around us.

Similarly, a genetic code is a set of rules used by living materials to translate information encoded within DNA into proteins, and into life. The development by Sir Francis Crick and others transformed the world of medicine, leading to breakthroughs such as personalised medicines, and phenomenal businesses like 23andMe.

More generally we have codes, like codes of conduct, as guidelines for the way we work and live. They are principles for doing better, non-prescriptive or definitive they are broad and flexible, approaches which we can adopt in our own personal ways.

The 49 codes create a new framework on which to move forwards.

Recode your future	Recode your growth	Recode your market	Recode your innovation	Recode your organisation	Recode your transformation	Recode your leadership
1 What's your future potential?	8 Ride with the megatrends	15 Explore the market matrix	22 Be ingenious	29 Do human, inspiring work	36 Transform your business	43 Step up to lead the future
2 Have a future mindset	9 Find new sources of growth	16 Disrupt the disruptors	23 Search for better ideas	30 Work as a living organisation	37 Exploit the core, explore the edge	44 Have the courage to do more
3 Imagine a better business	10 Embrace the Asian century	17 Capture the customer agenda	24 Embrace a designer mindset	31 Collaborate in fast projects	38 Outside in, and inside out	45 Develop your own leadership style
4 Find your inspiring purpose	11 Embrace technology and humanity	18 Create new market spaces	25 Create unusual connections	32 Align individuals and organisations	39 Engage people in change	46 Achieve your peak performance
5 Create your future story	12 Start from the future back	19 Build trust with authenticity	26 Develop new business models	33 Create energy and rhythm	40 Build rocket ships to the future	47 Build endurance and resilience
6 Deliver more positive impact	13 Accelerate through networks	20 Develop brands with purpose	27 Experiment with speed and agility	34 Be an extreme team	41 Create a circular ecosystem	48 Create a better legacy
7 Be the radical optimist	14 Build a growth portfolio	21 Enable people to achieve more	28 Dream crazy	35 Build a butterfly business	42 Have strategic agility to never stop	49 Be extraordinary

FIGURE 0.2 The 49 codes of the new business DNA.

THE NEW DNA OF LEADERSHIP

What kind of future do you want to create, shape and lead?

The future business will only emerge with your leadership. Leaders need the courage to step up, to envision and implement this future.

Having spent many hours with leaders, one to one, and with their teams – teaching, coaching and advising them on strategies and change – and explored the many leadership theories, and insights from today's most inspiring leaders – it became clear that there are some common attributes.

These attributes form a pyramid, somewhat analogous to Maslow's hierarchy of needs (see Figure 0.3). At the foundation are the essentials required to operate, and deliver performance.

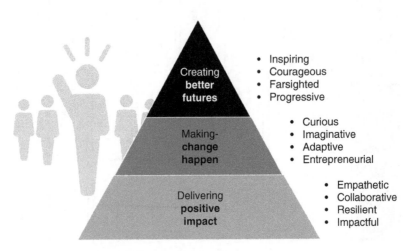

FIGURE 0.3 The new leadership DNA.

Above these are the attributes required for progress, to make sense of change, to find new growth, and drive innovation.

At the top are the attributes required of leaders who want to transform their organisations, guided by purpose beyond profit, to create a better business, and a better world.

These 12 attributes collectively make up the "new DNA of leadership", with three levels from the top to the bottom:

"Creating better futures" attributes:

- **Inspiring** … being guided by a purpose and passion
- **Courageous** … daring to do what hasn't been done before
- **Farsighted** … looking ahead with vision, foresight and intuition
- **Progressive** … pioneering, embracing challenge, seizing opportunities

"Making change happen" attributes:

- **Curious** … making sense of new, complex and uncertain environments
- **Imaginative** … envisioning a better future worth working towards
- **Adaptive** … having emotional agility to survive and drive relentless change
- **Entrepreneurial** … the creative spirit to explore new ideas and think differently

"Delivering positive impact" attributes:

- **Empathetic** … engaging people, tapping into their human qualities
- **Collaborative** … working together, embracing diversity, to achieve more
- **Resilient** … sticking to the task, enduring turbulence, motivated and optimistic
- **Impactful** … making a positive difference to business, stakeholders and the world

HAVE THE COURAGE TO LEAD THE FUTURE

The implications for business are broad and significant: a better approach to people and the jobs they do, organisation structures and how people work, a different approach to strategic development and innovation, how brands develop and engage customers, and a more enlightened approach to how businesses grow to create and share value.

The new codes of business challenge our deeply engrained assumptions and practices, some extending and strengthening what we already do, others replacing the old ways.

There is no magic formula for business success, although plenty of concepts and models, frameworks and tools which can help. Developing leaders in today's world is much more of a mindset, a way of thinking, opening your mind to a new world of possibilities, and the many ways to succeed in it. Most importantly it includes the inspiration to do it.

Inspiration, for me, comes from real people – ordinary people who have applied themselves to make dreams come true, turn challenge into opportunity, bring others together to achieve incredible results. I am most inspired by people around the world, who are leading, shaping and creating the businesses of the future right now.

INSPIRATIONS TO CHANGE YOUR WORLD

Here are seven characters who give me inspiration to change my world:

INSPIRATION 1: ELIUD KIPCHOGE
The humble Kenyan says that "no human is limited" and, despite his Olympic gold medal and world record, set himself a much more audacious goal.

"I don't know where the limits are, but I would like to go there," said Eliud Kipchoge as dawn broke over the Danube river in Vienna.

Two hours later he stood in the middle of the tree-lined Hauptallee, having just sprinted to the finish of the Ineos 1:59 Challenge, the first human to break two hours for the marathon. "That was the best moment of my life," he said, standing exhausted but still smiling at the finish line. The clock above him stopped at 1 hour 59 minutes and 40 seconds.

Having followed the Kenyan runner throughout his 20-year career, I watched his iconic record attempt in awe. Around him, some of the world's greatest athletes, from Olympic 1500m Champion Matt Centrowitz to rising star Jakob Ingebrigtsen and the highly experienced Bernard Lagat, cheered and took selfies with the record breaker, pacemakers to the great man, happy to be part of history.

"Today we went to the Moon and came back to Earth," he said.

Back at home in Kenya, people were crowded around televisions, cheering for their runner. But Kipchoge lives a humble life, with the greatest clarity of purpose.

Every morning, just before 5 am, in the small village of Kaptagat in western Kenya, he rolls out of bed, wipes the sleep from his eyes and gets ready to run. By the time the sun rises over the ochre red, dusty roads of the Rift Valley, he is well into his stride. Joined by dozens of ambitious young local runners, he strides past farmers heading for their fields, children waiting for their school buses.

This is just his first 20 km, his first run of the day. Every day.

On returning to his training camp, it might be Kipchoge's turn to make breakfast. Most likely it will be a simple bowl of ugali, a Kenyan staple made each day in a big pan from maize flour and water, plus whatever fruits are in season. Afterwards, he will probably hand-wash his running kit, ready for the afternoon session, and then take a nap. On other days, it might be his turn to head to the local farm for provisions, or to clean the communal toilets.

It is a frugal existence, particularly for a global champion, and self-made millionaire.

Yet for Kipchoge, the Olympic champion and world record holder, it is the only way of life that he has known. His wife and young children live in a much more spacious house in the town of Eldoret 40 km away, but during his most important training periods, he prefers the simplicity of his spartan camp.

For 15 years, Kipchoge has been chasing a dream. I remember first seeing him run as a teenager, his bulging eyes fixed on the path ahead, always with a smile on his face. He showed early promise, beating world record holders Kenenisa Bekele and Hicham El Guerrouj to become the 1983 5000 m world champion whilst only 18 years old. Over the next decade he won many medals but couldn't call himself the best. As he reached his 30th birthday, he decided to move up to the marathon. To astonishing effect.

In the marathon, he became unbeatable.

Kipchoge's first attempt to break two hours was a failure. In 2017, his sponsors Nike created a project to see if it would be possible to break the 2-hour barrier. They searched the world for the perfect location, choosing Monza's Formula 1 motor racing circuit in Italy, the perfect conditions, the perfect pace set automatically by a Tesla car, and the perfect shoe. He missed the target by a mere 25 seconds. Yet he was unphased, delighted but determined to do better. He went back to Kenya and set about improving himself.

Listening to him, dressed in a dark suit and tie, as he addressed the Oxford Union later that year, it struck me that he is perhaps one of the most thoughtful, intelligent athletes you will ever meet. Constantly seeking to challenge himself as a way to progress. Always curious, always listening, wanting to read more and learn from others.

He is even a fan of motivational business books. He regularly rereads Stephen Covey's *The 7 Habits of Highly Effective People* saying it taught him the importance of working hard, treating your profession as seriously as you can, and how to live alongside other people. He also likes John Maxwell's *15 Invaluable Laws of Growth*.

Why does he think he has become the best? Because of his mental toughness, he says. "Many of my peers train just as hard as I do. But success is more about having the right attitude." Maybe unexpectedly for an African marathoner, he likes to quote Aristotle. "In any profession, you should think positively. That's the driver of your mind. If your mind is really thinking positive, then you are on the right track. 'Pleasure in what you're doing puts perfection in your work.'"

Kipchoge is sometimes called the philosopher, sometimes even the Buddha. "No human is limited," says the rubber band that he wears around his wrist. "The mind is what drives a human being," he says. "If you have that belief – that you want to be successful – then you can talk to your mind. My mind is always free. My mind is flexible. I want to show the world that you can go beyond your thoughts, you can break more than you think you can break."

What keeps him motivated, having achieved Olympic titles and world records? It was actually when he visited Iffley Road, the small Oxford running track where Roger Bannister had broken his 4 minutes for one mile, back in 1954, that Kipchoge became truly fixated by 2 hours, as a challenge and a legacy. He says "The world is full of challenges and we need to challenge ourselves. For me it is to run faster than anybody else in history."

You might assume that once he found a winning formula, he would keep doing what he does. Not Kipchoge. A surprising supplement to his training schedule before Vienna was the introduction of aerobics and pilates. Seeing the highly tuned athletes working out to Pharrell Williams' *Happy* soundtrack seemed almost surreal. "Constantly seek and embrace change," he says. "I know it is not really comfortable to adopt change but change in life of a human being or life of any profession is really important."

He constantly asks himself what he could have done better, and what can he do in the future. He describes a tree planted near where he lives. "There is a sign next to it saying that the best time to plant a tree is 25 years ago. The second-best time is today."

At the end of his 2-hour barrier-breaking run in Vienna, Kipchoge talked selflessly about how he hoped his moment would inspire others, not just to also beat the 2 hour barrier, but also for people to believe in the spirit of humanity, to rise above conflict and doubt. "We can make this world a beautiful world, a peaceful world, a running world."

INSPIRATION 2: DEEPMIND
Whilst we marvel at extreme feats of human performance, we also know that technology has the potential to outperform humanity.

The game of chess has long served as a benchmark for AI researchers. John McCarthy, who coined the term "artificial intelligence" in the early 1950s, once compared it to the way in which the fruit fly is used to understand genetics.

In 1996, IBM's Deep Blue supercomputer embarked upon a series of chess games against Garry Kasparov, the world champion. Deep Blue eventually beat Kasparov, marking the first time a machine had defeated a world champion.

Within a few years computing technology was consistently beating chess grandmasters.

However, AI developers knew that they needed greater challenges, searching for more complex games to test their increasingly sophisticated algorithms. They turned their attention to the ancient Chinese strategy game of Go, which is both deceptively simple to play, yet extraordinarily complex to master.

The game was invented in China more than 2500 years ago and is believed to be the oldest board game continuously played to the present day. It was considered one of the four essential arts of the cultured aristocratic Chinese. Go has a larger board than chess, a 19×19 grid of lines containing 361 points, and therefore with many more alternatives to consider per move.

It took another decade of machine learning development until scientists were able to create a truly competitive AI-based Go player.

In 2014, a team at London-based DeepMind Technologies started working on a deep learning neural network called AlphaGo. Two years later a mysterious online Go player named "Master" appeared on the popular Asian game platform Tygem. The mysterious player dominated games against many world champions.

Eventually it was confirmed that the "master" was in fact created by DeepMind, since acquired by Google, and now a subsidiary of Alphabet.

The master was replaced by a grandmaster in 2017. AlphaZero, an enhanced version of the original system, embraced an even more sophisticated algorithm designed to learn as it progressed through games. The system simply plays against itself, over and over, and learns how to master whatever game it has been pro-grammed to work with. Searching through 80 000 positions, a fraction of what other predictive software had used, it had per-fected the game in 24 hours using an AI-type of intuition.

AlphaZero achieved two things: autonomy from humans, and superhuman ability. Scientist and futurist James Lovelock calls this "the novacene", translated as "the new new" in Latin and

Greek, where a new form of intelligent life emerges from a human-initiated AI-based machine into one which no longer requires human intervention.

He calls AlphaZero, and other such beings, cyborgs.

In his book *Novacene: The Coming Age of Hyperintelligence*, Lovelock suggests that AI-based entities can think and act 10 000 times faster than humans (and to put that in perspective, that humans can think and act 10 000 times faster than plants). He then reflects that maybe AI-based life would be rather boring, considering that a flight to Australia using physical transport would currently take 3000 AI-based years.

The real point of a cyborg, a term first coined by Austria's Manfred Clynes to describe an organism as self-sufficient as a human but made of engineered materials, is that it is able to improve and replicate itself.

Of course, we already have many devices that learn and improve continually. Take Google Maps, for example, which constantly learns from all its users about realtime traffic situations, and the more users it has the better the information becomes. Or consider Google Nest, an intelligent thermostat which takes control of the temperature in our homes. For now, they are useful tools, to help us live better.

Hungarian John Van Neumann described "the singularity" as a point at which intelligent technological growth becomes uncontrollable and irreversible. Both physicist Stephen Hawking and entrepreneur Elon Musk have warned of the profound implication of autonomous AI.

INSPIRATION 3: TAN LE
The Vietnamese boat refugee who found a new beginning in Australia, qualifying as a lawyer, then creating Emotiv, a world-leading neurotechnology company.

Tan Le was only 4 years old when she fled Vietnam with her mother and sister, crowded on board a fishing boat with 162 other people, in search of a better life. It was a difficult choice, leaving her father behind and heading out to the uncertain seas.

For 5 days they sailed, and then after losing power, drifted across the South China Sea. She remembers the long dark nights and rough seas, and everyone becoming desperate once food and water ran out.

Fortune came in the shape of a British oil tanker, which offered to rescue them. After three months in a refugee camp, the family were offered a flight to Australia. As the plane flew across the unknown country, she was struck by the huge emptiness of the land, and later reflected on it as symbolising the new opportunities which she could never have imagined.

At 8 years old, her mum says, she was a dreamer, and particularly liked to pretend she had the power of telepathy, as inspired by a movie she had seen. In reality, she called herself a curious nerd, desperate to work hard and seize her opportunity. At the same time, she was very conscious about being different – her looks, her accent, her background.

Then, when she was 20, she won Young Australian of the Year for her work in helping other immigrants to settle locally, to learn the English language, and to find jobs. She was astonished that somebody like her could win such an award. It was the moment that really opened her mind.

She started to look beyond her mum's dream of her becoming a doctor or lawyer. She qualified as a lawyer, but quickly turned her attention to software engineering, exploring how brainwaves can control digital devices. It was all about understanding the brain in context, and how it could be directed to do more productive work, to engage consumers more deeply with brands, to help people with disabilities. Her early work included the development of EEG (electroencephalography) headsets enabling people to control a car, or drone, or game, with their mind.

"When the neurons in your brain interact, they emit electrical impulses, which we can then translate into patterns that become commands, by using machine learning," she explained.

She founded Emotiv, a bio-informatics company focused on understanding the brain in context, and how it could be directed to do more productive work, to engage consumers more deeply with brands, to help people with disabilities.

Chosen to be part of the World Economic Forum's Young Business Leaders in 2009, she sat at a dinner held in Buenos Aires with fellow participants. Opposite her sat a wheelchair-bound Brazilian called Rodrigo Hübner Mendes. He introduced himself as a Formula One racing car driver, who used a specially developed brain interface to control the vehicle.

Mendes explained how he would turn left by imagining eating tasty food, turn right by imagining he was riding a bike, and accelerate by imagining he had just scored a World Cup goal for Brazil. He explained how the technology for the car was developed by a small innovative company called Emotiv. She smiled, deeply moved by his story.

Today Emotiv is a world-leader in brain interface software, with technology that is cheaper than a gaming console, but has the ability to fundamentally disrupt and improve our lives. With offices around the world, she spends much of her time in Hanoi, where her ground-breaking technology is being developed by young Vietnamese technologists.

Le reflects on her personal journey, saying, "Like my mum, I took a leap of faith into the world of technology, and particularly into a completely new area for which I had no qualifications or experience."

She freely admits that she doesn't have all the answers, with "I try to make the right choices, but you never know exactly where you are going, or if you're doing your best" but also has an infectious optimism: "The future is not here yet. We have the chance to create it, to co-create it."

As for Mendes, he recently found himself at a conference in Dubai listening to world champion F1 driver Lewis Hamilton. When it came to questions at the end, Mendes's hand immediately sprung up. He challenged the world champion to a race, using brainwave-controlled cars. Hamilton, a lover of new technologies, accepted. The race awaits.

INSPIRATION 4: SATYA NADELLA
The Indian-born CEO says he doesn't want to be cool, but to make other people cool, inspiring Microsoft to become the world's most valuable business, again.

Technology's impact on our lives is still in its infancy. From mobile phones to social networks that bring new connections and instant gratification, to the reinvention of every industry. This is where Microsoft sees its future.

After 15 years of Bill Gates's visionary leadership in the emergent technological world, "putting a computer on every desk", Microsoft declined under the heavy-handed control of Steve Ballmer, until 2014 when Satya Nadella took over, and in his words, "hit refresh".

His first speech as CEO did not even mention the word "Windows", the company's proprietary operating system and cash cow. Instead he said "the world is about cloud first, mobile first" setting out his new priorities for growth.

Within five years he had more than quadrupled the company's value, and with a focus on how a new generation of technologies, most significantly AI, can enable other companies to transform themselves, with the help of Microsoft.

"We don't want to be the cool company in the tech sector," Nadella says, "We want to be the company that makes other people cool." By which he means that his mission is to build Microsoft as the enabling force behind today's business world. Whilst his predecessors burnt their fingers trying to create branded hardware, most notably acquiring Nokia's mobile business, Nadella is happier to create the smart insides of other people's solutions.

To be the partner, the enabler, to empower others to be great.

At Microsoft's huge Redmond campus, just outside Seattle, there is a revolution in attitude and practice. Gone is the ego-driven, insular thinking of old. Boardroom strategies are replaced by hackathons where anyone can shine. Elitist developers are usurped by ideas that can come from anywhere. Collaboration with partners, even Apple and Amazon, is the new normal. And big human and ethical dilemmas are top of the company's agenda, how to control intelligent machines, how to address global healthcare and inequality.

But this is not a cult of leadership, or a hierarchy of command. Nadella is a very modern leader, recognising that his role is not to be the expert, or the hero, or the decision-maker – but to be the facilitator, the connector, the enabler. Behind that behaviour is his belief in the idea of a "growth mindset." Nowhere will you find this approach to leadership more clear, applied and powerful than in today's Microsoft.

"Growth mindset" is a simple but powerful concept that I use constantly in my work with business leaders. One of the biggest problems companies run into, and the successful ones even more so, is that they keep trying to perfect their existing world.

Instead, it's probably time to let go. As the world changes, ever more dramatically, leaders need to change too – looking forwards not back, experimenting with new ideas, rather than seeking to optimise the old. Efficiency savings won't create your future, but ideas and imagination just might. Move from diminishing returns to exponential opportunities.

"Don't be a know-it-all, be a learn-it-all," Nadella loves to say. "In 2014, we cancelled our company meeting where our leaders would tell employees what was important, in favour of having a hackathon that lets our employees tell our leaders what's important," recalls Jeff Ramos, head of the Microsoft Garage, where employees with a bright idea can come and experiment, build, hack, and see if their ideas have potential.

I recently watched Nadella take to the stage at Microsoft Envision, a huge event where the company brings together many of the world's leading CEOs to explore the future. There was a real energy in the room. From him – a great beaming smile, an uplifting speech, an entirely positive demeanour – but also from his team too. He believes in a new business world – one where teams beat hierarchy, where collaboration beats competition, where humanity is always superior to technology, and where dreams outperform numbers.

In November 2018, Microsoft became the world's most valuable company again, after a gap of 16 years. Seven months later the business soared through the trillion dollar market capital mark.

At the end of 2019, Nadella was named Financial Times' Person of the Year, the Financial Times saying that Nadella has presided over "an era of stunning wealth creation."

INSPIRATION 5: MARY BARRA
She challenged the traditional culture of GM (General Motors) in dramatic style, rejecting complacency and embracing new tech, on a mission to reinvent her industry.

Car-making is far from a luxury business, particularly in the decimated heartlands of the American car industry. The arrival of better, cheaper brands like Toyota from Japan, and more recently others from China and South Korea, fundamentally challenged local makers. Globalisation was killing the local industry.

Mary Barra grew up just outside Detroit, at a time when the city and car making were booming. Her father, Ray Makela, worked as a dye maker for 39 years at the Pontiac car factory, whilst Mary started working in the industry at the age of 18, checking fender panels and inspecting hoods to pay for her college education.

"My parents were both born and raised in the Depression. They instilled great values about integrity and the importance of hard work, and I've taken that with me to every job," she says.

When studying at the General Motors Institute, her tutor recalled how he taught her many aspects of car design, including how to make windscreen wipers work. He said she was always the leader, taking charge of mostly-male groups, balancing her strong technical knowledge with her easy-going communication skills.

She joined GM full time and worked through the ranks, becoming VP of Global Manufacturing in 2008, and then of Human Resources. In 2014, with the business increasingly struggling to survive, and uncertain about a future that looked electric and driverless, she became CEO.

She described her mission as "to save GM and to reinvent the auto industry".

In her first year as leader, GM was forced to recall 30 million cars due to safety issues that resulted in 124 deaths. She was called before Senate to explain the problems, and brand reputation plummeted to an all-time low. The recalls, however, also demanded significant change in work practices. She introduced new policies for employees to report problems, and a new culture of openness and determination to fight back was born.

Over the next five years Barra pushed GM to transform itself, to embrace innovation and new ways of working, both operationally and strategically. In particular she wanted to seize the leadership in new technologies such as hybrid engines and automated driving.

Asked by CNN what it takes to transform a traditional business she said "It takes a lot! You need the right people, the right culture and the right strategy. To be truly great, your team must have diversity of thought and be willing to collaborate constructively."

Your company culture should empower and inspire people to relentlessly pursue the company's vision, always with integrity. A strong strategy is the roadmap to achieve your vision, but you need strategies for this year, as well as the next five, 10, and 20 years — and they all may need to work in tandem. Our vision at GM is a world with zero crashes, zero emissions and zero congestion, and everyone on the team knows we are committed to putting the customer at the centre of everything we do.

At GM we live and work by a set of seven behaviours, one of which we call Innovate Now. This means "I see things not how they are but how they should be." So, we empower our teams to innovate and create, while also understanding macro trends.

In 2016 Barra splashed out over $1 billion to invest in Cruise, a software business for driverless cars. She put it at the heart of her revolution. Her acquisition gave the old business an injection of new capabilities, but also new courage and creativity too.

"My definition of 'innovative' is providing value to the customer," she adds.

Her move was worth $20 billion of market value in investor confidence alone. Soon revenues started to grow back, employees and customers both believed in a new future. The Chevy Bolt, a car with no steering wheel, suddenly made autonomous dreams real, and the GM brands started to become desirable again.

INSPIRATION 6: JACK MA
The Hangzhou teacher on $12 a month built Alibaba into a $400 billion global technology leader over 20 years, before retiring to become a teacher again.

Technology, of course, is not everything. Whilst machines might eclipse 30% of the human jobs of today, there will still be a need to achieve more than speed and efficiency. This demands that humans rise up to harness their more distinctive assets, to be creative and intuitive. To go beyond the technology.

Ma began studying English at a young age, spending time talking to English-speaking visitors at the Hangzhou international hotel near his home. He would then ride 70 miles on his bicycle to give tourists guided tours of the area to practice his English.

Foreigners nicknamed him "Jack" because they found his Chinese name too difficult to pronounce.

In 1988, he became an English teacher earning just $12 a month, and describing it years later whilst speaking at the 2018 World Economic Forum, as "the best life I had".

From teaching, he soon had ambitions to do more. He applied for 30 different jobs and got rejected by all. He wanted to be a policeman but was told he was too small. He tried his luck at KFC, the first one to arrive in China. Famously he retells the tale: "24 people went for the job. 23 were accepted. I was the only guy who wasn't." He applied to Harvard Business School, but was rejected 10 times.

He persevered. In 1994, he discovered the internet. One day, when searching online for the different beers of the world, he was surprised to find none from China. The world's most consumed beer brand, Snow beer, is of course Chinese. So he and a friend launched a simple Chinese language website called China Pages. Within hours investors were on the phone, and within three years he was generating over 5 000 000 Chinese Yuan:

> My dream was to set up my own e-commerce company. In 1999, I gathered 18 people in my apartment and spoke to them for two hours about my vision. Everyone put their

money on the table, and that got us $60 000 to start Alibaba. I wanted to have a global company, so I chose a global name.

Interviewed at the World Economic Forum he said, "I call Alibaba 1001 mistakes. We expanded too fast, and then in the dotcom bubble, we had to have layoffs. By 2002, we had only enough cash to survive for 18 months. We had a lot of free members using our site, and we didn't know how we'd make money. So we developed a product for China exporters to meet international buyers online. This model saved us."

Over the next two decades he built Alibaba into a $400 billion organisation. In 2017, to celebrate the internet giant's 18th birthday, Ma appeared on stage dressed like Michael Jackson, turning the event into a "Thriller" performance. His passion for his company, and for his audience of employees, shone through.

Looking back he reflected, "The lessons I learned from the dark days at Alibaba are that you've got to make your team have value, innovation, and vision. As long as you don't give up, you still have a chance. And, when you are small, you have to be very focused and rely on your brain, not your strength."

And about himself, often quoted as a supporter of the "996" work mindset (working from 9am until 9pm, 6 days a week), he adds, "I don't think I'm a workaholic. Every weekend, I invite my colleagues and friends to my home to play cards. And people, my neighbours, are always surprised because I live on the second floor apartment, and there are usually 40 pairs of shoes in front of my gate. We have a lot of fun."

On Alibaba's 20th birthday, himself now 54 years old, and worth over $40 billion, he decided to retire, saying, "teachers always want their students to exceed them, so the responsible thing to do for me and the company to do is to let younger, more talented people take over in leadership roles so that they inherit our mission 'to make it easy to do business anywhere'."

"Having been trained as a teacher, I feel extremely proud of what I have achieved," he wrote to his colleagues and shareholders, before adding "I still have lots of dreams to pursue. I want to return to education, which excites me with so much blessing because this is what I love to do. This is something I want to devote most of my time to when I retire."

He spoke passionately about the challenges for the future of education, saying, "A teacher should learn all the time; a teacher should share all the time. Education is a big challenge now – if we do not change the way we teach, 30 years later we will be in trouble. We cannot teach our kids to compete with the machines who are smarter – we have to teach our kids something unique. In this way, in 30 years' time, our kids will have a chance."

INSPIRATION 7: JK ROWLING

Harry Potter was the culmination of her own story from poverty and rebellion to fame and fortune. "It matters not what you are born, but what you grow to be."

The power of our imagination, to drive creativity and innovation, to engage people with empathy, and to inspire their dreams, was the theme of Joanne Rowling's speech to graduating students at Harvard University in 2008.

The bestselling author, better known as JK Rowling, told how she used her experiences of working as a researcher and bilingual secretary for Amnesty International to imagine the stories that became her much-loved books.

She conceived the idea for her *Harry Potter* books while on a delayed train from Manchester to London in 1990, and started imagining a story of a young wizard who went to wizard school. Without anything to note down her ideas, she rapidly set out an entire plot in her head, then tried to write it down on arriving home.

The next 7 years were tough, with the death of her mother, birth of her first child, and divorce from her first husband. Having lost her job, because she sat dreaming about her plots, she decided to move to Porto where she briefly married a local TV journalist, before heading to Edinburgh to be with her sister.

In 1995, she sent her manuscript off to every publisher she could find, but was rejected by all, being told that her story was too long, too elitist, and too complicated. Eventually the daughter of publishing firm Bloomsbury's CEO read the story and couldn't put it down. Her influence on her father resulted in a £4000 advance to Rowling. The only catch being that they felt her pen name needed more style, so she borrowed a middle initial from her grandmother, Kathleen.

Harry Potter and the Philosopher's Stone was published in 1997 to rave reviews. What really changed her life was when the publishing firm Scholastic offered to buy the American rights to the book for a sensational $105 000. The book sold 80 000 copies in the first year, and topped the New York Times bestseller list. Over the years since it has become the most financially successful novel in history, with 400 million readers, and generated $10 billion of sales.

Her own story, a little like Jack Ma's, was one of rags to riches, as she progressed from living on state benefits to being the world's first billionaire author. She lost her billionaire status after giving away much of her earnings to charity, but remains one of the wealthiest people in the world.

She wrote her first book, *Rabbit*, when she was six years old, about a rabbit who lived in her village of Tutshill in Gloucestershire, who got sick and was cared for by a bumble bee called

Miss Bee. She was convinced she could be a writer, even though she lacked confidence otherwise.

When Rowling was at school her parents didn't want her to pursue her dream of being a writer because they worried it wouldn't pay a mortgage. She ignored them, saying listen to your friends, family, and those who care about you, but remember it is your life. "If you have a gift, talent, dream, then pursue it. There's no way anybody knows how it will turn out, but if you love it and you put all your energy into it, your chances of success are great."

Her editor at Bloomsbury says that Rowling's great strength is that she has "a microscopic and macroscopic view of the world" which enabled her to tell such imaginative tales in such engaging detail.

"Passing exams," she said to the new Harvard graduates, "does not determine your success". Whilst she admitted to having a knack for taking tests and passing exams, she also said that it was her failures that had taken her further. "It is impossible to live without failing at something unless you live so cautiously, you might as well not have lived at all". Rather than seeking to avoid failure, we must be willing to accept that it is going to come and be ready to build our lives off it.

"To get through life without failing," she said, "would not be a life worth living."

"Imagination is the power that enables us to empathise with humans whose experiences we have never shared," says Rowling, proclaiming that imagination is crucial for life. Without it, we ignore the one truly unique quality that differentiates us from all other species, effectively claiming that we are human.

Perhaps we should also remember the words of Rowling's great wizard Dumbledore, headmaster at Hogwarts School of Witchcraft and Wizardry, who said, "It matters not what someone is born, but what they grow to be."

SO, READ ON ...

Do you have the belief of Kipchoge, to harness technologies like that of AlphaGo, that can transform businesses like Nadella, letting go of the past like Barra, creating the legacy of Ma, and realising dreams like Rowling?

And do it your way?

AURORA

Recode your future

HOW WILL YOU REINVENT YOUR BUSINESS FOR A BETTER FUTURE?

From profit machine to enlightened progress.

Aurora is the Latin word for dawn, originating from the ancient Roman goddess of the dawn. In meteorology it describes the luminous bands that occasionally form in the upper atmosphere when charged solar particles align with the Earth's magnetic field.

Consider the stretching aspirations of these companies:

- Adidas, the global sports brand, believes that "through sport we have the power to change lives".
- Bulletproof, which creates innovative foods, including great coffee, exists "to help people perform better, think faster, and live better".
- Google seeks "to organize the world's information and make it universally accessible and useful".
- IKEA rises above its flat-packed creations to say it is here "to create a better everyday life for the many people".
- Nike wants "to bring inspiration and innovation to every athlete in the world" and notes that "if you have a body, you are an athlete".
- Shopify seeks to "make commerce better for everyone, so businesses can focus on what they do best: building and selling their products".
- Tesla, for all its focus on fast and stylish cars, has a more worthy aim, "to accelerate the world's transition to sustainable energy".
- Whole Foods wants "to co-create a world where each of us, our communities and our planet can flourish," adding "with great courage, integrity and love".

What is the purpose of your business?

CODE 1: WHAT'S YOUR FUTURE POTENTIAL?
Rise above the chaos and complexity of today, let go of the obsession with what got you here, and instead focus on creating a bold, brave and brilliant future.

As 1999 ended, optimism was sky high as a new millennium of possibilities approached. For me it was particularly exciting as my first child, Anna, was born just weeks before the start of 2000. As clocks chimed to ring in the new millennium, my wife Alison and I stood outside our home at midnight, our new baby asleep in my arms, as the most dazzling fireworks display I have ever seen lit up the skies around us.

However, economies move in cycles, and within three months of celebrating a new century, I vividly remember the day of the dotcom crash. The starry-eyed dreams of many online entrepreneurs came crashing down. Some survived, but many others didn't, including my own venture. I realised that, now with a young family, I needed to be smarter at building a business, and at anticipating the future.

Most people took their inspiration from a Seattle-based start-up called Amazon. A few years earlier, in 1993, Jeff Bezos was working on Wall Street, a 30-year-old rising star of the hedge fund world. On his desk a report landed describing how the emerging internet could become a huge virtual marketplace, that could reach across the old boundaries of nations and markets. Tim Berners-Lee at CERN had just launched the World Wide Web earlier that same year, enabling anyone to start to build a business online, simply and cheaply.

Within a few weeks Bezos left his high-flying job, packed a campervan and drove west with his young wife, still asking huge questions. In Seattle, where most tech people clustered around Microsoft, he set out his business plan with a dream to create the world's largest bookstore. Initially he called it Cadabra, then considered Relentless, but eventually settled upon Amazon. Within three years, he took the business public with an IPO. Anybody who invested $5000 in Bezos's company back then would be worth around $5 million today.

At that same time, Anne Wojcicki, a 25-year-old junior investment analyst, was sitting at her desk on Wall Street, not far from Bezos's old office.

She read that the future of healthcare was all about data, genetic profiling of each individual enabling personalised medicines and care. No longer would people need to rely upon standardised drugs with limited effectiveness, seeking to address already-developed illnesses often too late. Instead, healthcare could be transformed to become personal, positive and proactive.

Like Bezos, a passion to create a better future was stirred inside her, and within weeks she quit her job and headed to San Francisco to start up a DNA profiling business, 23andMe.

At the time it cost around $300 000 to sequence an entire human genome. Wojcicki sought to dramatically reduce the cost by using a technology called genotyping, which spot checks specific parts of a gene for mutations known to be linked with certain diseases, instead of a creating a full sequence. They launched the brand to consumers in 2007, with testing packs available by mail order for $999, and later directly from the pharmacy's shelf.

The revolutionary genetics business combined ideas of new genome technology and crowdsourced funding, into a model that has since reduced the cost of DNA profiling to $99 and is likely to fall much further in the coming years. She now leads a healthcare revolution.

LOOK FORWARDS NOT BACK

Yet we spend too much time looking backwards, not enough time looking forwards. And as a result our future defaults to an extrapolation of what we have done, not what we could do. In a world of turbulent change, a future based on the past, can be quite limiting, and with diminishing returns.

Of course, we take comfort from looking backwards. It is much easier to define, to evaluate.

As an individual, when was the last time you went for a new job? You most likely tried to demonstrate your future potential by describing what you've done in the past. You proudly laid out your resume, eloquently describing your past experiences, impressive qualifications and previous achievements. It might well be impressive, but it's an old story.

As a business, you probably do the same. Daily schedules, meetings and reports, are spent poring over the past. Performance is all about what we have done, last quarter, last year, and compared to previous years. Strategy is too often based on what we have done, our existing capabilities and assets, and we limit our future by what we currently do.

Yet we all know that what got us here is unlikely to be what gets us to where we want to go.

As individuals, and as organisations, we know it is not what we have done that matters, but what we can do, could do, next. Yet what we do next is most likely to be a repeat of what we've done, unless we change something. What is that change that will unlock more than was previously possible? What is the key to our future potential?

Looking forwards is a rare luxury.

A few weeks in the year are typically allocated to future planning. And of that, only a few days maybe even hours, are allocated to a serious discussion of future possibilities, vision development, and plotting out new directions. Ideas for the future are captured on flipcharts, slides and slogans, before their magic is quickly lost in a furious round of budget negotiations focusing on limiting expenditures rather than unlocking new revenues. Inspiring ideas for tomorrow are quickly diminished by the machinery of managing today.

It shouldn't be like this. And in a turbulent world of relentless change, it can't be.

Business leaders need to have their heads up, not down.

Of course, we need success today in order to create tomorrow, but creating the future matters more. Most business leaders will claim they are powerless to jump out of this cycle, to spend more time looking forwards. They are slaves to quarterly reporting demanded by investors, and short-term attitudes of many analysts. But that is largely an excuse.

Paul Polman, when CEO of the British/Dutch consumer goods giant Unilever, famously decided to end quarterly reporting, arguing that he could never get anything else done, and that his projects to invest and develop future ideas were always compromised by an inevitable desire to make today's result look as good as possible. In a showdown with investors, he made the case that they too should be much more interested in long-term growth, rather than short-term glory. He won his battle, and Unilever began to thrive.

The challenge is to focus on the future, to engage everyone in exploring and creating your future potential. A business's economic value is measured as the sum of future cashflows, not past profits. These can only grow through more future-focused initiatives. The alternative is to squeeze ever more revenues and fewer costs out of the existing business with diminishing returns. That's not much fun, and certainly not the way to a better future.

Investors who understand, through better information and dialogue, the future potential of longer-term future initiatives, will reward the business with their confidence. This flows through to stock markets and market capitalisation.

Intangible assets, in the forms of everything from brands and patents, to contracts and customer bases, are the building blocks of innovation and future performance. Around 52% of the cumulative enterprise value of all publicly traded companies is intangible, worth $57.3 trillion according to Brand Finance's *Global Intangible Finance Tracker*. The majority of business value is therefore about its future potential.

If business leaders can more clearly articulate future strategies for changing markets, new business models for engaging customers better, and innovation portfolios to drive new ideas into action, then even more of this future potential can be captured in the value of their businesses.

WHAT'S YOUR FUTURE POTENTIAL?

Our potential is what lies ahead … how we can be more, do more, achieve more.

Think of some of the great people who have changed to realise their potential:

JK Rowling was a secretary at a publishing firm. On her way to and from work, she used to dream of writing a novel, sketching out plots in her head. As a secretary, her potential was conventionally limited to roles in administrative support. But then she threw in her job, took the bold step to write her first manuscript, and her potential was transformed.

Eliud Kipchoge was a very good runner. He was one of the hundreds of African endurance athletes who competed around the world, picking up medals at major events. But then, realising that his career was drawing to a close, he wanted to leave more of a mark. He switched to the marathon. Olympic champion, world record holder. The first man under 2 hours.

"Future potential" is the desire and ability to be more. Individually and organisationally, it is typically driven by three factors:

- **Future courage** … Do we dare to be more than we currently are? Future potential demands personal ambition and drive to go beyond our current world, to let go of what we know, to go further, to enter the unknown.
- **Future vision** … Do we know where we are heading, and is it the right direction? Future potential demands more scope, opportunity space, more fertile ground to support new growth, to stretch further and wider ahead.
- **Future capacity** … Do we have the talent, creativity and resources to get there? Future potential demands that we become more, dig deeper into ourselves, to develop new mindsets and future-relevant capabilities.

In a sense, it is moving from what might seem impossible to seeing them as possible, and then through our courage and capability, making them plausible.

I work with many organisations, and it is quickly apparent which have the greater "future potential". The organisations who do, typically see the future beyond the frames of today; they look to go beyond their sector, innovate new business models, disrupt the current game.

In 2017, Tesla reframed itself as an energy company not just an auto business, giving it so much more potential, and investors saw likewise, as its stock market performance rose. Orsted was a Danish coal-based electricity generator, but within 10 years had transformed itself from black to green, and is now a renewable energy business, with huge growth potential.

The companies who don't have future potential, compete within their existing space, seek improved products and operational efficiencies, but are essentially happy to play the old game. Vodafone, for example, is obsessed with being a telecoms business, focused on handsets and tariff plans, while the rest of the world is more interested in convergent platforms and the content on them. Or Ford, battling to survive in an auto sector that is quickly been redefined by new forms of mobility.

Similarly for individuals, it is quickly apparent who has the greater "future potential".

People who seek to be more than they currently are – not just ambitious to climb corporate hierarchies and attain greater positions, more power – but the ones who are constantly learning, curious and creative, they want to improve themselves, searching for new ideas, new initiatives, new ways to move forwards (Figure 1.1).

Future potential is closely aligned with change, and with growth. An organisation is unlikely to achieve significant change, unless people are prepared to change too. The future potential of leaders has a huge influence on their organisation's future potential. Without the right leaders, organisations are stuck in today.

Change in mindset, in activities, in capabilities. And as a result of that, organisations are unlikely to achieve significant growth, beyond just working-harder-type of growth, unless they see personal growth as a prerequisite.

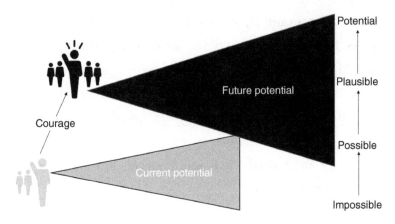

FIGURE 1.1 Realising your future potential.

How much "future potential" do you have?

- How farsighted are you to dare to look beyond the horizons of today?
- What proportion of time do you spend looking forwards, compared to looking back?
- Is your business purpose a limiting or liberating definition of why you exist?
- Does most of your innovation exploit the core, or seek to explore the edges?
- Is your business largely defined by your current products, and existing competitors?
- Do you typically think more in terms of probabilities, or possibilities?
- Are performance metrics driven by what you have done, or by what you could do?
- Is your market value a reflection of what you could do, or what you have done?
- Do you have leaders with the potential to unlock your future potential?

Finding your future potential requires a shift in your business, a more forwards orientation, a growth mindset, a reframing of where you are going and what is possible. And it requires a stretch to make the mental and physical shift. It needs a catalyst to open minds, it needs energy to break out of today, and it needs courageous leadership to take it to a place you don't yet know.

Without "future potential" you and your business are unlikely to find a better future.

LEADERS NEED TO BE FARSIGHTED

When I asked Jim Snabe, former co-CEO of SAP, and now chairman of Siemens and Maersk, how he makes sense of his business world, he paused. His first reaction was the obvious, to understand his specific industries, his customer and competitors, today. But then he reflected on the inadequacy of that current view. If what comes next will be different, then he needs to look differently for it, he said.

Seeing the bigger picture, is one way to change our viewpoint, but it's probably still not enough. We still put ourselves at the centre, and then explore the obvious adjacencies. Instead we need new perspectives, seeing the emerging patterns of change, the parallels and possibilities, how to react to them, to seize the best new opportunities first. Put simply it's about being farsighted.

Beth Comstock, former chief marketing and commercial officer of GE wrote about her leadership experiences as the business faced the challenges of rapidly changing markets. Her book *Imagine it Forward: Courage, Creativity and the Power of Change* is a call to action for all those executives who felt that they could continue doing what they had always done, and they and their company would be ok.

Comstock starts with a passion: "The pace of change is never going to be slower than today." She points out that 50 years ago the life expectancy of a Fortune 500 firm would have been around 50 years, whereas now it's 15 years.

Futurist Ray Kurzweil goes further in an article entitled *The Law of Accelerating Returns*, saying "We won't experience 100 years of progress in the 21st century, it will be more like 20 000 years of progress."

The ability to be forward-looking and focused on the future, the capacity to imagine and articulate future possibilities, sets the great leader apart from others. Whilst the rest of the organisation is focused on the shorter-term deliverables, they look to the leader to put what they do into the context of where they are going, and how it contributes to the journey.

Leaders as strategists are intensely curious about the future, looking beyond their own organisations and industries, to make sense of a changing world. They look to the changing dynamics of markets, of how organisations compete, but also at the shifts in macro-economics, politics and society. Indeed, the real catalysts for change are outside, not inside, an organisation.

The ability to look forwards, say Barry Posner and Jim Kouzes in *The Leadership Challenge*, is second only to honesty as the most admired trait in leaders. They found that 70% of employees say forward-looking is the attribute they most look to in their leaders. This is not just about communicating a compelling vision, but being able to make sense of complexity, connecting the dots into a bigger picture, and to anticipate events before they happen.

New research which I led at IE Business School, as part of my role as academic director of their leadership development programmes, explored the reality of farsighted leaders.

We found that forward-thinking escalates with levels of leadership. Frontline supervisors need to look months ahead, mid-level managers who lead complex projects need to look 1–3 years ahead. C-suite executives should be thinking 5–10 years forwards, even if they plan and focus their actions on a shorter timeframe.

Yet the research also showed that most senior executives currently spend around 5% of their time thinking about the future – which could be a few hours every week, or more likely one or two weeks every year.

Contrast this to some of the great business leaders. Talking at his annual Berkshire Hathaway AGM in Omaha, Nebraska, Warren Buffett claimed to have spent around 80% of his career reading and thinking. That seems extreme, but so is his performance as one of the world's great investors.

Richard Branson told me how he always tries to take a swim for around an hour each morning, often a lap around the shore of his Caribbean island, giving himself time to think before anything else in the day. He also famously drinks 20 cups of tea each day, saying it gives him time to pause amidst the daily chaos, and just think a little. Jeff Bezos schedules "thinking" meetings about future ideas at 10 am every morning, when he is fresh and alert, and never in the afternoon.

The future is an infinite array of possibilities – for you to decode as options and choices. Firstly, we need to make sense of what those options are, then explore what they could mean for us, and then decide how to make the right choices.

Forward-looking leaders embrace four important tenets:

- **The future is fast.** While the speed of change accelerates relentlessly, we shouldn't be intimated by it, or jump to knee-jerk actions in panic, but take our time to think longer-term, and about how to achieve progress.

- **The future is complex.** While the search for simplicity is admirable, it is not always possible or the best solution. Instead we need to recognise that today's world is not about reducing things to 2 x 2 matrices, or binary choices.
- **The future is unpredictable.** While we have a desire to be complete, and right, the future does not offer such precision. Instead we need to embrace uncertainty as a positive force, to define our north star then embrace the journey as it evolves.
- **The future is there to be created.** While we like to limit ourselves to what we know, what markets and sectors we are in, there are no boundaries or rules that limit where we can go. Imagination is our guide to write the future we want.

In his book *Farsighted: How to Make Decisions that Matter*, Steven Johnson asks, if the most difficult choices are the ones with most consequences, why do we spend so little time thinking about them. It is fashionable, he says, to argue that we live in an age of short attention spans, requiring quick thinking and rapid action. Yet he argues that we have become much better at holistic thinking – connecting multiple ideas together, connecting the dots, systems-based approaches. Speed of change requires bigger thinking, he says.

Adam Grant, a pyschologist at Wharton Business School, reflected on Johnson's challenge. He argued that a good way to think bigger is by reading novels, enabling us to transport our brains into new spaces and gain new perspectives – including exploring ideas for the future, through science fiction. Star Trek, for example, is a lifetime obsession of Jeff Bezos.

The IE research suggests that many leaders are averse to future thinking because there are no absolutes, no detailed analytics on which to base decisions. Indeed, over the last decade we have embraced scientific method into our business to such an extent that we now feel exposed without it. Instead, making future choices requires intuition and imagination, and courage.

Psychologist Ellen Langer's advice for making difficult choices about unpredictable futures, is: "Don't make the right decision, make the decision right". Her point is to think about how we might explore the opportunities ahead of us, and their implications. Given you are never likely to have as much information as you'd like, don't search for the perfect answer, consider how you can make the best choices from what you know.

CODE 2: HAVE A FUTURE MINDSET
Open your mind to new possibilities, reach higher and further to embrace the unknown with curiosity and courage, to shape the future on your terms.

"Shoshin" is the Zen Buddhist concept of the "beginner's mind" and embraces an attitude of openness, eagerness and lack of preconceptions.

In his book *Zen Mind, Beginner's Mind*, Shunryu Suzuki explains the framework of shoshin, saying "in the beginner's mind there are many possibilities, in the expert's mind there are few".

As a father, I was always struck by the clarity of my two daughters' questions, particularly in their early years. They would question everything they saw, like a test of my education to try to explain the actions of nature, and even people. In the early days, they asked why; as they grew older and more challenging, they would demand why not.

Their questions often stopped me in my tracks, making me realise that I had grown acceptant of what I had learnt, I had embraced a mindset built on conventional education and personal experience, but this did not necessarily equip me to answer their most simple questions, and share their often penetrating curiosities.

OPEN YOUR MIND TO NEWNESS

Langer says, "It is not primarily our physical selves that limit us, but rather our mindset about our physical limits".

Mindsets are the beliefs, attitudes and assumptions we create about who we are and how the world works, and how we can achieve progress. Or as Mahatma Gandhi said, "Your beliefs become your thoughts, your thoughts become your words, your words become your actions, your actions become your habits, your habits become your values, your values become your destiny".

Mindsets should not be confused with mindfulness which is about having a heightened awareness. With its roots in Buddhist meditation, mindfulness is about acceptance without judgement, about living in the present rather than future or past. Whilst this is useful in staying alert to our current situation, to connect ourselves to our outlooks, it is our mindset that moves us forwards.

Coca-Cola's former CEO Roberto Goizueta described the mindset of his leaders as a competitive advantage, visible when they could "find opportunities which others cannot see". During a 16-year tenure, the company's market value increased from $4 billion to $145 billion. He described four types of mindsets that determine a leader's ability to explore new opportunities for innovation and growth:

- Zero Mindset: you don't see change
- Passive Mindset: you see but fear change
- Active Mindset: you embrace and deliver change
- Creative Mindset: you see and do what others don't

James Quincey replaced Goizueta as CEO in 2016 saying that he wanted to go further, to embrace a "growth mindset". This included different ways of thinking, beyond the single-minded pursuit of selling the same drink to more and more people.

Quincey wanted his people to embrace new agendas, such as health and wellness, together with responsible and sustainable practices. Whilst he valued the "performance-based culture" which valued "urgency, speed, agility, accountability and entrepreneurship", he argued that consumers expected Coke to be "both thoughtful and fast" which might even mean "doing fewer things better", and even selling fewer better things.

I had a very similar experience when meeting a group of business leaders at Microsoft recently. Walking into their offices at their sprawling Redmond campus just outside Seattle, I was struck by a child-like wonder in what is a relatively old technology company. In the past they would accept the technology in their hands, and focus on sales; today they constantly challenged themselves as to why they did it, and how they could do better.

Culturally this was no longer a technology company, but a business with a much bigger imagination, and a deeper conscience. As Microsoft leads the way in the latest AI-based innovations, they are as interested in the ethical implications of such human-redefining capability, as they are in what it could practically do to increase business performance.

I realised that Satya Nadella, CEO of the business which, after a near 30-year gap, had just become the world's most valuable company, had instilled a new mindset. As the executives talked, it became clear that this "growth mindset" had had a profound effect on them as individuals, and their business practice.

Gone was the head-down obsession with selling at any cost, characterised by the Steve Ballmer years. Now they were much more interested in doing what was right, creating progress for their customers, but equally for society. They wanted to explore and experiment with new ideas, to pause and consider alternatives, to embrace diversity, ethics and sustainability. It felt enlightened.

Nadella says we need to move from trying to be expert "know it all" to being constant students, or "learnt it all". Whilst the past can give useful insights, it is a focus on the future that matters, he says. "If you keep your eyes focused on the rear-view mirror, you're going to crash. You need to keep focused on what's ahead."

GROW YOURSELF, AND YOUR BUSINESS

When Carol Dweck was a graduate student in the early 1970s, she began to study how children cope with failure. She quickly saw that *cope* was the wrong word, they *realised*. Now a psychology professor at Stanford, she has spent several decades studying this dichotomy, which she initially termed "incremental theory".

She eventually found a better language – the "fixed" and "growth" mindset. Her book *Mindset: The New Psychology of Success* became a bestseller.

Dweck applies the concept to every walk of life – from children's education and parenting, to sports coaching and mental performance. She argues that a growth mindset leads to higher achievement, whilst a fixed mindset actively plateaus an individual's progress. She also applies the idea to teams and organisations. Those who, for example, like to single out star performers are more fixed in their mindsets, rather than embracing everyone with their different contributions over time.

A "fixed mindset" suggests that some people are creative and others not, some are intelligent and others not. As a result, we become more concerned about how we look to others, we avoid failure at all costs for fear of exposing ourselves, we play safe and avoid risks, we feel threatened by others success, and we become obsessed with our fragile reputations.

- We become trapped in a black-and-white world of success and failure
- We seek easy options, because we fear failure
- We accept mediocrity, and reject change
- We blame others and avoid responsibility
- We play it safe

A "growth mindset" recognises that our personal and collective progress is achieved through development and learning. We embrace change as an opportunity, we seek out challenges to stretch us, we work through obstacles to find new solutions, we listen to alternative opinions and criticism, we embrace fear and risk as part of moving forwards, we accept failure and success as equally important parts of our journey, and we value effort, not just accomplishment.

- We live in a world of potentials, of new opportunities and possibilities
- We seek challenges, without fear of failure
- We embrace change, and reject mediocrity
- We take responsibility and listen to other viewpoints
- We seek progress

Of course, mindsets are not black and white, and we might find ourselves fluctuating between them in different aspects of our lives. We should also recognise that everyone is different, in their strengths and capabilities, and in how they project themselves. The role of a team still matters, with its strength in combining differences. The role of a leader matters even more, creating a context for growth mindsets to thrive.

CREATE THE FUTURE IN YOUR OWN VISION

"Exponential" is a word thrown around when talking about the future, and particularly about the influence of new technologies. All around us we see how companies embrace the network effects of connected markets to multiply their impact reach and richness, influence and impact, rather than just growing them incrementally.

Alphabet's innovation lab, X, famously champions the idea of seeking solutions that are "10x not just 10%" better. Astro Teller, X's leader says, "To create exponential value, it's imperative to first create an exponential mindset. The incremental mindset focuses on making something better, while the exponential mindset makes something different. Incremental is satisfied with 10%. Exponential seeks 10x."

Personally, I find the "10x" challenge incredibly simple and useful. Imagine, for example, that you want to create a better-performing car, say, a car that currently drives at 50 mpg. Most car brands would be happy with an incremental 10%

improvement, to 55 mpg. The exponential mindset, however, seeks 10x, or a 500 mpg solution. That forces you to think differently, change perspectives, try new approaches. Even if you end up failing, and a car that drives at 200 mpg, it would be a significant breakthrough.

Teller argues that, without an exponential mindset, organisations would not be able to leap forwards in dramatic ways, to create newness and progress in the world. Google, he argues, would not have been able to create its ambitious vision to "organise the world's information", or Airbnb to seek a world where "7 billion people can belong anywhere." Like a scientist seeking to prove a new hypothesis, it starts with a leap of imagination.

A "future mindset" is a growth mindset with a strong future orientation. You could argue that a leader needs the mindset of a true futurist – to be visionary, to make sense of change, to define what has not been articulated.

The future isn't like it used to be. Safe, predictable, certain.

What got you this far in your market, in your business life, is unlikely to take you to where you want to go next. Continually using, or extending, the old models of success will have diminishing returns. Instead we have to embrace new futures, and new ways to get there.

The future mindset therefore enables a leap of imagination, it enables a business leader to envision a future business beyond what others can see. A better view of the future enables leaders to shape it in their own vision, to their advantage.

CODE 3: IMAGINE A BETTER BUSINESS
Seize the power of business as a platform for change, to engage colleagues and society in solving big problems, to grow and do good at the same time.

Over the last 30 years, our world has seen huge social improvements and technological progress. We have experienced unprecedented economic growth as hundreds of millions of people have risen out of poverty.

Today we are benefiting from a digital revolution that is transforming lives, giving people access to education and healthcare in ways we could never have imagined. As a result, we can embrace the diverse cultures, creativity and capabilities across the world to solve many of the most pressing social and environmental challenges. Yet despite these successes, our model of progress is still deeply flawed.

THE DEEP FLAWS OF CAPITALISM

Signs of capitalism's failure and imperfections are everywhere.

Natural disasters triggered by climate change have doubled in frequency since the 1980s. Extreme weather has affected most of the world – forest fires to freak tornadoes, increasing desertification and declining farming land, diminished melting ice caps and rising sea levels. Violence and armed conflict cost the world the equivalent of around 10% of GDP, while lost biodiversity and ecosystem damage cost an estimated 3% and rising.

We continue to invest in high-carbon infrastructure at a rate that could commit us to irreversible, immensely damaging climate change. Stagnant growth only makes us more determined to continue with the old ways, rather than shifting to the new. The recent direct medical costs and associated economic costs of 2020's global pandemic could have paid for a full-scale transformation to a renewably energised world many times over. Social inequality and youth unemployment are worsening in countries across the world, while on average women are still paid 25% less than men for comparable work.

Mark Thomas, a British economist and former colleague, has founded the 99% Organisation. In his book *99%: Mass Impoverishment and How We Can End It*, he says that the median wage earner is poorer today than they were in 2007. This, he says, is mass impoverishment. He argues that if you are part of the 99% – and there is a 99% chance that you are – then you are one of the first generation in living memory who can expect to be poorer than your parents, even as the economy continues to grow. And you could be quite a lot poorer. "If we continue as we are going, the civilisation we enjoy today will not last until 2050. For most young people, buying their own house is a distant dream; wages are failing to keep pace with inflation; more and more people rely on food banks," he says.

Inequality also generates deep anxiety about the impact of globalisation and automation on all types of jobs, from factories to call centres. That has directly impacted on politics with a rise in nationalism, protectionism and trade wars. Real interest rates are historically low, even negative, in several major economies, while total debt remains uncomfortably high.

Economic views diverge between optimism and political pessimism, and stock markets become increasingly volatile. The resulting uncertainty makes it even harder to predict the future. It is easy to understand why many companies seem to be paralysed by uncertainty – sitting on cash, buying back shares, paying high dividends – rather than committing to longer-term investments.

The 2020 Edelman Trust Barometer reveals that a majority of respondents in every developed market do not believe they will be better off in five years' time, and 56% believe that capitalism in its current form is now doing more harm than good in the world.

BUSINESS AS A PLATFORM FOR CHANGE

"The great miscalculation of the age is the idea that businesses have to make a choice: to become profitable or become platforms for change. This is not the case," says Marc Benioff, CEO of Salesforce, in his book *Trailblazer*.

His point, of course, is that business is deeply embedded in the everyday lives of every one of us. How we eat, drink, talk, connect, meet, travel, work, laugh and love. We are all consumers, seeking brands that we emotionally love and trust, products and services that we need and desire, business models that can operate at huge scale.

If these everyday transactions, and all the activities that enable them, could be harnessed in a way that is good for the world, to address the many challenges we face socially and environmentally, then they could be incredibly powerful. Far more powerful than any non-profit could achieve, because they simply lack the resources and infrastructures.

Business has the power be the greatest platform for change.

This is not some crazy, utopian ideal. We already see how an everyday cup of coffee from Starbucks can help the subsistence farmers of Columbia to escape poverty, where buying the latest cool sneakers from Adidas can help reduce the environmental damage of the beautiful places where you run, or how Danone's Grameen micro-financed home dairies across Asia allow people to grow their ways to a better livelihood.

The *Blueprint for Better Business* was developed by The Blueprint Trust, an independent charity, seeking a better business. It proposes that a "better" business:

- Has purpose beyond profit … believes that profit is not its purpose, but the outcome of an effective business that seeks to achieve a better purpose for society.
- Acts for broader society … acts beyond self-interest, demonstrating respect for people and building relationships that benefit business and society.
- Enables good … becomes a platform for change, and force for good, to deliver clear benefits to society as well as delivering long-term sustainable performance.
- The blueprint is built on "Five Principles of a Purpose Driven Business," creating a picture of what a company that is guided and inspired by a purpose that serves society might look like (see Figure 1.2).

Similarly, a group of business leaders, including Jochen Zeitz (Kering), Paul Polman (Unilever), Richard Branson (Virgin), Emmanuel Faber (Danone), Muhammad Yunus (Grameen) and Hamdi Ulakaya (Chobani), launched "The B Team" in 2013,

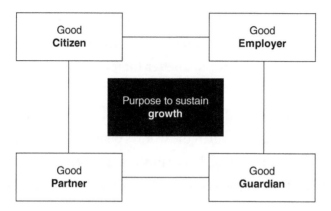

FIGURE 1.2 Blueprint for better business.

saying in a collective letter, "We believe that for a better tomorrow for our communities, our companies and our planet, we
need bold leadership now."

They set out to address 10 big challenges – from transparency to
collaboration, nature to communities, accounting to incentives,
fairness to rewards, diversity and long-termism:

> Our current economic model is broken. But it did not break
> itself. And it will not repair itself. We, as private sector and
> civil society leaders, envision the way forward as a better
> way of doing business. That's why we're working to shift
> the culture of accountability in business to include not
> only numbers and performance, but people and planet.
> We acknowledge that while we are part of the problem, we
> have the responsibility – and the power – to lead on the

solution. We will create new norms of corporate leadership that go beyond commitment and toward fundamental transformation today, for a better tomorrow.

P&G's top marketer Marc Pritchard recently described some of the profound ways in which the world's biggest consumer goods company is embracing sustainability to transform its brands. Or, as he puts it, to make P&G "a force for good and a force for growth".

As part of its new Ambition 2030 plan, P&G has pledged to make all its packaging fully recyclable or reusable by that year. It also plans to use 100% renewable energy and have 0% net waste by that point. Working with the Brands for Good coalition it seeks to use its $7 billion annual advertising spend to educate and inspire consumers to make sustainable lifestyles desirable.

P&G sought to make itself more sustainable, but also to help consumers adopt more sustainable lifestyles themselves. It's Head & Shoulders shampoo bottles are now made from waste ocean plastic (removing 2600 tonnes of plastics annually), whilst the surfactants in Tide washing powder enable cold-water cleaning, reducing household energy usage. It has also launched new products or is updating existing products with plant-based ingredients, such as Gain Botanicals and Downy Nature Blends. Such products are better for the environment but also align to the rapidly changing consumer agendas.

THE $12 TRILLION OPPORTUNITY OF THE SDGS

The United Nations' Sustainable Development Goals (SDGs) create a structured framework for developing better business strategies and transforming markets (see Figure 1.3).

Achieving the 17 goals, agreed by all member states in 2015, would create a world that is comprehensively sustainable, says the UN, which it defines as socially fair, environmentally secure, inclusive, economically prosperous, and more predictable. The goals are interconnected, like the world, so progress on them all will have much more impact than achieving only some.

Whilst businesses are clearly important to achieving the SDGs, they also create new opportunities for businesses to grow in a more positive way. The challenge, therefore, is to embed the 17 goals as a guiding framework for strategic development, as well as good operational practice.

Making the business case for the SDGs in 2017, the UN's Business and Sustainable Development Commissions estimated that they represent a $12 trillion opportunity, combining cost savings and new revenues. They particularly highlighted the opportunities for food and agriculture, cities, energy and materials, health and wellbeing – together representing 60% of the global economy.

FIGURE 1.3 The UN's 17 Sustainable Development Goals.

The commission said "to capture these opportunities in full, businesses need to pursue social and environmental sustainability as avidly as they pursue market share and shareholder value. If a critical mass of companies joins us in doing this now, together we will become an unstoppable force. If they don't, the costs and uncertainty of unsustainable development could swell until there is no viable world in which to do business."

The total economic prize from implementing the SDGs could be 2–3 times bigger, they added, assuming that the benefits are captured across the whole economy and accompanied by much higher labour and resource productivity. That's a fair assumption. Consider that achieving the single goal of gender equality could contribute up to $28 trillion to global GDP by 2025, according to one estimate. The overall prize is enormous.

In 2019, some of the world's leading companies – including ARM, Coca-Cola, Alphabet, Mastercard, Nike, Microsoft, SAP, Salesforce and Unilever – came together as the Business Avengers to better define the role that business can play in delivering the SDGs.

Each company agreed to apply the goal to its core business, financial commitments, employee networks, consumer activities and social influence, as ways to accelerate progress. They were also complemented by the World Business Council for Sustainable Development who added a Good Life

Goals framework which seeks to turn the SDGs into a set of personal lifestyle actions which are more relevant and tangible to every person.

CODE 4: FIND YOUR INSPIRING PURPOSE
Finding your reason for being, beyond products and profits, to capture the passion that guides you, and defines how you make the world a better place.

Yves Chouinard, founder of Patagonia, is a great purpose-driven leader. He is a dedicated nature lover who in the late 1950s started building climbing gear for a few people in the Yosemite mountains.

Today, Patagonia is a $200 million company, a certified B Corporation, and widely recognised as a leader in environmental sustainability. The company's success is largely due to some of the purpose-driven decisions Chouinard made along the way. This included an early decision to drop one of their best-selling products, pitons, the metal spikes climbers hammer into rocks, because of their damage to the environment.

Some years later Chouinard took a significant risk, insisting that all of the brand's clothes should be made of organic materials. This required new sourcing, building a new supply chain, and raising the cost of items. Both moves were good for the planet and aligned the company's work with Chouinard's own sense of purpose, but had he been driven only by profit, it's unlikely he would have made such choices. They were costly in the short run but helped the business to thrive in the long run.

Patagonia has long defined its purpose as to "build the best product, cause no unnecessary harm, and use business to inspire and implement solutions to the environmental crisis". However, for the elderly leader that was not enough, and in 2018 he redefined why the company exists, stating that "Patagonia is in business to save our home planet".

Chouinard says that the change in wording might look cosmetic but is far from it. He wanted to express urgency, in his business but also in society, that this is not just about climate change, but a climate crisis. "We're losing the planet because of climate change. That's the elephant in the room. Society is basically working on symptoms. Save the polar bear? If you want to save the polar bear, you got to save the planet," he says.

FINDING YOUR PURPOSE

So why does your business exist?

Purpose defines what the business contributes to the world, or equally, why the world would be a lesser place if the business did not exist. Purpose creates an enduring cause which the business is willing to fight for. For some this might be an urgent call to action, for others it might be a more personal inspiration.

Tesla exists to "accelerate the world's transition to sustainable energy", Starbucks to "inspire the human spirit", Dove to "help the next generation of women realise their potential", Microsoft to "empower people to achieve more", and Swarovski to "add sparkle to people's everyday lives".

Purpose creates a richer sense of meaning in your business, inspiring employees to raise their game, to transform and grow themselves and the organisation. It encourages a strategic focus, to rise above the distractions of today, to align on bigger goals and to innovate more radically. Productivity and performance typically follow.

It is a cause shared internally and externally, that investors want to be part of, partners want to align with, and customers want to promote through their consumption and loyalty.

Purpose goes far beyond the old mission and vision statements, which were largely internal mantras, about how good the company wanted to be – "the best", "the industry leader", "to maximise performance". Purpose is much more altruistic and inclusive. It is about what the inside does for the outside world. It sits above other ambitions, and should probably replace them, as an inspiring, single-minded intent.

If purpose is "Why we exist?", then mission is more about "What do we do?" and vision is "Where are we going?"

Mark Zuckerberg, the Harvard drop-out who spent his student years in pursuit of a Face Mash tool to explore the opposite sex, returned to the Boston campus recently with a new sense of purpose:

> Today I want to talk about purpose, but not some kind of grand speech on how to find it. We're millennials. We'll try to do that instinctively. Instead, I'm here to tell you finding your purpose isn't enough.

> The challenge for our generation is creating a world where everyone has a sense of purpose. One of my favourite stories is when John F. Kennedy visited NASA, he saw a janitor carrying a broom and he walked over and asked what he was doing. The janitor responded: "Mr. President, I'm helping put a man on the moon." Purpose is that sense that we are part of something bigger than ourselves, that we are needed, that we have something better ahead to work for. Purpose is what creates true happiness.

PURPOSE-DRIVEN COMPANIES DO BETTER

Of business leaders surveyed by Harvard's Beacon Institute, 90% believe that an organisation's purpose is central to business success, yet only 46% said that it currently informs their strategic and operational decisions.

The business case, however, is compelling. Purposeful companies are more profitable and valuable, attract customers who pay more and become more loyal, attract the best talent who become more engaged, and investors who support them over the long-term.

Such companies outperform the stock market by 42% according to analysis by the Corporate Board. Companies with purpose statements but who don't act on them deliver average performance, whilst those without a sense of purpose, underperform the market by 40%.

Edelman found that 80% of consumers believe that a business must play a role in addressing societal issues, whilst Accenture found that 62% of consumers want companies to "take a stand on issues like sustainability, transparency and fair employment".

66% of consumers would actively choose a purpose-driven brand, according to Cone Porter Novelli, whilst this rises to 91% of millennials. 67% said they were more willing to forgive companies who are trying to do better. 53% of people would complain if companies don't seem to care about social issues, and 17% would boycott them.

According to IBM, 70% of consumers would be willing to pay a price premium of around 35% for purpose-driven brands.

Purpose-driven companies are 2.5 times better at driving innovation and transformation, according to the Beacon Institute, whilst Deloitte says on average, they generate 30% more revenue from innovations launched in the last year.

Gallup found that only 34% of US workers were enthusiastic about or committed to their work. Millennials, in particular, seek out companies with more purpose, with Cone saying that 83% of young people are loyal to companies who do good for society or the environment. Deloitte found that purposeful companies have 40% higher retention.

Bank of America predicts a "tsunami" of capital flowing to "good" stocks in a boom of ethical investments. They say over the next two decades, $20 trillion in assets will flow into sustainable funds (similar to the current value of the S&P 500).

Coldwell Banker says that the "Great Wealth Transfer" of the next 30 years will see an estimated $68 trillion passed down from boomer parent to millennial children. By 2030 this new generation will hold five times as much wealth as they have today, with 77% of them stating that sustainable issues are their top priority when making investment decisions.

TURNING INSPIRING PURPOSE INTO PRACTICAL ACTION

Simon Sinek has a good definition of purpose in his book *Start with Why*, describing his golden circle, with "Why" at its centre: "All the great and inspiring leaders and organizations in the world, whether it's Apple or Martin Luther King or the Wright brothers – they all think, act, and communicate the exact same way and it's the complete opposite to everyone else. It's probably the world's simplest idea and I call it the Golden Circle … Why? How? What?"

Sinek believes that having a "Why" explains why some leaders and organisations are able to inspire people whilst others fail. Everyone knows what they do, most people know how they do things, but surprisingly few people can explain why they do what they do.

The "Why" needs to pervade the whole organisation, and its multitude of activities. It needs to be a "golden thread" that connects everything together. It needs to drive values and goals, strategies and everyday decisions, culture and communication.

The problem, however, is that a single statement can easily sound too simplistic, inspiring yet just a slogan. The challenge is to make purpose meaningful for each person.

Purpose drives you to make better strategic choices. In a world of infinite possibilities, where you could do anything,

FIGURE 1.4 The business purpose pyramid.

choices matter more than ever. And because of complexity and uncertainty they are harder to make. Purpose becomes a useful arbiter.

The secret is to make the "Why" more tangible, to build a bridge between high-level purpose and the strategies for practical action. There are three levels, as shown in Figure 1.4.

1. **Purpose – the Why:** finding your cause, that gives you an enduring and authentic direction, that aligns all that you do in an inspiring, meaningful way. It should be authentic, distinctive, coherent and enduring.

    This is built around your consumer audience, how you make their lives and the world around them better, and represented by your brand identity. Examples:
    - Nike: "expanding human potential"

- Kellogg's: "nourishing families so they can flourish"
- Starbucks: "inspiring the human spirit"

2. **Principles – the How:** defining the distinctive approaches by which you will deliver your purpose – high-level concepts, which flow through to your internal culture. Embedding such principles shapes leadership, culture and organisation.

    These make the purpose more tangible, but are still able to endure over time – they are conceptual platforms for differentiation and communication. Examples:

    - Nike is built on "achieving your best performance", through technically superior sportswear plus a range of services to help you perform better.
    - Kellogg's is built on "a portfolio of healthy breakfast cereals", including diverse brands and products to meet the needs of the whole family.
    - Starbucks is built on "human connections" which are achieved through coffee, and coffee shops which become "the third place" in people's lives.

3. **Practices – the What:** aligning purpose with your strategic choices which drive plans and processes, innovation and experiences, products and services:

    These become practical and evolve over time, delivering the purposeful concepts in ways that are distinctive, but also tangible and collectively profitable:

    - Nike's strategies might range from its Nike+ digital apps and online fitness clubs, to a new fabrics or shoe designs that enables you to perform better.

- Kellogg's strategies might range from new categories for an on-the-go lifestyle, through to more sustainable sourcing, production or packaging.
- Starbucks' strategies might range from new services like an online music sharing platform through to local neighbourhood initiatives.

An effective purpose is built on these strong and tangible foundations, rather than some one-liner that can easily sound too abstract and be dismissed as nice words. Purpose ultimately becomes a cause when it is embraced by the organisation and wider society outside. No longer just an intent, it becomes a collective movement for better. Great examples include CVS's move against smoking and Unilever's pursuit of sustainable living.

As Friedrich Nietzsche said, "He who has a why to live for can bear almost any how."

CODE 5: CREATE YOUR FUTURE STORY
Engage your people in a richer vision of the future, creating a narrative that captures hearts and minds, and defines a distinctive path for progress.

As a business leader you are a storyteller.

Not of fictional stories, but stories of your vision for the future, stories of where the business is headed, and what it will be like.

Stories that engage people in understanding those simplistic purpose statements in profound, human and inspiring ways.

Steve Jobs was a master of storytelling. In 2001, as the technology world was still in shock from the crash of the dotcom boom, Jobs mounted the stage for Apple's annual meeting. He was in his prime. His new iMac computers had been a success, the company had been transformed under his renewed leadership.

Jobs talked about his passion for music. How music inspires him, and every one of us. It marks the great moments, it defines moments in our lives, it can change our worlds. The Beatles. Dylan and more. By now, it felt like Apple could be a music business. And then from his jeans pocket, he pulled out a small white device, and held it up.

"A thousand songs in your pocket," he said with a huge grin.

WHAT'S YOUR FUTURE STORY?

Strategies and slogans are not enough. We need something more human and personal.

A story can resonate with people today and explain how tomorrow can be better. A story can bring a future vision to life, inviting people to imagine it with you, exploring its benefits. A story evolves, and shows a path from where we are, to where we could be. A story is more memorable and can be retold from person to person. People seek hope and want reasons to believe in better.

Elon Musk doesn't quite have the drama or fluency of Jobs, but he has become one of the best future storytellers of today's business world.

His businesses are founded on future ideas, building for future possibilities. They start with an inspiring purpose, be it SpaceX's desire to sustain life through a new civilisation beyond Earth, or Tesla's drive to accelerate the shift to clean energy.

SpaceX might have created a satellite launch business that is around 10 times cheaper than NASA, but he uses this capability to tell a far bigger story. They are just practice runs, for a much greater mission to Mars. Who can forget the dramatic moment when he landed his returning Falcon 9 spacecraft back on an incredibly small platform in the middle of the ocean? Or when the much more powerful Falcon Heavy launched a (Tesla) car into perpetual orbit playing David Bowie's *Life on Mars*?

Musk writes his Master Plan for his businesses, publishing them on his blog, and updating them every so often. His style is informal but informative, visionary but practical, combining scientific logic and technical facts. In 2006, he wrote his initial Master Plan for Tesla:

- Create a low volume car, which would necessarily be expensive
- Use that money to develop a medium volume car at a lower price
- Use that money to create an affordable, high volume car
- While doing above, also provide zero emission electric power generation options

In 2016 he continued his future story, with Master Plan "Part Deux":

- Create stunning solar roofs with seamlessly integrated battery storage
- Expand the electric vehicle product line to address all major segments
- Develop a self-driving capability that is 10 times safer than manual
- Enable your car to make money for you when you aren't using it

Musk can appear quite humble, quite nervous, when he speaks in public, but his bold ideas portray a great confidence.

When he first talked about the Hyperloop, he explained the concept relative to what we already knew, the magnetic levitating Bullet trains that speed between Tokyo and Osaka, and then went further. Imagine if it was in a frictionless tube, at 750 mph, taking 12 minutes from downtown San Francisco to Los Angeles. And then he showed us the video simulation. It almost felt real. We believed in the possibility, and how it would be better.

Strategies are stories. Brands are stories. Business cases are stories. Project plans are stories. When people say, "tell me your story" they are rarely asking about where do you, or your company, come from; more likely they are interested in where you are going.

PIXAR AND THE HERO'S JOURNEY

"Storytelling is the greatest technology that humans have ever created," said Pixar's former chief creative officer Jon Lesseter, in my book *Creative Genius*. He said storytelling involves a deep understanding of human emotions, motivations, and psychology in order to truly move an audience.

Luckily, storytelling is something we all do naturally, starting at a very young age. But there's a difference between good storytelling and great storytelling. Great stories start with human experiences, feelings that people can relate to. They have structure and process, typically taking a character on a journey. They have moments of joy and despair, surprise and the unexpected, appealing to our deepest emotions.

They are brought to life in words and pictures, polished in a movie or told one to one. But they are also incredibly simple and focused. Pixar's former story artist, Emma Coates, defined 22 rules of storytelling that are as relevant to business and its leaders as to Buzz Lightyear and his millions of followers.

Pixar always starts with a character, one who you admire, who you want to achieve something great, typically overcoming adversity, usually making the world better in some way. Or to fill in the blanks: "Once upon a time there was ___. Every day, ___. One day ___. Because of that, ___. Because of that, ___. Until finally ___."

That "adventure" type of narrative reflects a popular structure which we can see in many stories, from *The Wizard of Oz* to *Star Wars*. The Hero's Journey concept comes from Joseph Campbell's book *The Hero with A Thousand Faces*, which tells how the character, the hero, faces a crisis, achieves a great victory and comes home transformed. Campbell describes 17 stages in the journey, over three "acts" – departure, initiation, and return.

THE FUTURE STORY OF YOUR BUSINESS

For business, the "hero" is most typically the customer.

The future story for a business leader describes how we help the customer to overcome the challenges of today. The purpose reflects a positive cause, how good triumphs over evil, how the customer lives a better life.

Whilst stories might seem simple, they require thought. Framing is key to the initial stage, the context and way in which the challenge is presented. Equally important are some of the small details. A story is about emotions, hopes and dreams, love and friendship, fear and euphoria. It is about resonating with people.

There are many ways to tell the story. Some organisations turn to thought leadership, developing reports on the future of their industry, or maybe sending a letter to all stakeholders, like Larry Fink, CEO of BlackRock, sends each year. Elon Musk is particularly fond of visuals and videos, creating sci-fi-like movies that simulate his visions. These might evolve into the "We imagine" type of concept advertising, as Microsoft famously did, in portraying the future of work, or education, or travel. Another way is to create a manifesto, as companies such as Patagonia and Lululemon have done.

The best way to tell your story, however, is to stand up and talk. Authentically, personally and naturally. And be ready wherever you go to tell your "future story" in ways that inspire people to believe, to want to be part of that future, and to join you on the journey.

CODE 6: DELIVER MORE POSITIVE IMPACT
Redefine the meaning and metrics of success – the way in which you create and share value, deliver performance and progress, economic and social benefits.

Yancey Strickler, the Kickstarter founder, makes a passionate argument that we can, and must, redefine the measures of success if we want a stronger society than the one we have today.

He describes today's business world as one of "crumbling infrastructure, the dominance of mega companies, and the rise of offshore tax havens". He isn't opposed to money, or even wealth. "If businesses were optimised for the community or sustainability," he says, "the rich would still be rich, just not as rich," whilst the vast majority of people would be wealthier and happier.

In the global pandemic of 2020, the impact of a single-minded pursuit of profit was brought into sharp relief as the business world shut down and huge numbers of people lost jobs. The lack of healthcare provision and social safety nets plunged workers of all levels into turmoil. Similarly, hospitals lacked essential equipment because of a relentless drive for efficiency. As stock markets plunged, and trillions of dollars of value were wiped out, businesses started to realise the folly of their frugality and lack of compassion.

Business has sought to maximise financial performance for so long that it's hard to imagine another reason for companies to exist.

PROFITABILITY AND VALUE CREATION

Profits have become the predominant metric of success. Many people in business still think that market share and sales revenues are the goals, yet for some time we have seen that big is not always better. As customers and products have become less equal in their relative profitability, it is often more profitable to focus on less rather than more. Similarly, multiple channels with different efficiencies, and a drive to discounting, means that more sales don't always convert into more profits.

The notion of "value" is important. Businesses are often defined as value exchanges, creating value for customers and capturing value for the business.

Economists evaluate businesses based on the sum of future profits, adjusted for how likely these profits are to emerge. Strong brands, relationships and innovation pipelines make future profits more certain. Their sum is known as the enterprise value, reflected externally on stock markets, based on the judgement of analysts and behaviours of investors, as market value. Executives are incentivised to deliver profits. However, more thoughtful incentives will encourage their preference to sustain profits over time, often based around total shareholder return, the growth in market value plus a share of dividends.

Business leaders can decide how to design their value creation machine, in particular how to share value between all stakeholders over time.

As profits emerge each year, leaders decide how much to allocate to employees in salaries and bonuses, or as improved conditions, how much to allocate to customers through innovative products and services, or better prices, how much to allocate to investors in dividends or cash, and how much to share with society through social initiatives, or more generally through taxation. The relative allocations, and their purpose, determine how effectively the business invests for its future, to sustain the creation of value – or in other words, to grow a larger "value pie", from which everyone can enjoy a healthy share.

However, that ideology gets disrupted by greed, particularly by owners who are more interested in making a quick return, rather than seeing a sustainable long-term business.

James O'Toole, in his book *The Enlightened Capitalists,* explores the history of business leaders who have tried to combine the pursuit of profit with virtuous organisational practices – people like jeans-maker Levi Strauss and the Body Shop's Anita Roddick.

He tells the story of William Lever, the inventor of the Sunlight soap bar, who created the most profitable company in Britain, the origins of today's Unilever, and used his money to greatly improve the lives of his workers. In 1884 he bought 56 acres of land on the Wirral, near Liverpool, and built a new town for his workers, known as Port Sunlight, where workers and their families could live healthier and happier lives. Eventually, he lost control of the company to creditors, who promptly terminated the enlightened practices he had initiated. The fate of many idealistic capitalists.

FROM SHAREHOLDERS TO STAKEHOLDERS

In recent years the relationship between business and society has become increasingly fractured. Whilst there is nothing wrong with shareholders, and nothing wrong with profit, the culture of capitalism seemed increasingly out of sync with the world. A series of economic, social and environmental crises made it all the more obvious.

Of course, most businesses have woken up to the importance of sustainable issues, and their responsibilities to society over recent years, but they have largely seen them as a new component of capitalism.

Ten years ago, I wrote the book *People Planet Profit: How to embrace sustainability for innovation and growth*, which sold many copies, but little seemed to change. Yes, we got the sustainability report as an appendix to the annual report, the foundation that operates at arm's length from the core business, and a host of initiatives to reduce emissions and waste. At the same time, social enterprises emerged – indeed, I was a CEO of a $50 million non-profit business myself – but such organisations were still seen as a different breed from commercial businesses. Core business didn't change.

And then three things happened.

- In January 2018, BlackRock's Larry Fink wrote a letter to the CEOs of all the companies who he invests in, saying that he would not continue unless they could demonstrate that they were delivering on a significant "purpose before profit". BlackRock is the world's largest investment firm, a $6 trillion asset manager. This was seismic.

- In August 2019, The Business Roundtable, the most influential group of US business leaders, said they would formally embrace stakeholder capitalism, built on "a broader, more complete view of corporate purpose, boards can focus on creating long-term value, better serving everyone – investors, employees, communities, suppliers and customers."
- In January 2020, the World Economic Forum (WEF) launched the Davos Manifesto for "a better kind of capitalism", saying "the purpose of a company is to engage all its stakeholders in shared and sustained value creation" with "a shared commitment to policies and decisions that strengthen the long-term prosperity of a company."

Klaus Schwab, founder of WEF, called it "the funeral of shareholder capitalism", but also as the bold and brave birth of stakeholder capitalism.

Marc Benioff of Salesforce added that "Capitalism as we know it is dead. This obsession with the pursuit of profits just for shareholders does not work". IBM's Gina Rometty said that there are now two types of business – "good and bad".

Jim Snabe of Maersk said, "companies need to start making the change right now, to the way they work, the resources they use, the taxes they pay, and the decisions they make."

SMARTER CHOICES, POSITIVE IMPACT

The ideology sounds compelling. The challenge is to ensure that it changes how businesses work, the choices we make, and the impacts we have.

"Smarter choices" is the first challenge. A key role for the business leader is to make decisions, yet this has become much harder in a complex world of many trade-offs. Strategy is also about choices, the directions and priorities for the business, short- and long-term.

"Smart" lies in the ability to align the business purpose with all its stakeholders, and to find an effective way in which together they can sustain enlightened value creation.

"Positive impact" is the second challenge. Long have we heard the mantra "what gets measured gets done". Therefore, leaders need to underpin their stakeholder ideology with a new set of performance metrics, which drive behaviours, define progress, and rewards.

"Positive" lies in the ability for the business to create a net positive contribution to the world in which it exists, some of which will be financial, but also non-financial.

Stakeholder capitalism needs a set of metrics for sustainable value creation.

To seek a coherent model for this across the business and investment communities, the WEF brought 140 of the world's largest companies together, supported by the four largest accounting firms – Deloitte, EY, KPMG and PwC.

Their starting point was to align the existing approaches to measuring Environmental, Social, and Governance (ESG) performance and the Sustainable Development Goals (SDGs). They agreed to seek common metrics for greenhouse gas emissions and strategies, diversity, employee health and wellbeing as factors to publish in annual reports alongside financial metrics.

The proposed metrics and recommended disclosures have been organised into four pillars that are aligned with the SDGs and ESG domains. They are:

- Principles of Governance, aligned with SDGs 12, 16 and 17, and focusing on a company's commitment to ethics and societal benefit
- Planet, aligned with SDGs 6, 7, 12, 13, 14 and 15, and focusing on climate sustainability and environmental responsibility

- People, aligned with SDGs 1, 3, 4, 5 and 10, and focusing on the roles human and social capital play in business
- Prosperity, aligned with SDGs 1, 8, 9 and 10, and focusing on business contributions to equitable, innovative growth

There is some way to go in getting close to "integrated reporting" – in particular, connecting financial and non-financial metrics which enable the more difficult trade-off decisions – and understanding the genuine long-term health of an organisation.

One approach, developed by BCG (Boston Consulting Group), is Total Societal Impact (TSI), which is a defined basket of financial metrics and non-financial assessments brought together as one overall score. This enables leaders to consider the relative overall impact of different strategic options.

The challenge, of course, is that any private company's total value will always be financial, as long as it is possible for a buyer to come along and pay a certain price for it.

CODE 7: BE THE RADICAL OPTIMIST
Be the catalyst of change – the leader who others want to follow on a journey into the future – be imaginative, be inspiring, and believe in better.

"The world will never be slower than it is right now. To thrive, everyone has to make change," says Beth Comstock in her book *Imagine It Forward*. The former GE executive believes that every business leader needs the courage to defy convention, the resilience to overcome failure and the creativity to reinvent what is possible.

Comstock says "What holds all of us back, really is the attachment to the old, to what we know. We need more people with imagination and the courage willing to take risks and fight for the future."

Change might rage across our markets, across society, across our environment. But business change starts with you, as a business leader. It starts by giving yourself permission to look forwards, to believe in more than today and unleash your curiosity to discover what's next. It demands that you imagine a future others can't yet see, then have the courage to make it happen.

BELIEVE IN BETTER

Hans Rosling, the late great Swedish doctor who mesmerised people with his TED Talks, used fast and simple statistical analysis to explain our changing world. His message was that "the world is better than you think", and that we constantly underestimate how much progress has been made.

He also challenged some of our biases, engrained in our language, such as the descriptions of the "developed" and "developing" world. Such terminology is outdated when most of the world's growth comes from the so-called emerging markets, whilst mature markets are largely stagnant. If we look at where ideas come from, where the most rapid progress in science and technology is happening, then it is increasingly in the east not the west.

Indeed, the world is getting better every day, according to the Cato Institute's Johan Norberg. Whilst economic uncertainty, climate crisis, political extremism, and health pandemics might occupy your mind, data shows the past decade has been a story of human flourishing and progress.

Here are eight facts about human progress in the decade from 2010 to 2019, that give us reason to be optimistic about the journey ahead:

- 28% of all the wealth mankind has ever created, measured as GDP per capita, was created in the last 10 years, according to the World Bank.

- Life expectancy increased from 69.5 to 72.6 years, which means that every day over the last decade, our average lifespan increased by almost 8 hours, says the UN.
- Extreme poverty, defined as living on less than $1.90 per day, has halved in the last decade, from 18.2 to 8.6%, equivalent to 158 000 fewer poor people per day.
- Child mortality has reduced by a third, as education and healthcare standards improve in developing countries, with 2.1 million children's deaths prevented each year.
- Democracy might seem fragile but is growing. The share of people living in "not free" countries has declined from 34 to 26%, according to Freedom House.
- Countries in which the law actively seeks to protect women from violent partners have increased from 53 to 78%, says the World Bank.
- Despite global warming, extreme weather and uncontrollable wildfires, deaths from climate-related disasters have declined by a third, to 0.35 per 100,000 people.
- Many rich countries have reached "peak stuff", according to a US Geological Survey, which shows that consumption of 66 out of 72 tracked resources is declining.

Indeed, we live in an incredible time, with more change likely in the next 10 years than in the last 250 years. Change brings emotional challenges, but it also delivers opportunities like never before. The capabilities of technology, together with the creativity of people, allow us to imagine futures beyond our wildest dreams, and make them real.

BE CURIOUS AND OPTIMISTIC

The world moves forwards through curiosity. Most of society's major breakthroughs, from penicillin to self-driving cars, are the results of an impulse to ask new questions, to see new possibilities, to try new ideas.

Our curiosity drives us to think more deeply, both logically, to understand why things happen, and creatively, to solve problems and find new applications. Asking questions, rather than just seeking answers, allows us to keep exploring, to keep our minds open, rather than be satisfied with what we know.

Francesca Gina, a Harvard behavioural scientist, says that curiosity leads to better decision-making, because it helps us to avoid confirmation bias (seeking to confirm our existing beliefs, that might be wrong) and stereotyping people (because we are more interested, and make fewer broad, sweeping judgements). Curiosity also helps us to collaborate and communicate better through better listening, and be more creative and innovative as we look for new insights and inspirations.

Curiosity is best enhanced by being more interested in your world, and the worlds around you. This might mean spending more time with customers, understanding their broader worlds beyond their needs for your own products and services. Sharing insights with peers from other sectors, particularly those with similar challenges, can be mutually inspiring. As a team, seek to hire people who are different, who bring new experiences and perspectives, encourage people to explore more diverse interests, and keep asking open questions – "Why?", "What if?", and "How could we?".

Optimism, on the other hand, is a more innate quality. You choose to be optimistic, in terms of how you see the world, and respond to it. Optimism is infectious, so can be a powerful quality in leaders, although pessimism can be equally contagious.

Psychologist Martin Seligman believes that the most successful business leaders are inspired by a sense of optimism. Those who see life and work through a positive lens are far more likely to be successful, he suggests. Being optimistic does not mean ignoring the facts or the challenges required to make progress, but it does avoid getting lost in all the reasons not to progress, and a spiral of negativity.

An optimistic leader starts from a position of possibility, and then finds ways to overcome the most significant obstacles.

They communicate a positive vision with energy and inspiration. They relate better to people, championing benefits over constraints, rewards over risks, and they have a resilience to persist over time, to reach a better place.

One of the most optimistic people I have ever met is Virgin's founder, Richard Branson. In his organisation, he is better known as Dr Yes, for his insatiable positive attitude to new ideas. He chose "Screw it, let's do it" as the title of his autobiography, one of his favourite phrases. When I interviewed him, I asked him where he found his drive. He replied, "The brave may not live forever, but the cautious do not live at all."

BE THE CHANGE

Johan Berger, in his book *"The Catalyst: How to change anyone's mind"* says that successful change agents know that change is not about pushing harder, or providing more information, but about being a catalyst. Catalysts remove roadblocks and reduce the barriers to change. Instead of asking, "How could I change someone's mind?" they ask, "What's stopping them?"

Mahatma Gandhi, throughout his life in South Africa and India, was a fearless campaigner for the rights and dignity of people. His unwavering promotion of non-violence as a tool to win hearts and minds has forever left its mark on the world. He, of course, said "be the change you want to see in the world".

Maybe that is the point. It is not about changing others, which is never easy. It is more about changing yourself. That is within your reach. By changing yourself, it is much more likely that others will follow, and inspired by your leadership, your belief and optimism, they are more likely to want to change themselves too.

Gandhi went on to say, "If we could change ourselves, the tendencies in the world would also change. As a man changes his own nature, so does the attitude of the world change towards him. We need not wait to see what others do."

Which brings us to business leaders who seek to change their worlds. It doesn't take superheroes, it takes genuine, authentic people with a belief and passion to do better. It's about leaders stepping up in a world of incredible change, a world that sometimes feels like it is on fire, but also a world of opportunity.

The world is waiting for ordinary people to do extraordinary things.

SUMMARY: HOW WILL YOU RECODE YOUR FUTURE?

5 questions to reflect on:

- Look forwards not back … What's your future potential?
- Be farsighted … How much time do you spend on shaping the future?
- Find your inspiring purpose … Why does your business exist?
- Have a better vision … What's your future story?
- Creating positive impact … How do you measure success?

5 leaders to inspire you (more at businessrecoded.com):

- Anne Wojcicki, 23andMe … creating a personal and predictive future of healthcare
- Elon Musk, SpaceX … transforming future visions into audacious realities
- Patrick Brown, Impossible Foods … creating plant-based food that tastes better
- Larry Fink, BlackRock … the investor demanding that purpose drives profits
- Yves Chouinard, Patagonia … from passionate climber to B Corporation activist

5 books to go deeper:

- *Hit Refresh* by Satya Nadella
- *Find your Why* by Simon Sinek
- *Trailblazer* by Marc Benioff
- *Reimagining Capitalism* by Rebecca Henderson
- *Catalyst* by Jonah Berger

5 places to explore further

- Futurism
- Institute for the Future
- Future Timeline
- B Corporation
- World Economic Forum

KOMOREBI

Recode your growth

WHERE ARE THE BEST OPPORTUNITIES TO GROW FURTHER AND FASTER?

From uncertain survival to futuristic growth

The Japanese term komorebi *has no translation into English but describes the effect of sunlight streaming through the leaves of the trees. Looking up at the midday sun can be blinding, yet from other perspectives the effect becomes beautiful and inspiring.*

Consider some of the innovations reshaping markets:

- In Shanghai, Chinese police wear augmented reality glasses, with AI-enabled facial recognition software, able to identify every citizen and their social credits.
- On Wall Street, AI-based Fusemachine software is helping Citibank investors to make better investments, minimising risks and maximising returns.
- At DeBeers' head office in Johannesburg, Tracr is a new blockchain-based system that tracks the life of diamonds, ensuring their authenticity and ethical practices.
- In London, MedicalChain uses blockchain to create and maintain a single version of medical records for every patient, enabling better care from any doctor.
- In Indonesia, homeless charity New Story is working with Icon to create thousands of new homes after natural disasters, each being 3D-printed in 24 hours for $4000.
- In San Diego, Organovo 3D-prints human tissue. Currently synthetic skin is the bestseller; however, 3D-printed hearts and other organs could soon transform life.
- At the University of South Denmark in Odense, a unique running track with hills and spirals is used to test robotic exoskeletons for Paralympians and extreme jobs.
- In Seattle, Amazon's warehouses are dominated by 10 000 Kiva robot platforms carrying purchases from stockroom to delivery points faster than humans can run.

Where are your best opportunities?

CODE 8: RIDE WITH THE MEGATRENDS
What will shape your future? How will you ride the waves of change, be farsighted to turn disruption and discontinuities into innovation and impact?

Some of the best ocean surf in the world lies just along the coast from Lisbon in Portugal. The beautiful fishing village of Cascais seems a world away from the dramatic waves, and extreme surfers who seek to catch the ultimate ride.

Sitting in one of the many fish restaurants, calamari then seabass, a glass of *vinho verde*, I look up to the imposing citadel which towers above the small harbour. It has probably seen much change since its construction, a few years before Christopher Columbus passed by on his way to seek new lands. Yet it has remained largely unchanged.

In a similar way, we rarely have time to pause and look at the bigger picture of our changing world, the tectonic shifts that are likely to transform our world in the coming years. Threat or opportunity, we ignore them at our peril.

Surfing the waves of a changing world enables us to keep pace with change, to see the opportunities ahead, and to prepare to embrace them.

Megatrends, a term first used by John Naisbitt in 1982, are the huge changes – social, economic, political, environmental or

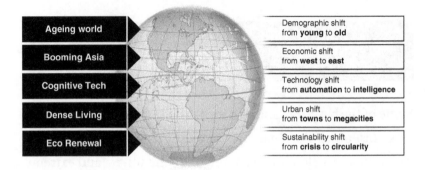

FIGURE 2.1 The five megatrends shaping your potential future.

technological – that are slow to form, but once in place can influence a wide range of activities, processes and perceptions, possibly for decades.

They are the underlying forces that drive change in global markets, and our everyday lives. Whilst it might feel like technology is the primary megatrend, with new science and devices grabbing headlines, it is the broader implications of it that create most change. McKinsey analysis shows that riding the right waves of change, created by industry and geographic trends, is the most important contributor to business results. It says that a company benefiting from such tailwinds is 4–8 times more likely to rise to the top of future performers.

Five megatrends – the "ABCDE" of our future – are shaping our potential futures right now, shifting the way we will live and work:

1. **Aging World** ... *the demographic shift from young to old*

   Social changes are primarily driven by people living longer, healthier lives throughout the world, as healthcare, education and lifestyles improve.

2. **Booming Asia** ... *the economic shift from west to east*

   Consumer affluence is rising, particularly across Asia. So-called emerging markets will represent 6 of the 7 largest economies by 2050.

3. **Cognitive Tech** ... *the technological shift from automation to intelligence*

   Technological breakthroughs unlock new possibilities, and exponential progress – 125 billion connected devices by 2030.

4. **Dense Living** ... *the sociological shift from towns to megacities*

   Rapid urbanisation. 65% of the world will be concentrated in urban environments by 2050, today in the megacities of Asia, tomorrow in even larger cities of Africa.

5. **Eco renewal** ... *the environmental shift from crisis to circularity*

   50% of the world's energy will be sustainable by 2050, as we seek ways to combat climate change, and also the stress on natural resources.

50 years ago, in his book *Future Shock*, Alvin Toffler identified the watershed of a new post-industrial age, pinpointing the enormous structural change afoot in the global economy, and the acceleration of technological advances towards a "super-industrial society" in an information era. Now we see much of what he predicted has come true. In much less time, 10 or 20 years, we will see the true impact of these new megatrends.

Using a range of data sources, including United Nations (UN) and Organisation for Economic Co-operation and Development (OECD), and most usefully Max Roser's fantastic website, OurWorldinData.org, we explore these five trends and their implications for business:

Megatrend 1: Aging World ... *the demographic shift from young to old*

Socio-demographic changes, particularly the aging of populations throughout the world, will have a huge impact on every nation:

- **Asian boom.** The global population will likely increase to 8.5 billion by 2030, from 7.2 billion in 2020 – made up of 5bn Asians, 1.5bn Africans, 750m Europeans and Latin Americans, 400m North Americans, and 50m in Oceania.
- **Declining youth.** Birth rates are declining, particularly in wealthy nations, resulting in fewer young people, and 90%

of the world's population under 30 now living in emerging markets.

- **Living longer.** Most profound is a likely 45% increase in the world's over-60s population by 2030, with 80% of them living in Asia by 2050 (Asia's over-60s already outnumber the entire US population).
- **Global citizens.** 4% of the world's population are migrants, not living in the country of their birth. Some individual countries are much higher – UAE 85% due to migrant workers, but also Australia 29%, Canada 22%, and US 14%.

The implications for support include:

- **Healthcare.** As populations age, demand for healthcare and home support will grow rapidly. US healthcare spending is set to rise by 8% of GDP each year over the next two decades, around $3.4 trillion every year.
- **Pensions.** A $400 trillion gap in retirement funding will likely emerge by 2050, as pension funds prove insufficient, people live longer than expected, and need more support. Young people will need to meet this shortfall and be less well off.
- **Robo workforce.** As people of working age decline, we will turn to automation to do more, machines and robotics becoming a necessary rather than unwelcome substitution within the workforce, taking manual jobs, as humans add more value.
- **Consumption.** Age and health will significantly shape markets from travel and entertainment, to food and

fashion. In terms of food, we will demand products that are fresh and organic, functional and medical, convenient and delivered.

Megatrend 2: Booming Asia ... *the economic shift from west to east*

From west to east ... population growth drives a significant global shift in economic power, and the rise of a huge new middle class of consumers:

- **Made in Asia for Asia.** "Emerging" economies have shifted from being producers for developed countries, to becoming the primary consumers of the world. They now account for 80% of the world's growth, and 85% of growth in consumption

- **Chinese superpower.** 15 years ago, China's economy was 10% of the US economy, but will surpass it by the late 2020s. China expects to have 200 cities with over a million people by 2025.

- **ASEAN tigers.** South East Asia's growth will outpace China, in particular Vietnam and Thailand. India has the world's 10 fastest growing cities. Delhi will soon displace Tokyo as the world's largest city, whilst the port of Surat grows fastest.

- **New consumers.** Asia's new middle class has boomed in recent times and will represent 66% of the world's 5.3

billion mid-income consumers by 2030. 70% of Chinese will be in this group, a $10 trillion consumer market.

The implications for markets include:

- China's economic power will be consolidated in coming years, despite being driven by high debt levels and property market valuations. China has also grown astute in developing "soft power" using culture and business for global influence.

- Chinese business growth is relentless, with over 100 unicorns and over 7500 new companies registered per year, and more patent registrations than any other nation. Its support to start-ups help them survive infancy and accelerate scale-up.

- Intra-Asian markets will dominate the global economy. 15 of the world's 20 largest air travel routes are within Asia, led by KUL–SIN with over 30 000 travellers per year (compared to LHR–JFK with half as many, the 13th largest).

- The E7 (as Goldman Sachs termed the emerging economies of China, India, Brazil, Mexico, Russia, Indonesia and Turkey) will be larger than the G7 by 2030 and double their size by 2050 (E7 already outperforms G7 on purchasing power parity).

Megatrend 3: Cognitive Tech ... *the technological shift from automation to intelligence*

The "fourth industrial revolution" sees a shift to connected and intelligent technologies that underpin every other trend:

- **Exponential change.** This will occur as digital platforms connect markets, IOT connects everything and network effects multiply the impacts, robotics displace manual workers, and artificial intelligence outthinks our minds.
- **Liquid media.** The concept of digital v physical is rapidly evolving into a fused state, in which every experience is both real and technically enhanced. Augmented reality and holographic 3D displays accelerate this, as does gaming and movies.
- **Data is the new oil.** 90% of the world's data was connected in the last 2 years, with 1 trillion connected objects by 2025, over 90% of stock trading is now done by algorithm, and around 66% of the world's population is online at any one time.
- **Intelligent life.** 60% of all occupations could see at least 30% of their component activities automated. Robotics and AI can enhance are human capabilities, free us from repetitive tasks, enhance sporting prowess, and release our creativity.

The implications of fast tech progress include:

- **Ideas unlimited.** The speed of technological advancement accelerates beyond the shifting behaviours of consumers, or the needs of business. The creative challenge is not the technology development, but how to apply it most usefully.

- **Beyond the singularity.** Ray Kurzweil describes a hypothetical future point, around 2045, when intelligent machines are no longer controllable by humans. Elon Musk shares his fear and is a critic of Alphabet's DeepMind.
- **Sustainable tech.** Many of today's environmental challenges will ultimately be addressed by technology, through new approaches to additive manufacturing and renewal, or the capture of carbon and conversion of waste.
- **Ethics and security.** The growing intelligence of machines pose many ethical dilemmas for business and society. Security and privacy issues will only be addressed by considering new approaches to authenticity and regulation.

Megatrend 4: Dense Living ... *the sociological shift from towns to megacities*

More than half of the world's population now lives in towns and cities, and by 2030 this number will grow to about 5 billion, mostly in Asia and Africa:

- **Megacities of 10 million.** In 1990 there were only 10 such cities, by 2025 there will be 45, with 33 of them in Asia. Many large cities are building secondary overflow cities, like Xiongan New Area, which is 100 km from Beijing.
- **Migration to cities.** Globally, more people live in urban than rural areas. In 1950, 30% of the world lived in cities, today it is 55%, growing to 66% by 2050. Cities disproportionately attract young people in search of work and prosperity.

- **Life is better in the cities.** Cities typically have better services, schools and hospitals, and better access to sports and culture. People are healthier, better educated and wealthier. In China, urban income per capita is triple that in rural areas.
- **Smart cities.** Cities are first to adopt new technological infrastructures, from free connectivity to driverless cars, intelligent homes and renewable energy. The "smart city" market will triple in 10 years to $1.2 trillion by 2030.

The implications of this urbanisation are:

- Cities are driven by modern urban populations that demand advanced infrastructures, and quickly embrace technology and innovation. New cities are able to build from plan, whilst older cities have to adapt legacy structures.
- Health and safety will drive new levels of surveillance, as authorities seek to overcome crime and improve traffic flows, sanitation, and emergency response. Alibaba's "CityBrain", for example, is deployed in many Chinese cities.
- Consumer aspirations change, as traditional symbols of progress, like a car or larger house, are infeasible. Instead new priorities emerge, such as fashion and entertainment, product miniaturisation and personalisation of services.
- Virtual communities replace the more traditional forms based on location and neighbours. Resources become

increasingly shared, from energy suppliers to mobility solutions. Virtual, group behaviour dominates in new ways.

Megatrend 5: Eco renewal ... *the environmental shift from crisis to circularity*

The impact of climate change is all around us – rising temperatures and sea levels, forest fires and food prices:

- **Population strain.** Growing numbers of people drive huge demand for energy, water and food, testing the planet's finite resources. The population of 2030 will demand 35% more food, 40% more water, and 50% more energy.
- **Carbon emissions.** Greenhouse gases, primarily carbon dioxide from fossil fuels, will drive warming above 2 degrees by 2036 at current rates. That could cause sea levels to rise by 2 m by 2100, flooding the homes of 250 million people.
- **Extreme weather.** Global warming drives more unpredictable and extreme weather, hot summers driving desertification and loss of agricultural land, storms threatening cities. Extreme weather caused $148 billion damage in 2018.
- **Industrial strain.** Food production has depleted the land and oceans of natural stocks, damaged ecology and reduced biodiversity. Technological products have stripped the earth of precious metals, and oil is increasingly a limited resource.

The implications of these environmental impacts are:

- **More from less.** Meeting the population's demands requires innovation to improve production with less resource. Detecting weeds with sensors and spot sprays could reduce herbicide usage by up to 95%.
- **From oil to renewables.** Converting to sustainable energy, particularly solar and wind, will accelerate as battery storage develops rapidly. Government policies and taxation will be key drivers of business, alongside consumer demand.
- **Electric travel.** The shift to non-carbon fuels in road vehicles will accelerate rapidly, seeing carbon-fuelled vehicles eliminated by 2040. The same shift is now required in all modes of transport. (Road drives 70% of emission, air and sea 14% each).
- **Consumer demand.** 66% of consumers would pay more for environmental-friendly products, rising to 73% for millennials. This will be the biggest driver of businesses adopting more sustainable and circular economic models.

CODE 9: FIND NEW SOURCES OF GROWTH
Markets are incredibly diverse and dynamic, offering many more opportunities beyond the boxes and boundaries by which we currently limit our growth ambitions.

In the summer of 2019, fires ravaged the Amazon rainforests, causing alarm around the world. For Brazil's João Paulo Ferreira, CEO of Natura, one of the world's largest cosmetics companies, with a passion for sustainability, it was a disaster. Natura is committed to working with 35 local communities in the Amazon region, including more than 4300 families, to help develop products and sustainable business models that benefit the forest and its inhabitants.

Natura is also seeking to accelerate its growth, looking for new ways to grow across the world, helped by the acquisition of brands such as Australia's Aesop luxury cosmetics, the UK's Body Shop, and Avon, the network-marketing business with 6 million representatives across the world.

Ferreira's growth model seeks to bring together three important shifts in the market – the consumer's demand for more sustainable products, the drive for accessible luxury, particularly in the wellness sector, and the shift to peer-to-peer communities and business models. On top of this, his notion of growth is not simply the sales revenue, but the increasing positive impact for all its stakeholders, including his Amazonian partners, who desperately need his help to recover their livelihoods.

FINDING THE FUTURE FIRST

William Gibson, the sci-fi author, said, "the future is here – it's just not very evenly distributed." Much of what will create the future, therefore, is already in front of our eyes. Our challenge is to make sense of it, to see how it fits together, to imagine how it can be more.

Newness occurs in the margins not the mainstream. We need to look to the outliers, the early adopters and extreme users, for emergent behaviour in markets. We need to look to the smaller, specialist innovators for the new solutions. Finding newness is less about waiting for a completely new technology, such as quantum computing, more about connecting the dots of what is already here, then using imaginative fusions to understand how they will be shaped into a new reality for many.

As new ideas gradually catch on, they begin to spread more rapidly, a bit like how ice melts from the edges almost imperceptibly slowly, but then much more perceptibly faster. Sometimes these ideas can seem cool to the geeks, but then get shunned by the mainstream, because they are not practical or desired. Geoffrey Moore calls this "the chasm", which new ideas need to leap to reach most people.

How can you see the megatrends, and how they will affect your business and customers, before they arrive?

Seeing around Corners by Rita McGrath focuses on the inflection points in our changing markets. If we think of market evolution as a series of s-curves, then a market takes off slowly, but then accelerates where it inflects. Malcolm Gladwell termed it the tipping point. The inflection is typically caused by external factors, such as new capabilities or attitudes, or economic or regulatory change.

The challenge is to be ready for these inflections. Indeed, much of future thinking is less about predicting with any certainty, but about being prepared for uncertainty. We can search for clues that an inflection is close or upon us. We can look to adjacent markets for parallel behaviours. Food trends tend to lead drinks trends, sportswear trends lead couture, gaming leads entertainment.

McGrath observes that inflection points don't happen instantly. They take a long time. The original title for her book was taken from Ernest Hemingway's novel *"The Sun Also Rises"*. One of the characters asks another: "Well, how did you go bankrupt?" And the response was: "Oh well, gradually and then suddenly." Which is how inflection points feel. When they are upon you, they feel as though they've emerged from nowhere and they're just disruptive and difficult. But if you really look at the roots of them, they've been coming on for a really long time.

Nike's shift to direct-to-consumer (DTC) channels has been evolving for some time, but now it has become the norm. Perhaps by watching start-ups who have created direct relationships with consumers, like Casper mattresses or Harry's shaving products, Nike gained the confidence to switch away from traditional channels and create a better shopping experience of their own, both in their flagship stores and online. By using the consumer relationships built up through Nike+ fitness trackers and membership, the brand can have a one-to-one dialogue, offer personal incentives, and a truly individualised experience directly with consumers. Competitors don't get a look-in. Nike acquired new capabilities such as data analytics company Zodiac to support it, and Invertex to create Nike Fit whose 3D remote scanning of shoes enables consumers to ensure they get the perfect fit. $16bn of sales flowed through Nike's DTC channels in 2019.

However, too many leaders resist change. Too many leaders have grown to love their status quo. Stability brings more certainty and efficiency. Constant change requires more effort and turbulence. Carefully made plans need to be written, production lines adapted, new products and packaging developed, new talents recruited and partners forged, new ads created.

As McGrath says, "Leaders turn a blind eye quite deliberately because it is just more convenient not to take in news that things might be changing."

SEEING THINGS DIFFERENTLY

Airlines are one of the worst industries to work in. Every time an economic downturn comes around, their businesses are hit worse than most. I remember working for British Airways through economic downturns. Within days, bookings would have evaporated, and planes would be grounded. The problem was that they saw themselves as an operator of aircraft, and little more.

An alternative frame of thinking would be that they are in the business of connecting people. For travellers on vacation, they help them to explore the world, to meet up with family and friends. For business travellers, they are in the business of facilitating trade, finding new partners, reaching new markets, doing new deals. If they framed their business around the customer, and what they seek to achieve, there could be many alternative options to sustain their business, even in a downturn.

Similarly, Adrian Slywotzky, author of *How to Grow When Markets Don't*, says that too many companies over the last decade have stagnated because they have forgotten how to grow. Whilst their businesses grew rapidly in their entrepreneurial years, they then become fixated on their existing products and services, framing themselves in these ways, and thereby in markets which have matured and stagnated. He says that most companies have relied on traditional "product-centred" strategies for growth.

"Reframing" therefore becomes an incredibly powerful way in which to see your opportunities differently. By redefining the boundaries of what market you are in, you immediately escape the limitations of the old thinking, you jump to uncontested spaces which are no longer fought over by the same competitors, and you potentially engage customers in new, more inspiring and valuable ways.

CVS famously reframed their pharmacy business into a health business. Whilst a pharmacy is seen as a slightly negative place, a store to go to when you are sick, in search of a specific product transaction, health is a more positive idea, where you might go more often for a wider range of wellness-based products and services, and even pay more. In other cases, you might even find that you see a significant change in stock prices, as analysts apply different P/E (price-to-earnings) ratios, for example in shifting from a communications to media business.

Whilst one way is to reframe your market, another is to understand what else is inside your business that could add value to customers and differentiate your proposition.

Chris Zook worked with Slywotzky on another book, *Unstoppable*, which encourages companies to understand what their hidden assets are and find ways to leverage them to generate new opportunities for profitable growth. Hidden assets include undervalued business platforms, unexploited customer assets, or underused capabilities.

THE 12 SOURCES OF GROWTH

Growth remains the overarching pursuit of a business, even when it embraces a more socially engaged economic model where value is shared more equally between all stakeholders. Growth creates a bigger pie which can be shared amongst everyone, and that growth can be driven in a way that is efficient and has more positive impact as it is created, not just as a result. Positive growth, if you like.

You could argue that Igor Ansoff still has the answer to growth. His "product/market expansion grid" from the 1950s explores the opportunities and risks of growth – a simple 2x2 matrix that explores new and existing markets, and new and existing products and services. The limitation of course, is that it encourages thinking based around products and the existing frames of markets.

Finding growth is an increasingly creative and multi-dimensional process that combines the ideas of searching for new opportunities based around changing attitudes and behaviours, new capabilities and aspirations, and creative ways to frame, connect and define them. This gives us at least 12 sources to explore:

- **New audiences** ... reaching new customer segments, or those which have not been explicitly addressed in the past, through the same or adapted products and propositions. Example: Nivea's skincare for men.
- **New propositions** ... exploring the new or different needs and aspirations of customers, or new price points, such as line extensions, or a low-end or luxury version. Example: Mini, Mini Cooper, Mini Clubman, Mini Countryman.
- **New channels** ... reaching underserved or inaccessible audiences, either with direct channels, or through new types of intermediaries. Example: Bolthouse Farms selling carrots as snacks through vending machines.
- **New geographies** ... taking the existing business to new geographies – new locations, cities, nations – in the same or adapted forms. Example: Hershey's have five different chocolate formulae for different parts of the world.
- **New products** ... this is largely driven by new capabilities, that are embraced to better meet new and existing needs and aspirations, new varieties and formats, and new applications. Example: Innocent's smoothies, juices, snacks, water.
- **New services** ... adding chargeable services, such as support to enhance the use of the product, or shifting from

products to charging for access, like SaaS, software as a service. Example: Eataly's cookery classes, Beyond stores and restaurants.

- **New experiences** ... combining products and services of your own, and potentially partners, into a richer added-value experience for customers. Example: Airbnb Trips, adding flights, car rental and activities to accommodation.

- **New categories** ... creating new market spaces that emerge from new needs, or fusions of existing needs, with distinctive products and services to address them. Example: Red Bull's energy drinks.

- **New partners** ... collaborating with partners who enhance the offer, from affinity brands to competitors and complementors. Example: Clothing brand Supreme partnering with Louis Vuitton to enhance brand reputation.

- **New business models** ... developing new operational or commercial models for businesses – subscriptions, freemium, one for one, and more. Example: Microsoft 365 cloud-based subscription.

- **New acquisitions** ... enhancing your portfolio, your capabilities or reach by acquiring new businesses that complement your existing ones. Example: Facebook acquiring Instagram to reach people more actively and intimately.

- **New possibilities** ... developing entirely new markets based around novel capabilities and solutions which have no precedence. Example: Virgin Galactic developing its space tourism business.

Growth of course is easy if only measured by sales – any fool can discount a product. The challenge is to find sustainable, profitable growth. This list is not exhaustive, nor are the approaches mutually exclusive. Many growth initiatives will use a combination of these approaches, and will focus as much on accelerating existing sources, as finding new ones. Growth accelerators range from new brands and propositions to exploiting network effects, such as social media and distribution platforms, that multiply reach.

CODE 10: EMBRACE THE ASIAN CENTURY
The 21st century belongs to Asia. As economic power shifts from west to east, from nations to cities, and to a new middle class, so political and cultural power shifts too.

Some years ago, my Chinese father-in-law, who had grown up in the countryside north of Hong Kong, just over the border in mainland China, went back to the village of his birth. I remember him telling me stories of a simple life, playing in the rice fields, and faded photographs of him riding water buffalo as a young boy.

Having moved to Europe he wanted to retain some presence in the small place. He bought some land and built a small block of apartments which he hoped might grow in value, as a form of pension for him and his family.

Over the past 30 years, the fishing village of Shenzhen has been reborn as a futuristic metropolis bursting with factories. It is the heartland of China's tech revolution, dubbed the Silicon Valley of hardware.

In 1979, the Chinese government turned it into an experiment to grow capitalism in a test tube, designating it as the country's first Special Economic Zone. The city is driven by an influx of workers from the countryside. Huawei was founded in Shenzhen in 1987 by Ren Zhengfei and is now the world's second largest smartphone manufacturer after Samsung. The city is also home to Tencent, the huge digital platform, to the world's largest electric car business BYD, and to the world's leading drone maker DJI.

Shenzhen and the surrounding Pearl River Delta is now known as the world's factory floor.

It is now a megacity of over 12 million people. It has also become an incubator for cutting-edge design, a city of futuristic urbanisation, and a symbol of China's economic progress. The Chinese government is using Shenzhen as a showcase for its move from "Made in China" to "Designed in China", to rebrand the country as a place that can invent, not just copy and mass-produce.

INCREDIBLE ASIA

While the 19th century belonged to Europe, and the 20th century to America, the 21st century is Asian – 5 billion people, two thirds of the world's megacities, one third of the global economy, two thirds of global economic growth, 30 of the Fortune 100, six of the ten largest banks, eight of the ten largest armies, five nuclear powers, massive technological innovation, the newest crop of top-ranked universities.

Asia is also the world's most ethnically, linguistically and culturally diverse region of the planet, eluding any remotely meaningful generalization beyond the geographic label itself. Even for Asians, Asia is dizzying to navigate.

China is the world's second largest economy, a huge new and growing consumer market, and home to many of the world's fastest growing companies: Alibaba to Baidu, BYD and Bytedance, China Mobile to Didi Chuxing, Haier to Huawei, SAIC to Tencent, Dalian Wanda and Xiaomi. China has shifted from imitator to innovator, fundamentally driving new technologies, new applications, and the new agenda for business.

And while China's growth is huge and sustained, many other Asian countries will grow even faster through the next decade: India, Bangladesh, Vietnam, Malaysia and the Philippines. Collectively these are known as the 7% club. Indeed, we could add another list of great non-Chinese Asian companies like DBS and Grab in Singapore, Samsung and LG in South Korea, Uniqlo and Softbank in Japan, Reliance and Tata in India.

As the new superpower of China spars with the fading power of the US, it is the "Eurasian" market axis, connecting Europe and Asia that is set to grow most significantly. Portuguese political scientist Bruno Maçães argues in his book *The Dawn of Eurasia* that the distinction between Europe and Asia has disappeared, that China's new "Silk Road" projects are more important than the G20, and that Europe is missing out on this new opportunity.

Asia is home to the world's fastest growing markets, and it is also where many of the best new ideas for business come from – both what to do, and how to work – applicable to every business leader anywhere. Western business leaders seeking new inspiration should perhaps look east rather than west, as they did centuries ago.

How to embrace the new technologies like AI and robotics? The best examples are probably companies like Alibaba and Samsung. How to engage customers in new and faster ways? Take a look at the incredible popularity of Jio Phone or WeChat.

How to reorganise your business for smarter and more agile innovation? Be inspired by the likes of Haier or Huawei.

Go shopping in Shanghai, and stores are unlikely to accept your cash or cards, instead expecting you to buzz their QR code with your mobile phone. Sit down in a Dalian Wanda's movie theatre and you are invited to immerse yourself in the story with your VR headset. Anything you need at home in Shanghai, Meituan Dianping will deliver it within minutes, and in fact probably know so much about you that they can anticipate your need before you request it on WeChat.

THE NEW SILK ROADS

The Silk Road was a network of trade routes connecting the world from the second to eighteenth centuries, enabling economic trade, but also cultural, political and religious exchanges. It takes its name from the lucrative trade in silk carried along it, bringing in China's Han dynasty. However, the "silk" name is a more recent creation, whereas it is believed spices were the largest trade in earlier times.

In 2013, China's President Xi Jingping launched the Belt and Road Initiative (BRI, or in Chinese, 一带一路, which translates as One Belt One Road), a huge infrastructure development project involving 70 countries and three continents – Asia,

Europe and Africa. The "belt" refers to the overland routes for rail and road transport, largely following the ancient Silk Road, whilst "road" refers to the sea routes.

The Chinese government's stated objectives are "to construct a unified large market and make full use of both international and domestic markets, through cultural exchange and integration, to enhance mutual understanding and trust of member nations, ending up in an innovative pattern with capital inflows, talent pool, and technology database."

The BRI's first phase focuses on infrastructure development for transportation, but also communications, and power. It is regarded by many as the largest infrastructure project in history, with development planned over 30 years, whilst in reality it is more of an aggregation of many projects, from roads and bridges to ports and railways. The second phase will involve "softer" initiatives in healthcare, education, and financial services.

Its total cost is estimated to be $4 to 8 trillion, compared to China's annual trade potential along the route, which is put at around $3 trillion. At the same time, it has faced criticism for the huge amount of lending to small nations who contribute to the development, but then face huge debt, which in effect brings them into Beijing's political sphere of influence.

As a businessperson, it means that I can step on a train at London's St Pancras station bound for any major city across Asia. In 2017, the "East Wind" freight train started a new service carrying a huge cargo of textiles and electronics, travelling 12 000 km from Hangzhou, retracing the old Silk Road through Kazakhstan, Russia, Belarus, Poland, Germany and eventually to London. Meanwhile the sea route includes the world's largest ports and nations such as India, and those in the Middle East and East Africa.

LEARNING FROM GROWTH MARKETS

The *I Ching* is probably the oldest surviving text on how to deal with uncertainty. Also known as *The Book of Changes*, it dates back over 4500 years, and is considered the source of Chinese culture, science and medicine.

The *I Ching* embodies three principles of change:

- Everything changes (变易) meaning the world is in constant change.
- Change can be simplified (简易) meaning everything is connected.
- Everything, and nothing, changes (不易) meaning there is an equilibrium.

In practical terms what this tells us is that Asian culture is based on change. It tells us to constantly look for new ways to solve problems, to look for connections between things outside of our normal frames, and to view the world, society and business as a system.

This philosophy sits at the heart of a very different leadership mindset which I find in Asia, compared to the west. Look at the leaders like Alibaba's Jack Ma or Wang Jianlin, who is often called the "the Walt Disney of China" and is founder of Dalian Wanda, which brings together an empire of shopping and entertainment. These leaders have a much more connected way of thinking; they see connections, they embrace systems thinking, and create incredible ecosystems of partners.

Asian companies have been learning management practices from the West for the last 30 years. Now western companies could learn much from Asia. Why? Most significantly because of the environment in which Asian companies are working:

- **Culture:** the unique characteristics of Asian markets and customers – fast growth, urban concentrations, large families, huge aspirations, controlled and uncontrolled markets.
- **Competition:** the fierce competition from Asian companies is shaking up every market globally – thirst for technology, leapfrogging infrastructures, incredible work ethic, success focused.

- **Control:** the private ownership structure of many organisations, built around entrepreneurs who stick with organisations as they grow, and family ownership, enabling longer-term thinking.
- **Collaboration:** the search for new investment or partners, locally and globally – ecosystem and platform models are normal, recognising the power of collaborations, and desire to be more global.

In India, for example, consider Mukesh Ambani or Rata Tata, who have a far more purposeful leadership style. Indeed, Tata's company, which produces everything from steel to trucks, Tetley Tea to Range Rovers, is primarily owned by a non-profit social foundation. And of course, many of the west's best-known businesses are now led by Asian leaders too – most notably Satya Nadella at Microsoft and Sundar Pichai at Alphabet. Both have brought a very different style and priority to their leadership compared to predecessors Steve Ballmer and Sergei Brin.

So, what can we learn from Asian companies?

- **Values.** The Confucian approach is often quoted by Chinese premier Xi Jinping – a philosophy founded on social harmony and collaboration, frugality and hard work, and education – values shared across much of Asia.
- **Agility.** Taoism is about going with the flow and adapting to change. The yin and yang symbolise the ability for opposites

to coexist in a positive way, communism and capitalism, centralisation and decentralisation, fast and slow.

- **Long game.** Private ownership gives Asian companies stability to take a longer-term view. Softbank takes a 30-year investment view. Governments work to a 5-year plan, enabling strategic initiatives to thrive.
- **State.** Whilst this is often seen negatively, government support enables companies to grow with long-term loans, to develop new capabilities together in dedicated zones, and to develop shared infrastructure like ports and rail.
- **Digital first.** A desire to create the future is combined with a willingness to let go of the past, and not be hampered by legacy structures, jumping to the digital world. Look at DBS in Singapore, the world's best bank.
- **Fast and intuitive.** Fast decision making is a hallmark of companies like Alibaba, typically leaders in small groups, acting less democratically, and with much more intuition rather than being bound by spreadsheets and business cases.
- **Research.** Huge investments, partly state-funded, go into new science and technologies, in particular fields such as AI, robotics, biotech, and sustainable energy. Three Chinese electric car companies, led by BYD, now outsell Tesla.
- **Experimentation.** The fast and intuitive approach lends itself to constant experimentation. Companies like Xiaomi continually try new ideas to see what takes off with its huge consumer audiences.

- **Scale.** The huge size of Asian markets, 5 billion people compared to 1 billion on every other continent, means that even niche ideas have significant audiences, and can then be scaled rapidly though networks and give efficiencies.
- **Entrepreneurial.** Many western companies struggle with how corporations can act like start-ups. Haier transformed its business into 10 000 micro businesses under one roof, calling it its Rendanheyi model.
- **Copying.** This is another seemingly taboo subject, but still what Chinese companies excel at (as does Apple). Meituan Dianping was recently ranked the world's most innovative company yet copies and tweaks business models.
- **Ecosystem.** Asian businesses are not afraid to openly work together. Alibaba and Tencent are like "Google plus Amazon plus Facebook plus eBay plus payment plus logistics plus wholesale" all in one. Platform models are the norm.
- **Relationships.** Famously, the Asian concept of *guanxi* plays a huge role in many of these aspects, a relationship based on face and trust, where businesses and individuals commit to collaborate without hustle or strong-armed deals.
- **Leadership.** We probably know more CEOs of Asian companies than western companies. Why is this? Because trust in companies comes through people, and particularly in ecosystems of employees, partners and customers.
- **World view.** Many Asian companies see the world, rather than local markets, as their home. Xiaomi for example sees

natural affinity and rapid growth across similar emerging markets, from India to Brazil and Mexico.

- **Education.** Back to the Confucian idea at the beginning, education becomes key to future success. China has four times more STEM (science, technology, engineering and maths) students than the US, and 33% of all students study engineering compared to 7% in the US.
- **Frugal.** Whilst rich young Asians have a huge appetite for partying and designer brands, overall they have a frugal attitude and most people save hard. Net household savings in China are 38% compared to 18% in the US and 4% in Europe.
- **Hard work.** Jack Ma swears by the "996", which means working long hours, 9 am to 9 pm 6 days every week. Whilst the west has taken life easier, the Asians are working hard.

CODE 11: EMBRACE TECHNOLOGY AND HUMANITY
Digital technologies do more than automate the existing world, they will transform every aspect of life and work, from AI to smart cities, augmentation to immortality.

Peter Diamandis is best known as the founder of the X-Prize Foundation, which offers seven-figure cash prizes as an incentive for technology to solve the big problems of humanity. Recent contests have focused on water abundance, genome sequencing, women's safety and adult literacy. His new book,

The Future is Faster than you Think, argues that the already rapid pace of technological innovation is about to get a whole lot quicker. He says that in the next 10 years, we're going to reinvent every industry on this planet, but the change is one that is primarily for the benefit of humanity.

Computing power has been the foundation of progress over the last 30 years, and will continue as it evolves into quantum computing, becoming ever faster and cheaper, and converging with many other technologies. Sensors and robotics, virtual reality and artificial intelligence will all develop exponentially as machines become more intelligent and networks more prolific. As prices fall and applications increase in areas such as education and healthcare, then more people will embrace it, and it becomes more core to everyday life. Add to this, more capital to invest, drive more radical experimentation, and faster and more dramatic breakthroughs.

THE 4TH INDUSTRIAL REVOLUTION

Technology is transforming the worlds of education and health-care, agriculture and hospitality, as well as the more obvious communications and entertainment, retail and finance. Once technology could be left to technologists. Now, despite its enormous complexity and intimidating language, it is a core topic for every business leader.

Consider the industrial revolutions that have led us to today, from the iron smelters of Ironbridge in Shropshire, England through to the digital entrepreneurs of Silicon Valley and Shenzhen. In each instance, the inflection points that marked the new revolution were the emergence of new technologies that reshaped key aspects of the world, from manufacturing to healthcare, society and the environment.

- **1st Industrial Revolution** (1760–1840): used water and steam power to mechanise production
- **2nd Industrial Revolution** (1870–1940): used electric power to create mass production
- **3rd Industrial Revolution** (1940–2000): used electronics and information technology to automate production
- **4th Industrial Revolution** (2000–): uses digital technologies, converging with the physical and biological worlds

Our current technological revolution is at an inflection point right now. The technologies and applications emerging have three capabilities that are different, more advanced, and likely to have more impact on our world than the technologies of past revolutions:

- **Intelligent …** New technologies are intelligent, with the ability to sense or predict an environment or situation and act on that knowledge. This extends far beyond knowledge; it is the ability to make sense of things.

- **Integrated ...** The technologies connect with humanity, with the ability to align with the physical and mental capabilities of humans, and the natural environment. They embrace voice and gestures and can enhance human capabilities.
- **Immersed ...** They are embedded in everything and everywhere, from people and machines to physical and natural environments. This creates a connected world of intelligence that can operate independently and collaboratively.

MIT recently identified a number of fundamentally important technologies for the next decade. Each is already recognised as powerful in its own right, yet together they can be much more. Increasing development and connections, will give rise to a new generation of super technologies, that will transform business in ways that we cannot yet imagine. Whilst this might fill us with trepidation, it should also fill us with hope, that they solve many of the huge social and environmental challenges which we face today, to enhance humanity, and our everyday lives.

Tech 1: Pervasive Computing ... embedded, accessible computing

Pervasive, or ubiquitous, computing delivers information, media, context, and processing power to everyone, wherever we are. It is characterised by vast networks of connected microprocessors embedded in everyday objects, the internet of things (IOT). Instead of data stored centrally, it is continually updated in open networks, or blockchains, safer and more accessible.

Example: Vital Patch is a biosensor on the arm with sensors to detect heart rate, body temperature, and breathing, with data connected in realtime to health professionals.

Tech 2: Biotechnology ... enhanced life-forms and systems

Biotech is the use of living systems and organisms to develop products. Humans have been bioengineers since we first planted crops, now enhanced by genetic engineering, informatics, and chemical sciences. CRISPR enables geneticists to edit genes, which allows us to tackle diseases like breast cancer before it attacks. At the same time, the engineering of living cells in humans or agricultural brings new ethical dilemmas.

Example: Biometrics, using retinas or fingerprints, but soon body odours and vein patterns, create a new level of security and access.

Tech 3: 3D Printing ... digitally designed, chemically manufactured

3D printing, or additive manufacturing, is a revolution built on chemistry that is transforming the world's factories and supply chains. Rather than ordering a spare part for your car, you download the digital blueprint, then 3D print it on demand, often through local networks like 3DHubs based in the Netherlands. As materials as diverse as human tissue are able to be printed, it may transform life too, with new organs printed to order.

Example: Customers might subscribe to a fashion brand's digital design catalogue, enabling them to customise and then 3D print any dress they desire on the day, and then repurpose the material into another design a few days later.

Tech 4: Machine Learning ... fast, automated and intelligent analytics

Machine learning can most simply be thought of as computer programs that "learn", however it also includes pattern recognition, statistical modelling, and analytics for decision-making. This is underpinned by three technologies. Cloud computing separated storage and processing capability from devices, creating ubiquitous access to software, data and collaboration (e.g. games like Pokémon Go). Big data aggregates and interprets huge amounts of data, enabling new insights and decisions. AI-based algorithms enable devices to use this data to learn and act on it.

Example: Customer analytics, powered by loyalty cards, enables suppliers and retailers to supply goods, and incentivise purchases, based on a deep understanding of target audiences, their influences and behaviours.

Tech 5: Nanotechnology ... engineered, super-materials

Nanotech is based on molecular engineering, which builds incredibly small devices the size of molecules, typically 1–100 nm (there are 100 million nanometers in 1 metre). The highly engineered materials are the foundation of innovations such as Nike's Dri-Fit sports clothing, odourless socks, water-repellent shoes, stop-smoking patches.

Example: Nanotech will support the development of molecular structures that replicate living cells, enabling doctors to regenerate body parts that are lost to infection, accident, or disease.

Tech 6: Robotics ... precise, agile and intelligent devices

Robotics is the development of mechanical systems (essentially, a frame, electrical components, and software code) that can operate autonomously or semi-autonomously. Whilst simple robots are not new, witness factory production lines, they have been transformed in recent times by their precision, agility and intelligence.

Example: in healthcare, Intuitive's Da Vinci surgery system has reduced highly trained surgeons to joystick operators, as their hand movements translate to ultra-precise robotic actions. Enhanced vision and controls allow surgeons to operate on patients with minimum invasion, reducing risk and damage, and enhancing recovery and success.

AI IS ROCKET FUEL FOR GROWTH

Working in the UAE recently, I was invited to meet some of the nation's leaders to discuss the impact of technology on future trends. I arrived at UAE's new Ministry of Possibilities in Dubai to be greeted by a robot, and was soon immersed inside a merged reality space, combining governance, a diversity of collaborative innovation projects, and tech education.

Omar Sultan Al Olama, the UAE Minister of State for Artificial Intelligence (how many nations have one of those?) had just launched BRAIN, the National AI Program, with an ambition for the UAE "to become world leaders in AI by 2031" and boost the local economy by $182 billion. A leap to the future, maybe, but a practical growth strategy too.

From Siri to self-driving cars, AI has the potential to transform our human capacity to embrace the power of technology, and solve the most complex problems, from climate change to eradicating disease, cybersecurity to neuro-controls. Whilst we image AI taking the humanoid form of Sophia, the human-like robot created by Hong-Kong based Hansen Robotics, AI comes in many forms, from Alphabet's DeepMind to Tesla's autonomous cars.

Today's AI is more formally known as narrow (or weak) AI, meaning that it is designed to perform a narrow task, like playing chess or searching online. We see this embedded in our everyday lives, from anti-lock brakes in cars to fraud protection of payments, email spam filters and autocomplete forms. Future AI, however, seeks to take a more integrated form, known as general (or strong) AI, with the ability to do any task, and having far more autonomy.

In healthcare, for example, AI can already interpret scans, sequence genomes, and synthesise new drugs within minutes, whilst also powering virtual nurses and robotic surgeons.

"Everything invented in the past 150 years will be reinvented using AI within the next 15 years," says Randy Dean of Launchpad AI and, maybe not surprisingly, PwC estimates that it could add $15.7 trillion to the global economy by 2030.

However, AI brings many ethical questions and risks associated with inbuilt biases, and has inconsistent regulation. Gender, race and ethnic biases can wrongly negatively influence the criminal justice system; fake news and misinformation can spread rapidly through bots and social media. It threatens privacy and security; and it could displace many humans from jobs.

AI is the new rocket fuel for business innovation and growth. Here are some examples:

- **American Express** processes $1 trillion in transactions and has 110 million cards in operation, relying on AI-based algorithms to help detect fraud in near realtime, thereby saving millions in losses. Its data analytics also enables apps to engage cardholders with personalised offers, and merchants to manage performance.

- **Burberry** uses AI to combat counterfeit products and improve sales and customer relationships. Its loyalty programs go beyond rewards using that data to personalise the shopping experience online, and to augment the physical store experience using intelligent devices, from smartphones and biometric sensors.

- **Darktrace** Enterprise Immune System slows attacks on computing systems by emulating the way humans fend off viruses. An AI-enabled platform embeds in a network, learns what behaviours are normal, and flags anomalies, automatically slowing or stopping compromised networks and devices.

- **Lemonade** is reinventing insurance to be instant, easy, and transparent. It offers home insurance powered by AI and behavioural economics. By replacing brokers with bots and machine learning, Lemonade promises zero paperwork and instant policies and claims. As a B-Corp, it also has a Give Back scheme to non-profits.

- **Microsoft** has put AI at the core of its service. Cortana is a virtual assistant, chatbots run Skype and answer queries, Office includes intelligent features such as weather, traffic and personal schedule intelligence, and business customers can use the Microsoft AI Platform to create their own intelligent tools.

- **Netflix's** incredible growth is largely due to its AI-driven personalisation, bringing together the viewing histories, searches and ratings of viewers to offer recommendations to you and others like you. It then uses this intelligence to develop new preference-matched content, such as House of Cards.

- **Rare Carat** is disrupting the diamond market. Its platform uses blockchain technology to track provenance and verify certification, massively improving authenticity and ethics of diamond sourcing; it then uses AI-based analytics to compare the price of diamonds, connecting buyers with appropriate retailers.

HUMANISING TECHNOLOGY

Evan Spiegel sits in his loft-sized office, taking up the top floor of Snap's head office in Santa Monica. On the beach outside, young people chat and surf, sunbathe and play. Inside, his Snapchat platform enables those same teens and young twenty-somethings to stay connected day and night. Spiegel is one of the them, still in his twenties, but also a multi-billionaire tech entrepreneur founder of what Fast Company in 2020 called "the world's most innovative company".

A little like his hero Steve Jobs, Spiegel studied design at art college, followed by an internship at Red Bull, which taught him much about consumer culture. At Stanford he launched a start-up with classmate Bobby Murphy, initially called Picaboo, which evolved into Snapchat in 2011, and dropped out as the app reached 1 million daily users a year later. In 2014, Mark Zuckerberg offered him $2 billion for the business, which he turned down, instead choosing an IPO in 2017, which valued the business at $30 billion.

Then everything went wrong. Spiegel rapidly grew his team to thousands, putting himself at the heart of all technology development, yet Snapchat was haemorrhaging users, losing 5 million in 2018, and losing most of his senior team. The stock price dived by 90% and most people thought it was all over. However, Spiegel wasn't finished, knowing that he needed to fix his business, and his internal workstyle. With Murphy he reimagined the app around what people loved and invested heavily in augmented reality (AR) tools. Adding crazy rabbit ears to photos, or cool backgrounds mattered to his young audience.

Whilst Apple and Alphabet see the future of the smartphone eventually migrated to some form of headset device, Snap focused on its cheap and fun Spectacles, cool designs with built-in AR cameras. The team drove for new types of content, developing a Netflix-style platform for short 5-minute movies with teen-specific content, and a second app called Bitmoji which allows users to make Simpsons-like caricatures of themselves, and then place their avatar into animated movies alongside their friends, in Bitmoji TV.

What emerged was a very human approach to technology. Whilst many older audiences might trivialise those rabbit ears, Spiegel knew they could make his technology business cool, desirable and incredibly human.

Making technology "more human" will be a key step to its progress in forthcoming years. This could be like Pokémon Go embracing augmented reality in gaming or using gaming itself to transform activities such as shopping, like Alibaba's gamified incentives to attract shoppers with its 11:11 Shopping Festival, or Kahoot making education more fun.

"Humanising" technology takes many different forms – from the design ergonomics of an Apple iPhone to the controls that make it more intuitive to use, from the ability to integrate or augment existing human capabilities such as strength or intelligence, to the ability to make life, society and the environment better.

Interfaces will be more personal, language less technical. Authenticity enhances trust, whilst machines learn to interpret emotions. AI will evolve to recognise what is right and wrong, fake and real, ethical and not. Robotics will take the drudgery out of repetitive work, whilst also developing emotional intelligence and empathy to better support people, be that supporting elderly people living alone, or being driverless cars that become intelligent personal spaces.

CODE 12: START FROM THE FUTURE BACK
Jump to the future, beyond short-term distractions. Work backwards to connect to the priorities of today, then forwards to make the future happen in your own vision.

Zacco is a Danish IP firm, one of the largest in Europe, specialising in the protection of intangible assets like patents, trademarks and designs. With a team of over 500 expert technologists and lawyers it is a business focused on detail and process. However, when CEO Mats Boström asked me to work with the business to help his people think more imaginatively about the future, it was not easy. The future isn't logical, or absolute, or certain. The team found it hard. But in reality, they are in the future business, helping organisations to imagine better futures, and then make them happen in practical and profitable ways.

We started from the future, and then worked backwards.

Leaping out of today's business world is incredibly liberating. Gone are the pressures and priorities for short-term deliverables, gone are the limitations of being able to judge right and wrong, suddenly everybody can have a viewpoint, nobody is wrong. Starting at 2030, we imaged the worlds of their clients, how they will have used those protected assets to create incredibly innovations and made a difference to the world. And then we worked backwards to today. Administrators were transformed into visionaries, fundamentally thinking differently about why they do what they do, and how to do it better.

JUMP TO THE FUTURE

The future isn't like the future used to be. We cannot just evolve or extrapolate the past. Today's future is discontinuous, disruptive, different.

It is imagination that will move us forwards – unlocking the technological possibilities, applying them to real problems and opportunities to drive innovation and growth in every industry, in every part of our lives.

The best place to start is the future. The best entrepreneurs think "future back" rather than just trying to move forwards with the limitations and distractions of today. Elon Musk grabs headlines with his bold "Humans on Mars by 2030" vision, but then that makes everything else more purposeful, and more possible. Tesla to Hyperloop to SpaceX, all seem more possible, and even stepping-stones to a greater destination.

"Future back" thinking also means you are not limited by your own capabilities.

Richard Branson had a fantastic vision for a better airline, a consumer bank, a space travel business. But no idea how to make them happen. But then he found partners who could help make them happen. Partners with the expertise on tap, to connect with his ideas, and together innovate further and faster.

This is not about prediction, but possibilities. It is a stretch of imagination beyond intelligence. It is about building ambition, having courage, and building a future orientation. Once you have a strong sense of "future back" possibilities, then you can work backwards to today. With a new sense of direction, you start working "now forwards" with new awareness and ambition.

Like the mountaineer setting out on an expedition, you define the peak which you want to scale, and then you consider the potential paths to get there. There will be many – some shorter, some riskier, some unknown. As you set off towards the peak you will encounter many unexpected conditions – wild animals, fierce weather, difficult terrain. You change path, you improvise, you reevaluate, you may even change the goal. But you are going in the right direction.

EXPLORE FUTURE SCENARIOS

Imagining the future is fun, but also a serious challenge for every business today. What might the future market look like? Therefore which are the smartest choices of today?

Jumping to the future, we see dramatic change. For example, by 2050, the global population is likely to hit its highest point, then slowly reduce. By 2045, the much discussed "singularity" will be reached, where some machines have greater intelligence than humans. By 2040, a federated world government could be established, working with nations and tribes. And by 2035, a human population is likely to be established on Mars, perhaps by a Chinese-owned SpaceX.

By 2030 the average person in the US will have 4.5 packages a week delivered by flying drones. They will travel 40% of the time in a driverless car, use a 3D printer to print hyper-individualized meals, and will spend most of their leisure time on an activity that hasn't been invented yet. The world will have seen over 2 billion jobs disappear, with most coming back in different forms in different industries, with over 50% structured as freelance projects rather than full-time jobs.

Over 50% of today's Fortune 500 companies will have disappeared, over 50% of traditional colleges will have collapsed, and India will have overtaken China as the most populous country in the world. Most people will have stopped taking pills in favour of a new device that causes the body to manufacture its own cures.

Scenario planning is complex and easy. Infinite possibilities can create a rich diversity of possibilities and options, but also confusion and chaos. The challenge is not to predict the future, but to be prepared for it.

My first experience of scenario development was with Royal Dutch Shell, the oil business, which started using the technique in 1971, to understand the implications of oil shocks and, as we reach peak oil, the ways in which the world can shift to renewable energy. Shell's process is complex, although produces fascinating stories of possible futures.

A simpler approach, to stretch thinking and debate possibilities, can be achieved as a team within a few hours, largely using the insights and ideas in participants' heads, rather than requiring huge amounts of prepared data. The collaborative process, the rich discussion, the strategic stretch, are what matters. I use these steps:

- **Future drivers.** Consider the potential drivers of change that will shape the future of your broader industry, and the world of your customers. You could use megatrends as a stimulus, or develop your own drivers based around possible social, technological, economic, environmental and political (STEEP) changes.
- **Critical uncertainties.** Select a number of particularly interesting drivers and describe extreme opposite ways in which they might play out (polarities). For example, will retail shift primarily online with home deliveries, or into rich

social experiences on the high street? Consider the extremes, even if a balance seems likely.

- **Plausible scenarios.** Bring together some of the most interesting polarities. Do this most simply by creating 2x2 boxes built on any two polarities. For example, the retail shift, alongside economic boom or recession, or strong or weak sustainability focus. Each quadrant of each 2x2 is a mini scenario. Repeat, and discuss.
- **Strategic implications.** With a large number of mini scenarios from the group, bring them together in a rich picture of possible futures, sharing and discussing as you progress. Evaluate as a team the potential timeframes and certainties. How do they cluster? Which are most risky, and most rewarding? Which do we like most?

With a better understanding of possible futures, you can start to future-proof your business against the worst scenarios, but also choose the futures which you would like to create.

MAP THE GROWTH HORIZONS

Strategy used to be about setting out a vision and creating a plan to get there. Today strategy and innovation fuse together, and strategy becomes much more active, progressive and discovery-based.

There is no better way to align your leadership team, than to spend a few days imagining the future together. The problem is that we so rarely do it, we prioritise today over tomorrow, and because the future cannot be predicted, we don't explore it. The result is lack of vision, certainly a lack of shared vision, worse a multitude of differences and misunderstandings.

The key is to structure the process in a series of activities:

- **Leap to the future.** Imagine future possibilities, developing a rich picture of ideas and images. Use techniques like a futuristic news article, or a future consumer experience. Ask people to come with their visions developed alone, and then share them, building up a montage of possibilities. And then start to shape them into possible scenarios.
- **Explore possibilities.** Compare the future to today, the big differences and the possible journeys to get there. Talk about their implications. Consider your purpose statement. Is it aligned? Is the vision sufficient, or the purpose not bold enough? Then start to map out strategic horizons, working backwards towards today.
- **Map the horizons.** The best approach, for most industries, is to focus on "5–3–1" . Define a vision for 5 years, what it will be like, the key requirements, and the likely outcomes, including financial scale. Then work backwards to consider 3 years with the same details, then 1 year. A one-page journey map

emerges (see Figure 2.2). Stand back. Is it ambitious? Possible? Plausible? Profitable? Do we like it?

What emerges is a more practical roadmap to the future, or you could call it a "growth roadmap". What is significant is that you have developed it as a leadership team, with collective ownership and a rich discussion along the way. It doesn't matter if it's not perfect, it will change as the future emerges. Continual learning and adaptation will shape your journey as you progress, and you may even choose to accelerate the timeframes, to create the future faster.

Most importantly in developing the horizons is that the short-term will change more too. The temptation with "now

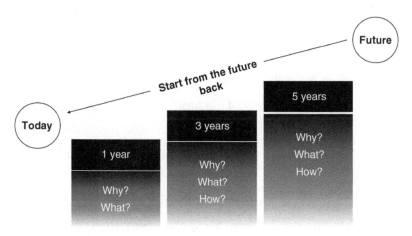

FIGURE 2.2 Strategy from the future back.

forward" planning is to iterate what you already have, to stretch the old world, and to pander to short-term priorities. By stretching yourself "future back", next year will be different, a step towards the future rather than a step from the past.

CODE 13: ACCELERATE THROUGH NETWORKS
Ideas and relationships are your most important business assets, multiplied through the exponential power of networks, enabling you to grow further and faster.

Kyle "Bugha" Giersdorf was only 16 as he stepped out to play at the Arthur Ashe stadium in New York City. His mother thought online gaming was something he just did in his bedroom, when he should have been focused on schoolwork.

But now here he was, one of 100 finalists in a global championship, competing for $30 million in prize money, and with 19 000 spectators packed into the stadium watching, plus another 2.4 million viewers joining live on YouTube and Twitch. A few hours later Giersdorf walked away with more prize money than the US Open tennis champion tucked in his jeans pocket, and winner of the inaugural Fortnite World Cup.

Around 2.2 billion young people now play online games, more than play all physical sports combined across the world. In 2019, eSports generated $1.1 billion in revenues, and is currently tripling each year, as its global network and competitions grow, and sponsors seek to reach the audience. This is not just kids playing in their bedrooms, it is redefining the worlds of sport and entertainment, and is a great example of the power of networks.

THE EXPONENTIAL VALUE OF NETWORKS

Network effects typically account for 70% of the value of digitally related companies.

Network effects were popularised by Robert Metcalfe, the co-founder of 3Com, which created networking cards that plugged into a computer giving it access to the ethernet, a local network of shared resources like printers, storage and the internet.

Metcalfe explained that, whilst the cost of the network was directly proportional to the number of cards, the value of the network was proportional to the square of the number of users. Or in other words, the value was due to the connectivity between users, enabling them to work together and achieve more than they could alone.

"Metcalfe's Law" says that a network's value is proportional to the square of the number of nodes in the network. The end nodes can be computers, servers and simply users. For example, if a network has 10 nodes, its inherent value is 100

(10×10=100). Add one more node, and the value is 121. Add another and the value jumps to 144. Non-linear, exponential, growth.

Network effects have become an essential component of a successful digital business. First, the internet itself has become a facilitator for network effects. As it becomes less and less expensive to connect users on platforms, those able to attract them in mass become extremely valuable over time. Also, network effects facilitate scale. As digital businesses and platforms scale, they gain a competitive advantage, as they control more of a market. Third, network effects create a competitive advantage.

This is not about the technology itself, it is about how the technology enables networks to work – how they enable people to connect with each other, to collaborate and influence, to build mutual affinity and trust. Communities emerge and where the power of peer-to-peer influence is the primary source of trust, recommendation and sales.

Movements are a step even further in making networks work, giving them purpose, values and momentum. This might sound obvious. But think how many retailers do nothing to connect their consumers, particularly those with similar interests. Even telecom brands, with billions of users, do almost nothing to add value beyond the basic connections they provide.

In 2015, three Chinese academics – Zhang, Liu and Xu – tested Metcalfe's Law based on data from Tencent and Facebook. Their work showed that Metcalfe's law held for both, despite the difference in audiences and services. They also look at every $1 billion unicorn business that has grown over the last 25 years. They estimated that 35% of the companies had network effects at their core; however, these network effects typically added up to 68% of the total value.

LINEAR BUSINESS VS. NETWORK BUSINESS

Linear businesses traditionally gained a competitive advantage by buying assets, controlling supply chains, and driving transactions.

Network businesses gain competitive advantages through the multiplying effect of the networks, and crucially what happens within its connections, relationships and interactions. Network-based businesses typically work much more collaboratively with customers and business partners, evolving into ecosystems that reach across traditional sector boundaries and can do much more.

As the network grows, its value multiplies. Think of a dating app. Initially a few users is very limiting, but as soon as the network grows, the opportunities to find a suitable match grow much faster. The value of the network to the user is in the number of connections possible, and for the business, the commercial value becomes the data that is generated through user-to-user interactions. This data can be captured and analysed, to drive more interactions between people, and becomes the real advantage. Jim Collins famously termed this the "flywheel effect", where having more customers creates a better experience, whose reviews attract more customers, who reduce costs or increase advertising incomes, which enables lowers costs, which attracts more customers.

Network effects, relationships and data, become the assets of a network-based business. They are "light" assets, typically in the form of intellectual property (compared to primarily heavy assets of linear companies), and drive "intangible" value financially.

There is a downside to network effects, in that exponentially growing networks become harder to control, coordinate or curate. The rise of unsolicited emails, fraudsters and fake news is one obvious consequence. And whilst Facebook and other networks employ huge armies of people to try to eliminate such factors, this is probably an old way of thinking. In reality it needs to leverage network-based solutions, such as peer-to-peer accreditation, as in the trust profiles which users give each other on platforms such as Airbnb, eBay and Uber.

15 TYPES OF NETWORK EFFECTS

As a starting point, network effects can be direct or indirect:

- **Direct** (same-side, or symmetric) network effects happen when an increase in users directly creates more utility for all of the users, that is, a better product or service. Consider, for example, Facebook or Tinder.
- **Indirect** (cross-side, or asymmetric) network effects happen when an increase in users indirectly creates more utility for other types of users. For example, Airbnb and Uber, where more hosts and drivers creates more utility for guests and passengers.

Different business models encourage different network effects. Dynamic pricing, for example, is used by Uber to encourage more drivers to join the network when demand is high, or more passengers when demand is low.

Many varieties of network effect emerge, depending on the types of business, each with strengths and weaknesses. Here are 15 types, where the first five are direct effects, the others indirect:

- Physical – infrastructure, typically utilities (e.g. roads, land-lines, electricity)

- Protocol – a common standard for operating (e.g. Ethernet, Bitcoin, VHS)
- Personal Utility – built on personal identities (e.g. WhatsApp, Slack, WeChat)
- Personal – built on personal reputation (e.g. Facebook, Instagram, Twitter)
- Market Network – adds purpose and transactions (e.g. Houzz, AngelList)
- Marketplace – enables exchanges between buyers and sellers (e.g. eBay, Visa, Etsy)
- Platform – adds value to the exchange of a marketplace (e.g. iOS, Nintendo, Twitch)
- Asymptotic Marketplace – effect depends on scale (e.g. Uber, OpenTable)
- Data – data generated through use enhances utility (e.g. Google, Waze, IMDB)
- Tech Performance – service gets better with more users (e.g. BitTorrent, Skype)
- Language – a brand name defines a market or activity (e.g. Google, Uber, Xerox)
- Belief – network grows based on a shared belief (e.g. stock market, religions)
- Bandwagon – driven by social pressure of fear of missing out (e.g. Apple, Slack)
- Community – driven by shared passion and activity (e.g. ParkRun, Harley Owners)

- Movement – driven by shared purpose or protest (e.g. Occupy, Black Lives Matter)

Most iPhone apps rely heavily on the existence of strong network effects. This enables the software to grow in popularity very quickly and spread to a large userbase with very limited marketing. The "freemium" business model has evolved to take advantage of these network effects by releasing a free version that affects many users and then charges for "premium" features as the primary source of revenue.

eBay would not be a particularly useful site if auctions were not competitive. As the number of users grows on eBay, auctions grow more competitive, pushing up the prices of bids on items. This makes it more worthwhile to sell on eBay and brings more sellers onto eBay, which drives prices down again as this increases supply, while bringing more people onto eBay because there are more things being sold that people want. Essentially, as the number of users of eBay grows, prices fall and supply increases, and more and more people find the site to be useful.

Stock exchanges feature a network effect. Market liquidity is a major determinant of transaction cost in the sale or purchase of a stock, as a bid–ask spread exists between the price at which a purchase can be done versus the price at which the sale of the same security can be done. As the number of buyers and sellers on an exchange increases, liquidity increases, and transaction costs decrease. This then attracts a larger number of buyers and sellers to the exchange.

CODE 14: BUILD A GROWTH PORTFOLIO
Growth amidst relentless change is a journey of many projects, innovations and transformations. See it as a balanced portfolio to be sustained over time (Figure 2.3).

Shigetaka Komori, CEO of Fujifilm has a mantra, "never stop transforming".

As a result, the Japanese business has created innovative solutions in a wide variety of fields, leveraging its imaging and information technology to become a global presence known for innovation in healthcare, graphic systems, optical devices, specialist materials and other high-tech areas.

In the 1960s, Fujifilm was a distant second place to Kodak in the photographic film market. But today, digitalisation has transformed how we take photos, Kodak is gone (bankrupt in 2012), and Fujifilm has shifted focus and resources into new areas.

In 2000, the film-related business accounted for 60% of Fujifilm's sales and 70% of its operating profit but fell to less than 1% within a decade. The traditional photographic imaging business, the core of the business, was largely replaced by other types of imaging, such as for healthcare.

"Whilst Kodak tried to survive in a declining market, Fujifilm looked to new futures," says Komori, when contrasting how the two companies responded to market change.

Imaging rapidly evolved into digital information, and a vast range of new businesses emerged in areas from medical system to pharmaceuticals, regenerative medicine to cosmetics, flat panel displays to graphic systems.

As an example, Fujifilm's cosmetics business started in 2006 with the launch of its Astalift skincare products, which then extended into make-up, and from them into other types of medical and well-being solutions. Whilst camera film and cosmetics might seem unrelated, camera film happened to be the same thickness (around 0.2 mm) as human hair. Collagen was used in its film to retain the material qualities, such as moisture and elasticity, over time. This expertise in manufacturing collagen is also fundamental to making skincare products.

Fujifilm introduced medical diagnostic imaging systems using its digital camera technology, which then gave it a platform for doing fundamental research into new medicines. Drug development is increasingly built on informatics, such as genetic analysis, fields in which Fujifilm could combine its expertise, giving it an advantage over traditional pharma companies.

INFINITE AND INVINCIBLE

In his book *The Infinite Game*, Simon Sinek explores how businesses can achieve long-lasting success, a relentless approach to transformation and growth, and sustained long-term value.

"In finite games, like football or chess, the players are known, the rules are fixed, and the endpoint is clear. The winners and losers are easily identified," he says. "In infinite games, like business or politics or life itself, the players come and go, the rules are changeable, and there is no defined endpoint. There are no winners or losers in an infinite game; there is only ahead and behind."

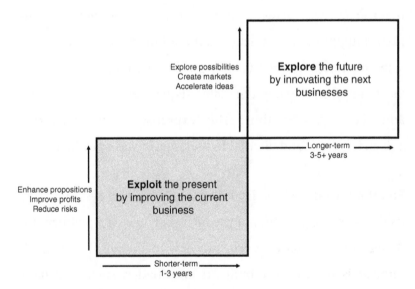

FIGURE 2.3 Building a growth portfolio.

Many businesses struggle because their business has a finite, or fixed, mindset. They set themselves an internal goal to be the best at something, or to launch a specific product, and they end up being a slave to it. Such narrowly defined, sales-targeted, product-centric businesses find it difficult to break out of their current approach. They only know how to do more of the same with diminishing returns. Sales stagnate, momentum is lost, innovation slows, energy dips, and they lag behind.

Leaders with an infinite, or growth, mindset – not just in terms of experimenting to find new ways forwards, but in terms of their whole approach to strategy and innovation – do much better. They are purpose-driven, growth targeted, customer-centric. This builds direction and alignment, momentum and energy. These factors drive them naturally to keep evolving, to adapt and innovate, to move with a changing world. They even create a rhythm of change ahead of the market, and so can shape the world to their advantage.

EXPLOIT THE PRESENT AND EXPLORE THE FUTURE

Alex Osterwalder and Yves Pigneur famously created the business model canvas, a one-page diagram in which to capture the essential components of any business model, and crucially to explore the connections and trade-offs which exist between different choices. However, they increasingly found that the best companies develop a series, or portfolio of business models, which can serve them over time.

Their new book is called *The Invincible Company* because companies who build a growth portfolio are sustained over time, not just in mindset, but also by a whole series of great ideas, innovations and business models that ensure its success today, and into the future.

Invincible companies manage a dynamic portfolio of established and emerging businesses – to protect established business models from disruption as long as possible, while simultaneously cultivating the business models of tomorrow. They need to "exploit" the present and "explore" the future:

- **Exploit the present:** requires leaders to manage and improve the existing businesses, focusing on their profitability, and their risk of disruption by new competitors, new technology, new markets, or regulatory changes.
- **Explore the future:** requires leaders to also search for new areas of growth, evaluating the potential profitability of new ideas which is drive by size and scalability, and also the risk associated with innovation, and how to make new ideas more certain.

To remain relevant and prosperous companies need to develop truly "ambidextrous" organisational structures which can create the future, whilst also delivering today. Innovation becomes just as important as delivery, but requires a distinctive culture, distinctive skills and metrics, in order to be explorers of the future.

LEADING FOR RELENTLESS GROWTH

Leaders, themselves, need to be ambidextrous – to be the delivers of today, and also the creators of tomorrow.

Komori's success has not come through creating one business, but a sequence of business concepts which keep building off each other. This sequence might take the form of leveraging distinctive capabilities with various applications into different sectors, as Alphabet has done, or it might be about taking more businesses to the same audience as Apple, or it might be a series of ways of working within the same sector as Microsoft.

Amazon is a good example of a company that intentionally manages a diverse portfolio of existing and promising new business models. The company continues to produce growth with its existing businesses (online retail, AWS, logistics), whilst also developing a portfolio of potential future growth engines that may become big profit generators one day (Alexa, Echo, Dash Button, Prime Air, Amazon Fresh, etc.).

Long-term sustained growth is built on a portfolio of short- and long-term innovative business models. Such "invincible" companies can better allocate capital and resources at each stage of development. A culture and process that drives a continuous flow of new ideas and innovation is much more likely to sustain your business in turbulent times and uncertain futures.

SUMMARY: HOW WILL YOU RECODE YOUR GROWTH?

5 questions to reflect on:

- Riding the megatrends ... Which trends will take your business further?
- Learning from Asia ... How can you learn from Asia's distinctive approaches?
- Technology radar ... Which new technologies will be most important for you?
- Using networks better ... How can use network effects to multiply your impact?
- Build a growth portfolio ... How balanced is your current and future portfolio?

5 leaders to inspire you (more at businessrecoded.com):

- Satya Nadella, Microsoft ... a leader seeking to make his customers cool
- Emily Weiss, Glossier ... turning her blog into a fast-growing beauty community

- Mary Barra, GM … from apprentice to leader, reinventing GM after years of failure
- Wang Xing, Meituan Dianping … delivering anything to China's new consumers
- Masayoshi Son, SoftBank … legendary investor with 300 year, $100 billion plan

5 books to go deeper:

- *Seeing Around Corners* by Rita McGrath
- *The Future is Asian* by Parag Khanna
- *The Invincible Company* by Alex Osterwalder and Yves Pigneur
- *Unstoppable* by Chris Zook
- *The Future is Faster Than You Think* by Peter Diamantes

5 places to explore further:

- Our World in Data
- McKinsey Insights
- Deloitte Insights
- Singularity Hub
- Visual Capitalist

SHIFT 3

TRANSCENDENT

Recode your market

HOW WILL YOU RESHAPE YOUR MARKET TO YOUR ADVANTAGE?

From marginal competition to creating markets

Transcendent comes from the medieval Latin word transcendentia. *It means to go beyond ordinary limits, surpassing and exceeding the normal, and once there to experience an unusually heightened level of perspective and purpose.*

Consider some of the challenges of our changing world:

- In the last 25 years, China's share of global manufacturing output has grown from 2 to 25%. Over that time China's GDP has grown thirty-fold.
- In the last two decades, 9.6% of the earth's total wilderness areas has been lost, equalling an estimated 3.3 million square km.
- 51% of job activities can be automated, only 5% of jobs entirely replaceable by machines. However, more new occupations will emerge than those lost.
- New digital technologies can enable a 20% reduction in global carbon emissions by 2030, equivalent to eliminating more than China and India's CO_2 emissions.
- Car sharing could reduce the number of cars needed by 90% by 2035, resulting in only 17% as many cars as there are today.
- CEO pay has risen 1000% over the last 40 years, however *average worker pay has increased by just 11%*, essentially stagnating when taking into account inflation.
- 72% of people feel that companies have become more dishonest. 93% of CEOs believe it's important to engender trust that their company "will do the right thing".
- 87% of millennials say that they base their purchasing decisions on whether or not a company makes positive social efforts.

Are you responding to your changing world?

Keanu Reeves described his 1999 movie *The Matrix* as a
wake-up call to the speed of our changing world. Two decades
later we can see many of the movie's themes in our everyday
lives – the primacy of the individual, disregard for the old
system, anti-corporate backlash, the blurring of fake and
reality.

Today's markets are a matrix of possibilities, where we could
say that almost nothing has changed in those last 20 years,
or everything has. The lens by which you see your market
shapes everything else about what you do, your strategy and
innovation, and how you work, your organisation and people.
Time for leaders to wake up.

BLURRED BOUNDARIES

We used to think of markets as defined spaces – industry sectors – with clear boundaries and categorisation, industry standards and predictable competition. And then markets started to
blur and fragment.

Amazon disrupts fashion, Alphabet disrupts travel, Apple disrupts healthcare, Tesla disrupts energy, Alibaba disrupts finance, Snap disrupts movies.

Sectors like telecoms and technology, communication and media, data and information, entertainment and gaming, converge into each other. Or pharmaceuticals and healthcare, wellness and food, fashion and sport, become a boundaryless continuum.

You can define your business any way you want. What kind of company are you? What market are you in? Anyone can frame their market "space" in this new market matrix.

The blur of boundaries has evolved in multi-dimensions:

- **The blur of digital and physical.** Fortnite's online games become a physical stadium event, Nike's flagship stores are navigated and enhanced by smartphones, L'Oréal's magic mirror customises your cosmetics and delivers to your home.
- **The blur of products and services.** Harley Davidson's holidays embrace bike hire plus flights and hotels, Adobe's software is delivered "as a service", Disneyland experiences can be planned and continued online at home.

- **The blur of categories and sectors.** Grab is a delivery company with a data and finance core, CVS is a pharmacy that reframed as a health and wellness store, athleisure-wear is sporting apparel made stylish for everyday fashion.
- **The blur of industry and functional roles.** IBM was the computer manufacturer who became trusted advisor, Amazon is a retailer but also a leading brand of own-label products and services, Casper mattresses are sold direct to consumers.
- **The blur of business and consumer.** Glossier is a cosmetics brand but equally a community of people who share and co-create, Avon is a brand of consumer sellers, Rapha calls its stores Cycle Clubs, meeting places as well as retail stores.

Taking advantage of non-linear value chains, and brands that have evolved beyond descriptors of products, manufacturers can think like retailers, creating direct to consumer (DTC) channels, with more trust and style than a commoditising intermediary. Think of Apple or Allbirds, Dollar Shave Club or Warby Parker.

Equally retailers like Carrefour and Target realised that private label products don't have to be inferior to the products of consumer brands like Heinz and P&G. Indeed, many are made by the same manufacturers. Retailers have many advantages, with more opportunities to engage consumers more intimately, to add adjacent services such as advice, and understand consumers personally. Target could be a stronger brand than P&G.

MULTI-DIMENSIONAL MARKETS

What are the major challenges for the markets of today, new business models, sustainable impacts, and rapidly changing aspirations of stakeholders?

- **Automotive.** The automotive industry is facing its most profound change in 100 years, with autonomous vehicles, electrification and other fuels, new models of ownership and connected ecosystems. Add to this, AI and smart road infrastructure, connectivity and entertainment. Issues like safety will still matter; Volvo, for example, is installing new sensors which will detect poor driving, intoxication or excess speed, and take action.
- **Beauty.** Personalisation and environmentally friendly products are key to the future of skin and colour products, with new science creating sophisticated functionality. Influencers like Michelle Phan rather than advertising shape attitudes, whilst the subscription models of Birchbox and the DTC models of Beauty Pie have transformed the traditional purchase experience from instore to bathroom.
- **Energy.** Decarbonisation, decentralisation and digitalisation are the key challenges for every power generator or distributor. As oil and gas, mining and fracking, give way to solar

and wind, there is also a shift to city and home management, from local generation to automated control. Typical disruptors are Lanzatech turning waste into clean energy, Fluence a huge battery business from Siemens, and Watty.

- **Fashion.** New materials, new business models and new technologies are transforming fashion. From Agua Bendita's beautiful bikinis made out of scraps to Bolt Thread's synthetic spider silk, from Unspun's custom-made jeans using a 20-second Fit3D bodyscan to ThredUP's resale platform, environmental impact has become the biggest issues in an industry which is one of the biggest polluters.

- **Finance.** Digital entrants and emerging technologies are transforming banking, from DBS transforming to become "invisible" inside other services, to Atom and Number26 seeking speed and simplicity. Lemonade has embraced AI to transform the business model of insurance, while AXA explores new applications of blockchain, and cryptocurrencies evolve.

- **Food and drink.** Wellness and sustainability have topped the agendas of major businesses like Danone, Nestle and Unilever, whilst animal- and dairy-based categories have been challenged by plant-based alternatives such as Impossible and Beyond Meat. New channels and business models have been driven by a huge rise in snacking and on-the-go markets, plus home delivery and meal kits.

- **Healthcare.** From positive health to personalised pharma, people are seeking to engage with healthcare in new ways.

Combine 23andMe genetic profiling with PatientsLikeMe's peer-to-peer advice, Babylon's AI-enabled diagnostics and wearable health trackers, Minute Clinic's simple consultations and Zipline's drone deliveries, Organova's 3D printed organs, gene editing and personalised medicines.

- **Media.** Playing games to streaming television, virtual reality and instant messaging, have transformed how we immerse ourselves in content. New business models, in particular subscription, enable access across platforms, as we now shift to content that is even more user-generated and interactive. Platforms like Twitch and Spotify will become more important in curating content and building community.

- **Retail.** In a sector dominated by Amazon, innovators like Shopify have helped direct brands to sell and deliver faster. Glossier has shown the power of community and pop-up stores, whilst Etsy has allowed artisans to reach the world, Alibaba embraces gamification to engage consumers more deeply, whilst intelligent delivery businesses like Meituan Dianping know consumers most personally.

- **Technology.** AI and cloud will embed tech ever further into our lives, enabling more intelligent and individual choices and behaviours. In telecoms the shift to 5G will enable realtime engagement like never before, video-based content will accelerate with particular application to education and work, whilst our primary user interfaces will continue to shift to voice, eye tracking, and ultimately the brain.

- **Travel.** AI will drive transportation to become automated, intelligent and efficient, health and environmental issues will continue to challenge airlines, hospitality and vacations. The shift to cleaner fuels and responsible tourism will be accelerated through innovations like those of Selina's nomadic places to live, Lilium's electric flying cars, and Ctrip in the huge Asian travel market.

WHAT BUSINESS ARE YOU REALLY IN?

Within the next decade, automotive companies will no longer sell cars, instead facilitating mobility on-demand, ride sharing and logistics services. They could also converge with other service providers such as scooters and trains, planes and hotels, energy and telecoms. Within the next decade we will subscribe to smart homes, which will manage our utilities, organise our shopping, stream our entertainment.

Who will provide these services? Tesla has long defined itself as an energy company, rather than an auto manufacturer. With "accelerate to renewable energy" as its defined purpose, it has a diversified business in batteries, energy systems and transportation. Indeed, it combines sales of cars with Powerwall charging systems, and even its solar roof tiles, creating an all-in-one subscription model that transforms value perceptions.

And there will be completely new markets too. Here are just a few examples of areas that are expected to be worth at least $100 billion by 2025: autonomous vehicles, IOT software and sensors, tissue engineering, smart grid technology and renewable energy.

The best way to "frame" your market space is around customers, and what you enable them to do. Just as we defined purpose, define your market around why you exist, rather than just what you do, or how you do it. The "Why" framing gives you a much richer space to play in, a broad range of market opportunities which by definition are desired, and more valuable to your customers.

Framing your market space is also a source of competitive advantage. By framing it differently from your competitors, you define your business and the value you offer in a more inspiring way. A new frame sets you alongside different alternatives, with different value perceptions and market models.

Consider other stakeholders too. Ask your employees, would they prefer to work in a telecom or tech company, a drug or wellness company? Similarly, alternatively framed markets will be seen as having different risks and rewards, directly affecting your market value.

CODE 16: DISRUPT THE DISRUPTORS
Start-ups are the cool companies, scale-ups are the profitable ones. Yet it is corporates who have many more advantages. How do you play a different game?

In the early 1960s, if you wanted a quality watch, you bought a Swiss one. Accuracy, craftsmanship and reputation had sustained Swiss watchmaking supremacy for over three centuries. Then came Seiko and Timex, Japanese innovators who used quartz technology to offer new features at a fraction of the price. Switzerland's share of the global market fell from 48% in 1965 to 15% in 1980.

The Swiss could have responded to the Japanese disruptors by also trying to compete on price, but they realised that disruption is not about playing the same game, it is about changing the game. Instead of going for cheap, they went for style and fashion. The Swatch watch was born with bright colours and ultra-modern design, a price cheap enough to accessorise every outfit or mood. They disrupted their disruptors.

EVERY MARKET IS DISRUPTED

The term "disruption" became popular with the publication of Clayton Christensen's *The Innovator's Dilemma: When Technologies Cause Great Firms to Fall*, which defined it as the process by which a simpler, more affordable product or service initially takes root at the bottom of a market and then relentlessly moves upmarket, eventually displacing established competitors – as Netflix did to Blockbuster, or the Ford Model T to the horse and cart.

Disruption can take many forms and is not limited to technology and price. The Beatles disrupted popular music, Brexit disrupted Europe, and the Covid-19 pandemic disrupted most of life on Earth.

Typically, disruption takes the form of a small insurgent taking on a much larger incumbent. David versus Goliath. The incumbent grows too familiar with its success and starts to rely on past glories, and forgets to move forwards. Meanwhile consumers grow tired of what is familiar, particularly if it becomes boring and diminished. An insurgent is new and exciting, it offers change and something better. It claims to be on the side of the people, fighting against the status quo, seeking a better world.

We see disruptors in every market, typically smaller start-up businesses who are trying to do things different and better. Often, they rise to become billion-dollar businesses, or "unicorns" as we call them. Compared to the impact of innovations between established competitors, Coke and Pepsi for example, where the new ideas can make marginal differences of 1–2%, disruptors can have a 30–40% impact:

- **Aerofarms** in agriculture … vertical, urban, intensive farming
- **Birchbox** in beauty … monthly subscription boxes of samples
- **Grab** in delivery … home delivery of anything on demand
- **Icon** in manufacturing … can 3D-print a house in 24 hours
- **Klarna** in online payments … simple, intelligent payments
- **Impossible** in plant foods … tastes better and good for world
- **Peloton** in fitness … the ultimate ride without leaving home
- **SpaceX** in space travel … cheap satellites and returns to Mars
- **Uber** in urban travel … shared, cheaper and trusted city travel
- **Udacity** in education … fast, online nanodegrees, linked to jobs
- **Xiaomi** in smart devices … low-priced electronics for emerging markets

Often these companies succeed by "decoupling" the traditional offerings of incumbents. They break up the conventional solutions into components and then choose to do only some parts, but much better, or a number of them, recombined in a better way. At the same time, they bring digital technologies to play, reimagining existing activities in simpler, faster, cheaper, more personal, more automated, or more convenient ways.

CB Insights, founded by Anand Sanwal, is a great resource for exploring how industries from healthcare to real estate are being decoupled and disrupted, reimagined and reinvented.

HOW CORPORATES CAN DISRUPT THE DISRUPTORS

In his book *The Phoenix and the Unicorn*, Belgian tech entrepreneur Peter Hinssen takes another perspective. As we had dinner in Seattle, he shared his idea: "Unicorn start-ups are brilliant. However, to be honest, very few of us will become founders or work for a billion-dollar start-up," he said. "Most of us struggle along in large companies trying to stay relevant to the ever-changing customer":

> The phoenix is just as magical as the unicorn, but perhaps a little more relevant. It represents all those companies that, just like this mythical bird, are able to rethink themselves in cycles: time and time again they rise from the ashes of the old and come out stronger than ever before. They are the Walmarts, the Volvos, the Disneys, the Apples, the Microsofts, and AT&Ts of this world.

Large, established corporates have many advantages – familiar brands and reputations, huge scale and customer bases, significant resources and talent, existing infrastructure and licenses to operate, a diversity of assets and partners, financial power and investors, and experienced leaders.

If only they could unlock them with the same foresight and creativity, energy and agility, of start-ups then they would be formidable incumbents. They have grown slow and lazy over their years of success, they have evolved with conservative cultures that seek to avoid change and risk, wedded to their physically based, full-service solutions, and struggle to innovate.

Start-ups are the "speedboats" that can zoom around evolving markets, seize new opportunities, partner easily with others, and adapt and evolve quickly. Corporates are the "supertankers" with power and scale but who find it hard to change direction.

CHANGE THE GAME TO YOUR ADVANTAGE

The "game" is your market, the framework in which you choose how to compete.

In my previous book *Gamechangers: How brands and business can change the world*, I explored many different strategies by which companies can change how they define that framework, the frame of their market, and the ways in which they compete.

We have also explored how the best organisations see the future differently, and this too is a distinctive advantage: Being able to:

- make better sense of the changing world, and prepare for the markets of tomorrow, rather than just competing in those of today.

- build a portfolio of innovations, exploiting today and exploring tomorrow, that will sustain growth over time.
- win by defining success in more inspired ways.

In the simplest terms, you can change the game by changing any, or any combination of, four strategic dimensions:

- Change the **why** ... your purpose, your vision, your brand
- Change the **who** ... your audience, your geography, your occasion
- Change the **how** ... your business model, organisation, process, partners
- Change the **what** ... your experience, products and service, costs and price

Great examples today of companies who have disrupted their disruptors include Disney, where Bob Iger led the fight back against the challenge of Netflix to create new types of branded content built on its Pixar acquisition and character franchises, and new business models such as the Disney+ platform to engage with customers. Similarly, Microsoft has fought back under Satya Nadella to reinvent itself, as have AT&T and Cemex.

Jujutsu is a type of Japanese martial arts which uses the strength of an opponent against them, rather than one's own. When faced with a disruptor, you would seek to learn from the new business model used against you, and then create a superior version of it yourself. More generally, jujutsu can inspire a business to scan a changing market for all possible new business models, then decode them to explore, challenge and build on them.

Jack Welch famously used the phrase "DYB" meaning disrupt your business as he encouraged his teams in GE to reimagine their own business in the same way that a young entrepreneur might seek to decouple and disrupt what GE did. Corporate venturing, working with entrepreneurs to develop new business and approaches under your own roof, is a more sophisticated way to embed this disruptive mindset within a large corporate.

One great example of changing the game comes from New Zealand, where Turners and Growers, a leading producer of fruit and vegetables started to cultivate the Chinese gooseberry in the 1950s.

Until that time, the fruit had only been grown in central and eastern China. Turners had the inspired idea to reimagine the fruit in a new way, calling it the "kiwifruit" and going on to position it as a superfood, high in vitamin C and antioxidants. It became popular locally, and then with a new brand name, Zespri, spread rapidly across the world.

CODE 17: CAPTURE THE CUSTOMER AGENDA
As audiences diverge and fuse, then geographies and demographics lose meaning. Sense and respond to uncover individual aspirations and evolving behaviours.

Pat Brown, the scientist who founded Impossible Foods, makers of plant-based burgers sausages and more, describes his product as alternative meat.

Whilst he recognises that his immediate audience will be vegetarians, who might compare his products to those of other plant-based solutions like Beyond Meat, his target audience is meat eaters, who compare Impossible to the real thing. He doesn't want to be compared simply on price and taste, but on the wider impacts which meat has, from the deforestation of rainforests to carbon emissions of cows.

Daniel Ek gives you unlimited streamed music on Spotify for a subscription fee of $9.99 a month, $4.99 if you are a student, $12.99 for a family sharing, or free if you are willing to listen only when connected by Wi-Fi, and with some ad interruptions. Compare that to the old transactional models, where you would buy an album of 12 tracks that tell a musical story and keep it forever, for the same price as accessing 50 million tracks today. But think further to the relative costs of production, payments to artists, and impacts on the environment.

Both examples illustrate the changing nature of "value".

THE NEW CUSTOMER AGENDA

In seeking to understand the longer-term agenda for customers, we need to combine our insight into customer priorities and aspirations of today with the broader "megatrend" drivers of the external world.

Eight "meta" priorities for customers emerge, which are likely to drive customer attitudes and behaviours through the decade to 2030:

- **My Identity.** I define myself how I choose, often rejecting conventional labels. Social media has democratised my ability to express myself. As a blogger or an influencer, amateur rock band or self-publishing author, anyone can build their own brand, often with more authenticity and empathy than glossy stars. Brands are platforms to help people share passions as new tribes, and do more together.

FIGURE 3.1 The new customer agenda: eight meta priorities.

- **My Wellbeing.** I embrace physical and mental wellness with a more personal and holistic approach that combines what is good for my health, my fitness and my future. More authentic, more natural, and more local solutions will become increasingly important. Brands, particularly in the areas of healthcare, nutrition and sport will become my new wellbeing partners.

- **My Access.** Smartphones and their derivatives, will be my access points to both physical and digital worlds, enhanced by collaboration, intelligence and augmentation. Gamification is really a shorthand for more intuitive, immersive and inspiring forms of access, as physical and digital experiences combine. I will seek easy, relevant and trusted brands as gateways to my preferred worlds.

- **My Community.** Instead of defining myself by locality or nationality, occupations or socio-demographics, I will choose which the communities I seek to belong to and be defined by, which I contribute to and care about. Digital lifestyles, geographic migration, and urbanisation will drive this. Social status will be less about wealth and more about quality of life. Brands will align with these communities.

- **My Value.** My personal success is still measured in economic terms, with some symbols of materialism and self-gratification. While sufficient incomes matter to achieve a sustainable lifestyle, my value in society is more quantified by contribution, through creativity and collaboration. I respect others who do more for our world, from small acts of kindness to ways to accelerate our progress.

- **My Rights**. I have the power to express my views, to actively stand up for what is fair, responsible and legal. I seek respect, to be protected, but also I have a powerful voice. Personal data and privacy are at the core of this, although I also recognise that this requires balance – to achieve more, I need to share more. I will respect and support brands and organisations who stand up for me and my principles.

- **My Responsibilities**. I care, and seek to do more, for "myself, my community and my world". As social and environmental issues become more tangible, reducing materialism, waste and resource use will be key environmentally. Socially, I will seek to support the most vulnerable people in local communities, and others globally. I seek brands and other platforms that can amplify my desire to contribute more.

- **My Portfolio**. I will build a portfolio lifestyle, around both my personal interests and professional activities. As lifelong careers give way to more fluid and freelance work, I will develop a portfolio of experiences and skills, alongside more personal hobbies and activities. My networks, socially and professionally, will be key to unlocking my portfolio through collaborative work and community life.

THE NEW CUSTOMER VALUE EQUATION

Customers look beyond product and price in today's world.

Economists used to simply define the "value" to the customer as benefits less costs, and a fair price would typically emerge out of a price elasticity analysis which judged what a reasonable share of customers were willing to pay. In today's world, customer value is a more complex story, although to the customer it is probably still an intuitive, emotional, split-second judgement.

For business, it starts with the changing nature of markets, how people purchase and consume products and services, brands and experiences. Three factors are key:

- **Customers are not average.** Individuals are more different in their needs and aspirations, and differ for business in the cost to sell and serve them. You certainly don't want everybody, and often fewer but better customers are better for business.
- **Alternatives are not equal.** Blurred boundaries in multiple dimensions, means that the choice of alternatives is far greater and comparisons are less equal. How to compare a soft drink and a live event, both offering "happiness"?
- **Products are not core.** Functionality used to be the starting point in seeking to understand what the customer values. But as offerings are built more around service and experiential attributes, products matter less.

Add to this the profound ways in which businesses have innovated, in particular as business models have shifted away from transactions to different patterns of value exchange.

Subscription models, auctions, freemium models, pay-per-use, all shape a new perspective on value.

- **Value enabled.** Focus on what you enable people to do, not just the immediate benefits of a transaction The "job to be done" reflects the bigger goal, be it living it a healthier life, or a business that is enabled to do radically more because of you.
- **Value beyond money.** Customers used to measure value as benefits gained relative to price paid, quantifying abstract concepts like quality and convenience financially. Today, the highest price increasingly does not reflect the most benefits.
- **Value over time.** As in the Spotify example, value over time becomes an important dynamic, in a similar way to buying or leasing a car. However, the choices and trade-offs are more complex, as in the upsides and downsides of fast fashion.

For customers, value is affected by their shifting priorities, which typically include broader issues in a changing world. Accessibility goes beyond convenience, fairness goes beyond producers, price goes beyond costs of production, achievement goes beyond themselves:

- **What I give, as well as what I get.** Customers recognise brands as platforms for good, where a purchase can benefit them and others. This might be explicit like Toms' original "one for one" or implicit like Juan Valdez's fairtrade coffee.

- **How it makes the world better.** Individuals will value sustainable benefits differently, supporting local or global causes, social or environmental issues, the ability to create a single or amplified impact.
- **The cost to me, and the world.** The total impact of a purchase, as for example measured by its carbon footprint, requires a systems-type of thinking, as in dairy farming, with global consequences balanced against health and happiness.

This new value equation for customers maps closely with the new value equation for business, for employees and investors, making a much richer and responsible value exchange both possible and desirable.

CODE 18: CREATE NEW MARKET SPACES
Markets can be defined however you want, framed in your own language, rejecting old models like B2C and B2B, focused on enabling customers to achieve more.

The Middle East is a fascinating yet bewildering place for many foreign visitors.

Whilst it is mostly welcoming and safe, it has grown over recent years, with a jumble of traditional culture and western influence. Working in Kuwait City recently, I ventured out from my hotel to explore skyscrapers mixed with traditional souq markets, cafés full of smoking locals, and small shops packed high with local delicacies.

Then I came across a minimalist single-floored glass building, % Arabica. It was full of young professionals, lined up for the best coffee and snacks in town, a meeting place that was an alternative to the crowded environs.

Japanese designer Ken Shoji told me that he had brought his Asian coffee concept to the Gulf state simply because it was so different. It was an inspiring fusion of multiculturalism – Asian architecture, African coffee roastery, and Arabic meeting place. One year after launching, "%" had become a cult brand.

CREATING NEW MARKETS

Chan Kim and Renée Mauborgne are both professors at the beautiful INSEAD business school based in Fontainebleau, 60 km south of Paris. It was founded in 1957 by Georges Doriot, often called the father of venture capitalism, which makes it a fitting place to explore new markets.

Blue Ocean Strategy published in 2004 has become a business text of our times. I first met Mauborgne in Istanbul, in the same year. She explained the concept incredibly simply, saying "red oceans are the crowded markets where everyone crowds in to compete, blue oceans are the unexplored markets which are quiet and uncontested".

For the last 15 years they have told the story of Cirque du Soleil, how it blended the ideas of opera and ballet with traditional circus, whilst eliminating animals and raising prices. Or Southwest Airlines, offering shuttle buses to secondary airports with limited service, the first low-cost airline. Or Nintendo Wii, taking the established concept of video games but adding multi-players and augmented reality to enable family participation.

Kim offers four ways to innovate the "strategy canvas" which maps out the attributes of a market, exploring what to reduce, what to enhance, what to eliminate, what to create. The results for Cirque's Guy Laliberté, Southwest's Herb Kelleher, and Nintendo's Shigeru Miyamoto, were innovative businesses that dominated new market spaces.

Creating a new market space, in my experience happens in one of three ways:

- **Forming markets**: the most radical, in that it creates a completely new business opportunity, responding to a new need and aspiration of the customer. Red Bull's Dietmar Mateschitz returned from Asia, tired after a long flight, with the inspiration to create an "energy drink", and the likes of Gatorade later followed.

- **Fusing markets**: combining the best ideas of two different markets, potentially to reach new audiences with new applications. Apple did this with the iPhone. When Steve Jobs launched it he described it as "a combination of a mobile phone, entertainment player and internet browser".

- **Framing markets**: redefining the boundaries, domain and descriptors of a market as trends shift, categories evolve, and new possibilities can be included. Shell, the oil giant, redefined itself as an energy company. Danone, the French food manufacturer, as a health company.

In three decades of working with hundreds of companies, these two latter concepts have proved the most enduring for me. More than any clever technique, name-checked model, or guru inspiration, the simple acts of "fusing" and "framing" have been most productive.

POWER TO THE PEOPLE

The most significant shift in business over the last 30 years has been from product-centred to customer-centred thinking. Many companies are still not there, but I suspect more has been invested in trying to make that transformation, than in anything else, even the digital transformations of recent years.

Thirty years ago, when I started my business career, all 30 000 staff in the company were asked to go on a two-day program called "Winning for Customers".

At the time, led by an inspired people-thinking CEO, Colin Marshall, it seemed radical and fresh. At the same time, for an airline, it seemed obvious. The primacy of the customer experience, rather than the functionality of any component – parking, check-in, boarding, seats, entertainment, food, transfers – seemed obvious. It was easy to think "horizontal" and follow the customer's journey, crossing over the "vertical" silos of internal functions and product and service components.

Customer-centric companies succeed in three ways:

- **Customer control.** The customer is the starting point of any transaction, determining when and how they want to do business. Technology empowers their choices and preferences, whilst imperfect responses are quickly challenged.
- **Customer creativity.** Increasingly customers want to be more active in the design and shaping of what they buy, be it through co-creation of personalised solutions, or more strategic involvement through partnerships.
- **Customer collaboration.** Customers trust and influence each other, advertising is largely background noise in today's marketing world, as customers seek to do more together,

sharing their passions and projects in communities enabled by brands.

Technology has finally made customer-centric thinking obvious for every type of business. Power is now unquestionably in the hands of customers. They have infinite choice, they can access your business or any other, with a simple click, and there is a surplus of supply rather than demand.

Businesses now even struggle to engage customers in a relationship, let alone gain their loyalty, as customers trust each other more than any brand, and are loyal to their community rather than any supplier.

EVERY BUSINESS IS A "CONSUMER" BUSINESS

This power shift from product to customer fundamentally changes the mindset and structure of businesses.

Businesses (B) are organised by customer (C) or segment rather than product or category, with internal alignment of capabilities giving way to an alignment of insight. In reality, a business needs to achieve both.

As supply chains become ecosystems, networks rather than linear flows, the relationships between businesses and customers change. Businesses can reach end-customers directly, by developing direct channels, giving them much more ability to self-assemble components, be it organising vacations or building their own homes.

As a result, the end customer, or the "consumer", becomes the lead actor in a reconfigured play. We can see the shifts here, evolving over time:

- **From B2C to C2B.** Empowered by technology, transparency and choice, consumers demand businesses and brands to act on their terms – when, where, how, what they need – they demand more, and influencers drive preference.

  Examples: L'Oréal personalisation direct; Netflix video on demand.

- **From B2B to B2B2C to C2B2B to C2B.** Enabled by technology, businesses no longer need to work through aggregators of solutions, or distribution intermediaries, instead the most "industrial" of businesses connect directly with consumers, again on their terms.

  Examples: Goldman Sachs' consumer bank; Cemex direct to consumer.

- **From C2B to C2C.** Enabled by technology, consumers find each other, seeking to share their passions, and possibly enabled by brands. Even if brands provide products and services, they are secondary to what the consumer seeks to achieve.

Examples: Glossier's beauty community; Rapha's Cycle Clubs.

Every business is a "consumer" business.

Alibaba's C2B model shows how to use the power of AI and machine learning to respond to customers' rapidly changing needs and aspirations. Ming Zeng, chief strategy officer, says that in a digital world, all successful companies use the latest tech, but Alibaba has taken the underlying principles of e-commerce the furthest, with a model based on machine learning and the comprehensive "datafication" of the consumer's experience.

The technology allows the company to put consumers at the centre of business, constantly collecting data on them and their purchase choices in realtime and using feedback loops to drive machine learning. When consumers log on, they see a customised webpage with a selection of products curated from the billions offered by millions of sellers.

The model requires several connected elements: a network that can dynamically adjust the supply and quality of service offerings, an interface where customers can easily articulate their needs and responses, a modular structure that can grow from an initial beachhead, and purchasing platforms than can provide agility and innovation.

Every consumer exchange supplies more data, which goes into the feedback loops required for machine learning. This system requires that a large number of actions and decisions are taken out of human hands. Algorithms automatically make incremental adjustments that increase system-wide efficiency.

For the brands of P&G, it means a new way of engaging, as demonstrated by L'Oréal. For industrial businesses like commodity miners, cement producers, agricultural farmers, it is a huge opportunity to connect directly with consumers, to add value in new ways and transform profitability.

It also means that there is no such thing as a "commodity".

CODE 19: BUILD TRUST WITH AUTHENTICITY
Customers engage more emotionally, they are human and empathetic. They trust each other more than any business, they influence and are loyal to each other.

Twenty-five years ago, Ray Davis arrived in the small Oregon town of Roseburg, where nothing much changed for the lumberjacks of the huge surrounding forests. His task was to transform the sleepy old South Umpqua State Bank with its 40 employees before it died.

Initially people poked fun at his insistence that employees, or colleagues as he called them, answer the phone with a cheery "Welcome to the World's Greatest Bank." However, over time, it became true. The bank was transformed, firstly by learning from other great customer service businesses, not banks. Banks become community hubs, interiors were opened up and modernised, products and language humanised. They served coffee, played music, and showcased great local businesses. Staff smiled, and customers loved it. Nowadays, Umpqua Bank, with over $25 billion assets and 350 branches across America, is one of the best banks.

However, Davis, now enjoying his retirement, or in "cruise" mode, as Umpqua calls it for customers who wanted to slow down and enjoy life, has a warning about change: "When we arrived in Roseburg, change was exciting, people loved progress. Today change is different, it has become relentless and dominated by technology. It scares the hell out of a lot of people," he warns. As change accelerates and technology dominates, many people lose faith in progress. The bond of trust can be lost.

TRUST IS A DEFINING ISSUE

Only one third of consumers trust most of the brands they buy or use, according to an Edelman special report in 2019.

According to the survey of 16 000 people in eight countries, 81% of consumers see brand trust as a deal breaker or a deciding factor when they consider a purchase. Trust is becoming more important because of growing concerns about the fast pace of innovation and automation, the use of personal data in tracking and targeting, and the impact of products and productions on society and the environment.

"Trust has always played an important role in brand purchase" says Richard Edelman, CEO of Edelman. "But consumers now have much larger expectations of brands, and their trust is predicated on how well a brand can pass through the three gates of trust – product, customer experience and impact on society."

When brands build trust, consumers reward them. Consumers who trust a brand are more than twice as likely to be the first to buy the brand's new products, to stay loyal in the face of new competition, to recommend it, and defend it when things go wrong. Also, a brand trusted because of its broader role in society, is almost twice as likely to gain such support, than if its trust is due to product aspects only.

Despite all of this evidence, brands are increasingly untrusted.

Most consumers believe that a brand has a responsibility to get involved in at least one social issue that does not directly impact its business, yet few see brands doing so. Indeed, most people think brands are using social good as a marketing tool, "trust-washing" if you like. This exacerbates their loss of trust.

However, people's trust in governments and other institutions is far less than in business, meaning that whilst many are unsure, they do see business as a better platform for addressing social and environmental issues than politicians and their agencies. Interestingly, people believe they have more influence on business than governments and can persuade them to take these issues more seriously.

"It's time for brands to take the next giant step," says Edelman. "They must accept the responsibility consumers have given them to effect change and welcome greater accountability and measurement of their impact."

BEING REAL, AUTHENTIC AND TRANSPARENT

In her book *Who Can You Trust?* Rachel Botsman asks: "If you can't trust those in charge, who can you trust? From government to business, banks to media, trust in institutions is at an all-time low." However, she argues that technology can enable trust in new forms, and that our main problem is a mismatch, saying "institutional trust was not designed for the digital age."

Originally trust was built locally between people, in local communities. Then as cities and business grew, we deferred to institutions as curators of trust – governments and corporations – trusting them to act on our behalf. Trust went from beng about people, to being built around hierarchies. Today, trust is built in networks, and flows between people enabled by technology. For a business there are three layers of trust:

- **Trust in the organisation**: the reputation of the business and brand, particularly in terms of ethics and responsibilities, openness and transparency.
- **Trust in the concept**: the relevance to customers, authentic and reliable, a positive way to solve a problem, and delivers on every promise.
- **Trust in the people**: the respect for people who lead the business, and deliver the concept, who are real and authentic, empathetic and caring.

Authenticity is closely associated with provenance, which is now a source of transparency for many manufacturers utilising the potential of IOT sensors and blockchain certification. Cult Beauty uses a transparency app to help users of its cosmetics to understand the sources of all products, from oils to colourings. Canada's Bridgehead Coffee was one of the first to set benchmarks for others in fairtrade and organic certification. Fishpeople can tell you which boat caught your fish and when. Tiffany & Co. can do the same with diamonds.

Whilst all of these matter, the most important is that people trust people. For most customers, they see two faces of the organisation – the leader who typically appears as the company spokesperson in times of challenge, and the everyday frontline employees who sell and serve customers in stores, on phones, or one-to-one.

As Botsman says "Most businesses that we interact with are built around money, and money only goes so far. Money is the currency of transactions. Trust is the currency of interactions."

PEOPLE TRUST PEOPLE

Satya Nadella, Microsoft's CEO, provided a model for business engagement with society when he gave his views on corporate responsibility, the pressing need for human oversight of artificial intelligence systems and a succinct description of how Microsoft has earned its social licence to operate in many countries around the world.

Nadella says every company is now a technology company and that brings with it a range of responsibilities, particularly in areas such as the ethics of AI, which he seeks to proactively take a lead in. "Technology is going to be so pervasive in our lives, and across all industries, that we'd better have one core currency around it which is trust. Without trust, we are not going to have a long-term business," he said at a recent Envision event.

Indeed, Microsoft has positioned itself as the world's "good tech" company, whilst Facebook and Alphabet are often seen by regulators and politicians as "bad tech", given their reluctance to address issues like privacy and fake news.

Leadership of trust, and trust in leaders, drive everything else.

We know that any form of change sparks fear in the human psyche. If not addressed early, proactively and directly, fear of job losses due to automation or globalisation can quickly take hold. In times of crisis, a leader brings urgency and compassion, but if there is not also direction and hope, then people lose confidence, and courage in their own actions.

Employees trust leaders who do what they expect them to do.

This requires an openness of leaders, so that people know what to expect. It means engaging people in the future direction, being honest about the need and implications of change, asking for ideas, and equally challenge, being visible and accessible, and being human.

Externally, there was a time when business leaders would never say anything controversial, when businesses were agnostic to the debates of society. Today, as people trust business more than politicians to show them a way forward, they seek business leaders to take a stand, to have a point of view.

This can be controversial, a viewpoint means that not everybody will agree, that some of your customers might feel alienated or even reject you. Apple is a strong advocate of diversity and human rights; Starbucks challenged the state on their actions against migrants. Leaders need to step up, to express their view, to fight what they believe is right.

In this way, brands develop a more authentic personality, business adopts a more meaningful role in society, and you gain the respect – and trust – of people.

CODE 20: DEVELOP BRANDS WITH PURPOSE
How to build a brand that has more meaning to people, by embracing the power of your purpose, delivering products and services in relevant, trusted and practical ways?

Emmanuel Faber believes that people want to have a vote in the world they live in.

"Each time people choose a brand they exercise their right to vote. They want that brand to be transparent, meaningful and responsible. Still, they also want the brands they choose to be playful, innovative, relatable, emotional and engaging. As a result, there is a new paradigm at play today: brands only exist through the power of people," he says.

Faber is CEO of Danone, the $25 billion food business, founded in Barcelona and now based in Paris, and serving 120 markets. It has transformed in recent years to become a B Corp, with a purpose that challenges itself, and the world, to do better. It says, "we expect more from our food".

Danone wants to change the way we eat and drink, the way the entire food system works, to "nourish lives and build a healthier world". It believes that the health of people and the health of the planet are interconnected. It issues a call to action for all consumers and everyone who has a stake in food to join "the food revolution", a movement aimed at nurturing the adoption of healthier, more sustainable eating and drinking habits.

BRANDS ARE ABOUT PEOPLE NOT PRODUCTS

The old idea of brands was that they were marks of ownership. Brand names and identities reflected where they came from, just as farmers burnt (i.e. branded) their distinctive markings onto their livestock. Most brands initially reflected family names and the activities of owners.

Over time, consumers became less engaged by origins of ownership, and responded much better to brands that reflected their own lives and aspirations. Names became more abstract as the concept became more important than the name, and the logo acted as a shorthand for distinctive attitudes and values. Concepts reflecting people, not products, could rise above functionality and enable brands to move beyond categories.

Digital media further changed the ways in which brands engaged with consumers, ultimately connecting consumers with each other. Whilst greater access to information drove scrutiny and demand for authenticity, consumers responded by trusting brands less. They switched off from listening to overtly commercial advertising and turned instead to trusting and engaging with friends and others like themselves.

A brand's story, and ultimately its reputation, became much less driven by what the business said about itself, much more by what people said to each other. In today's world, brand owners seek to nurture and curate what real people say to each other, tweets and posts, word of mouth, click to click, embracing it as an ongoing narrative which they cannot control, but which they still seek to influence and enable. Coca-Cola calls this "liquid and linked" story curation.

Brands today are about communities of consumers who share a common aspiration. The brand doesn't own the community, but it can be an effective and respected enabler of connecting people, not to buy products per se, but to share passions. Products and services then follow, as the brand becomes trusted and aligned to the activity which it enables. A brand purpose is the shared motivation of the community, and its enabler.

Brands are therefore defined more by what they enable people to do, rather than what they do themselves. Brands are more structures of collaboration to deliver this enablement and ongoing relationship, rather than the wrappers of products and transactions.

BUILD A MANIFESTO BRAND

Manifesto brands are about people. They are defined by what they enable people to achieve, rather than the means to achieve that. They are about:

- **People.** They achieve trust because they are built on human instincts, an emotional contract through which promises become reality.
- **Passion.** They share the interests and obsessions of their audience, they want more and give more, with energy and inspiration.
- **Purpose.** They share a guiding light, a common cause, to make personal lives, societies, and the world, better in some way.

Like all brands, manifesto brands are shorthand codes for bigger ideas that people believe in. They are built on a distinctive set of values, beliefs that they share, ideas to promote, causes which they want to support. In a sense, they are the consumer's interpretation of the company's purpose.

They are manifestos. Declarations for change, a belief in better.

Some brands even define their manifesto in detail. Not as an advertising narrative, but as a shared statement of intent. Brands, and the products and services which they bring together, then act as a platform from which business and consumers can promote good, and also do good.

Apple famously defined itself, not with a logo, but with a belief:

> Here's to the crazy ones. The misfits. The rebels. The trouble-makers. The round pegs in the square holes. The ones who see things differently … And whilst some may see them as the crazy ones, we see genius. Because the people who are crazy enough to think they can change the world are the ones who do.

Yes, it appeared as a memorable ad, in one form narrated by Steve Jobs himself. But it stirred an emotion in me. I wanted to be part of that. I wanted to be that.

Nike embedded its manifesto inside every pair of shoes, saying everyone is an athlete, striving to achieve their best, to find their own greatness. North Face is about "exploring", the world and ourselves, to understand both better, and to be more fulfilled. Fiat wants people to enjoy everyday life, to "celebrate the smallest of things with infectious excitement".

A manifesto brand typically is built around three components:

- **Brand manifesto and storytelling**: makes the purpose relevant to the consumer, built on insight and aspiration, communicated to or between people.
- **Brand activations and experiences**: delivers the manifesto through products and services, and broader initiatives, e.g. Coca-Cola's rural Ekocenters.
- **Brand ambassadors and community**: spreads the manifesto between people who share the cause, as it becomes a movement, e.g. Patagonia's climate protests.

Danone's manifesto brands are the means by which the business practically engages in the "food revolution".

Each of its brands is guided by a framework which defines and activates a specific cause, aligned with the company's overall purpose. This starts with a focus on people, identifying the tension between a relevant insight and the current reality, defining a legitimate gap to close, or paradox to resolve.

As a result, each brand has a strong point of view, a purpose, that justifies its existence in the world and relevancy for people, supported by a commitment to help improve the health of people, as well as to help protect our planet.

With over 40 manifesto-driven brands in its portfolio, Danone sees this as a more engaging and sustainable model to driving profitable growth, that is aligned with broader society and environment.

DELIVER BETTER VALUE PROPOSITIONS

Value propositions are devices to articulate your value to customers.

We have discussed the new customer value equation, and how it has adapted to the changing needs of people, but in essence it is still built around the distinctive benefits which you deliver and the total costs, or most simply the price, which the customer pays.

Whilst some people see propositions as creative slogans, they can be, as long as there is still thought into the value trade-offs which you are seeking to achieve. Propositions are also not products, they are more like a promise, on which a selected combination of products and services seek to deliver. Indeed, different products can deliver the same proposition.

A business, and a brand, can have one enduring value proposition, or many – for different audiences, for different occasions, for different solutions. These might endure or change over time, keeping the purpose, brand and proposition fresh, topical and interesting.

A proposition might also have a number of initiatives, beyond products and services, that support the delivery of its promise. For manifesto brands, these become particularly important as they are typically the most tangible aspects of the social and environmental contributions of the brand, enabling the customer to participate in doing more together with the business, or as a community.

A great example of a "better" value proposition is Eileen Fisher, the American women's clothing brand, founded in 1984 in New York.

Fisher says of her business "We believe in ethical, timeless, well-made clothes designed to work together, wear effortlessly and be part of a responsible lifecycle" and has set her business-stretching goals in order to deliver this ambition and the requirements for B Corp certification. Supporting this aspiration are three initiatives:

- *Renew* ... Begun in 2009, Renew is a take-back programme that gives Eileen Fisher clothes "life beyond your closet".

People bring back their old pieces, which are then resold as "gently used" alternatives, often desired because they are more distinctive from current season pieces.

- *Waste No More* ... This is part of a circular system designed to upend the conventional cycle of consumerism. The business takes back its old clothes, however worn, and "upcycles" the pieces that are damaged beyond repair into entirely new designs.
- *Women Together* ... Part workshop, part retreat, Women Together is a day of "inspiration, self-reflection and connection" that empowers women to find their inner strength and mobilise it for positive change. It often takes place in stores, and with store employees strengthening the brand's human bond.

CODE 21: ENABLE PEOPLE TO ACHIEVE MORE
Brands used to be marks of ownership, but today are built around the passions of like-minded consumers, enabling them to achieve more, and multiply their impact.

Cycling is a sport of connoisseurs. They love their coffee, in France they love their pastis, and they love their bikes and gear.

Riding at the heart of a Sunday morning peloton is as much social as physical, and so Rapha is designed to create premium cycling gear and coffee shops – or Cycle Clubs – where enthusiasts can meet.

Walk into a Rapha Cycle Club – in London or New York, Sydney or Osaka – and you can see, smell and touch a love of cycling. Rapha, founded in London's Covent Garden by Simon Mottram in 2004, has grown rapidly, building a direct relationship with consumers, through events and online community, as well as its coffee-shop stores. There are also line extensions into luggage, skincare, books and travel, plus a co-branded range with designer and cycling enthusiast Paul Smith.

Rapha is a brand that polarises opinion. For some it has created the ultimate in high-performance equipment, dedicated to a sport that breeds passion and perspiration. For others, it is overpriced and overdesigned vanity wear for middle-aged men who squeeze into their posh lycra for a weekend ride. Whichever your view, it gets talked about. Especially items such as the $450 pair of yak-leather cycling shoes, or the $150 pro-glide coffee tamper, to flatten your coffee like the best baristas after your run.

ENABLING MORE

Microsoft seeks to "empower every person and every organisation on the planet to achieve more", or as Satya Nadella says, "to make other people cool, not ourselves".

I worked with Microsoft to help them achieve this with business customers. Traditionally sales and technology experts had gone out to clients seeking to sell products, or in today's model, subscriptions. It was largely product push, with diminishing returns. We stepped back and asked how can we help clients to achieve more?

The transformation was to help them do what they want to do – to reach new markets, innovate new solutions, transform their own businesses. Instead of a relationship starting with a list of product options, we started by listening, and then together using the combined expertise and ideas of what is possible, to develop a new plan for growth.

If a brand is about what it enables people to do, rather than what it does, then it follows that a great brand enables people to achieve even more than they could imagine, or to do so in a better way, with greater success.

Enablement has become a key word in branding. Brands do more for their customers in three primary ways:

- **Educating people:** helping customers to learn how to use and apply their products and services in better ways, to get the best out of them.

- **Enabling people:** collaborating with customers to achieve more, using products better, changing how they work, to do more.
- **Enhancing people:** adding to the solution of customers, adding new ideas from other places, and transforming their own performance levels.

Apple stores are busier with education workshops – how to create better sales presentation, build a better website for your business, do your tax return correctly – than people seeking to buy or repair their devices. Lululemon yoga wear stores are transformed into yoga studios at regular intervals during the day, a place to do what you love, not just to prepare for it. M&C Saatchi ad agency has rooms for each of its clients, dedicated to their brands and campaigns, where they can work together as joint teams.

BUILDING A BRAND COMMUNITY

A brand community is a group of consumers who invest in a brand beyond what is being sold.

Think about some of the great examples of brand communities through which people engage with brands and businesses today, influencing what they buy, who they trust, and how they achieve more. From Lego Ideas to TED Talks, Xbox Ambassadors to

Nike's Run Club, Disney's D23 Fans to Bayern Munich's supporter's club.

Here are some of the most famous:

- **Harley Owners Group**: recognised that owners loved much
  more than the bike, it was the freedom to ride the roads, the
  thrill to ride together, to hang out at Ace Cafes, to share their
  passion for life.
- **Glossier**: became the world's fastest growing beauty business,
  emerging out of a Vogue editor's blog followers, to become a
  community where consumers share ideas and advice, but also
  co-create their products.
- **Lego Ideas**: about more than colourful plastic blocks, Lego is
  derived from the Danish for "creative play". It is about creative
  development and expression, which is why its online community is a vibrant space for contests, photos and new ideas.
- **Behance**: Adobe's platform for showcasing and discovering
  great creative work now has over 10 million participants,
  both professional designers and amateurs, including
  exclusive tools and project collaboration spaces.
- **Spotify Rockstars**: bringing together people who love
  music, encouraging discussion and recommendations,
  rewarding and ranking the most active, and also a platform
  for discovering new talent.

COMMUNITIES BUILT ON PASSIONS

From meaningful consumer retention to new sources of revenue, unfiltered consumer insight and predictable cashflows, branded communities offer many opportunities for a business to drive growth:

- Enhance consumer experiences – how people achieve more, collaborate and recommend, and create new content together.
- Ongoing engagement – how people engage with brands continuously, not just at moments of promotion or purchase.
- Know consumers better – 67% of businesses use communities to gain deeper insights to drive better focus and innovation.
- Increase brand exposure and credibility, making it easier to sell without selling – typically 35% increase in brand awareness.
- Reduce consumer support costs – 49% of businesses with online communities report cost savings of around 25% annually.
- Improve retention and advocacy – improving retention by 42%, tripling cross-selling, and people pay more too.

Building a great brand community has three foundations:

- **Consumer**: starting with your target audience, with a captivating reason for members to join the "tribe", be it a shared cause or interest, from hip-hop music, to a love of science fiction novels, or a desire to get fit.

- **Collaboration**: engaging with other people, facilitated by the brand and its community platform, which might take the form of discussions, co-creation and recommendations.
- **Content**: the glue that makes the community work beyond products. These might take the form of newsletters, events, videos, other products, discussion boards, merchandise, exclusive offers, and much more.

Underpinning this is a business model that ensures that the community adds real value to its members, but also commercially works for the organisation. For members, this means it adds value beyond the brand's conventional products and services, typically enabling them to use them better, and get more from them. For business, this means having a business model that drives incremental revenue growth. This might be in the form of consumer retention, selling more or different products, but also other types of content, and potentially a subscription to belong.

Communities are one of the most powerful ways a brand can grow, often exponentially.

SUMMARY: HOW WILL YOU RECODE YOUR MARKET?

5 questions to reflect on:

- Framing your space … How could you redefine your market space?
- Disrupt your own business … If you were a start-up what would you do?
- New customer agendas … What are the biggest changes in your customers?
- Manifesto brands … How could you embed more purpose into your propositions?
- Enable people to do more … What would a community of your customers look like?

5 leaders to inspire you (more at businessrecoded.com):

- Bernard Arnault, LVMH … building a portfolio of 70 brands, Dior to Dom Perignon
- Maria Raga, Depop … the very human Spanish CEO of "eBay for millennials"
- Ali Parsa, Babylon Health … the Iranian refugee reinventing access to healthcare
- Hooi Ling Tan, Grab … "the plumber" of the South East Asian super-app
- Mikkel Bjergso, Mikkeller … creating the world's largest craft beer business

5 books to go deeper:

- *Smart Business* by Ming Zeng
- *The Phoenix and the Unicorn* by Peter Hinssen

- *Blue Ocean Strategy* by Chan Kim and Renee Mauborgne
- *Who Can You Trust?* by Rachel Botsman
- *Digital Darwinism* by Tom Goodwin

5 places to explore further:

- CB Insights
- Edelman Trust Barometer
- Canvas 8
- Springwise
- Trendhunter

INGENUITY

Recode your innovation

WHAT DOES IT TAKE TO DRIVE MORE RADICAL INNOVATION?

From technology obsession to human ingenuity

Ingenuity is the quality of being clever, original, and inventive. Popular in the 1800s, and less so today, it also has a sense of nobility, of ingeniousness. It comes the French ingenieux *or Latin* ingenium *referring to the mind or intellect.*

Consider some more innovations, and their effect on people:

- Pokémon Go, the augmented reality (AR) game from Nintendo, was downloaded 500 million times globally in 2 months, and generated $600 million in revenue in 3 months.
- Tobii Pro, the world leader in eye tracking, allows advertisers to pinpoint which parts of advertising and packaging design attract the most attention.
- In initial tests, a machine-learning algorithm created at Carnegie Mellon was able to predict heart attacks four hours in advance, with 80% accuracy.
- Necomimi is a pair of cat-shaped ears that contain electroencephalogram (EEG) brainwave sensors, perking up when the brain is alert, flat when relaxed.
- The HiMirror, a smart mirror that uses an integrated camera to analyse your skin, track changes, and monitor the effect of skincare products.
- LiSA is a voice-activated social wellness platform helping older people who live alone by providing voice-based email, messaging, tips and reminders.
- Deep Space sells a line of low-pressure, eco-friendly propulsion solutions that use water to power small satellites on private missions into deep space.
- Celestis offers off-planet DNA storage enabling your genetics to be stored in a space craft, and eventually on a different planet for future analysis.

How can you be more ingenious?

CODE 22: BE INGENIOUS
Innovation does not come from technology but from how it enables humanity to be better. Ingenuity is driven by imagination and intuition, empathy and design.

Takashi Murakami is often called the next Andy Warhol, fusing high and low art, combining ideas from both Japan's rich artistic heritage and its vibrant consumer culture. But whilst the American icon created multi-million dollar works of art, Murakami is much more interested in creating everyday objects for everyone, from bubble gum and t-shirts to phone covers and limited-edition Louis Vuitton handbags.

He started in the traditions of Japan, then studied "Nihonga" art, which is a combination of nineteeth-century eastern and western styles, but became distracted by the rise of anime and manga in Japanese eighties culture. He loved the modern styles which connected with people, and with the issues and aspirations of today's society. He was fascinated by what made iconic characters such as Hello Kitty and Mickey Mouse so popular and enduring.

Japan has a centuries-long tradition of "flat" art, achieved with bold outlines, flat colouring, and a disregard for perspective, depth, and three-dimensionality. "Superflat" was a term Murakami started to use in 2001 and has evolved into one of modern art's most active movements, combining the tradition's flat art with anime and manga, and taking components of high and low culture to defy categorisation. He says that he uses the style to also reflect what he sees as the flat, shallowness of consumer culture.

Today Murakami is a rock-star artist, highly aware of his image and brand, and an avid user of social media. He loves fame and commercialism. His business has been helped by collaborations with celebrities, creating animated music videos for Kanye West and designing sculptures with Pharrell Williams.

If "ingenuity" is about thinking and performing in a way that is original and inventive, it is a good descriptor of Murakami. He is inspired by both the past and the future to create his own distinctive presence, to connect with and challenge his environment, to embrace personal insight and opinion to defy conventions and take his audience with him.

IMAGINATION, CREATIVITY AND INNOVATION

Imagination is often called the primary gift of human consciousness.

In a world of ubiquitous technology, which challenges our humanity, a world of infinite yet largely derivative choices, and a world of noise and uncertainty, there is nothing quite like being human.

Imagination move us forwards. It allows us to leap beyond the conventions, the limits of our current world. It takes us beyond the algorithms of AI-enabled robots who can create perfection out of the world which they know, but struggle beyond it. It inspires us to think in new ways, to shape hypotheses to test, and aesthetic designs to enjoy.

Sir Ken Robinson is probably best known for his self-deprecating sense of humour with which he delivers a very important message: "Imagination is the source of all human achievement." *The Times* said of his UK government report on creativity, education and the economy that "it raises some of the most important issues facing business in the 21st century. It should have every CEO thumping the table and demanding action."

His book *Out of Our Minds: Learning to be Creative* argues that our world is the product of the ideas, beliefs and values of human imagination that have shaped it over centuries. He says, "The human mind is profoundly and uniquely creative, but too many people have no sense of their true talents."

- Imagination explores new possibilities and captures them as new ideas
- Creativity shapes and stretches the potential of existing ideas

- Innovation takes existing ideas and makes them practical

Creativity is applied imagination, innovation is applied creativity, you could say.

I remember back to when my two daughters were young, the pictures they drew and models they built, the questions they asked and answers they imagined. Their's was a world unlimited by experience, by prejudice or conformity. Their brush strokes were simple, their colours bold, their questions were simple but disturbingly difficult.

As adults we shift to a productivity mindset, preferring to get things done, rather than explore possibilities. We seek to reduce complexity to its simplest form and describe ideas in the context of what we already know, squeezing out any nuggets of newness.

We are all born creative, but somehow lose that spark, or at least the confidence to allow it out. Some people, we say, are creative, and others not. Yet we all have the same neurons and synapses which drive the process. The reality is that no individual is as creative as even the dullest people once they start working together. If we could reclaim our creativity, we could discover our passion, allowing us to feel more alive and do so much more.

Harvard professor Howard Gardner identified eight "intelligences" or ways to solve problems. They range from linguistics (limited only by the words you use), logical (mainly through mathematics), spatial (as used by designers), musical, physical (like athletes), natural (like farmers), intrapersonal (within yourself), and interpersonal (with others).

The point is that we have many ways to be creative, or even through combinations of our mental and physical capabilities. As Leonardo da Vinci loved to say, inspired by his own polymath life as artist and musician, anatomist and sculptor, architect and engineer, creativity is ultimately about making new connections.

IMAGINING BETTER

The purpose of any business, and therefore any innovation, is to make life better. It drives human and social progress, as well as seizing new opportunities for business growth. Whilst it is a practical, technical and process-based challenge, it is also human and philosophical, strategic and futuristic.

The Royal Society of Arts recently published a document, *How to be Ingenious*, starting with a definition of ingenuity as having three components:

- an inclination to work with the resources easily to hand
- a knack for combining these resources in a surprising way, and

- in doing so, an ability to solve some practical problem

Another way to describe it is, "The ability to do unexpectedly more for less in the face of constrained resources." Given the social and environmental challenges facing every business today, that might be a useful addition.

Rob Shorter's "Imagination Sundial" is a design tool to help us imagine what we might seek from the future, and how. He believes that we are living in a time of imaginative decline at the very time in history when we need to be at our most imaginative, and describes his goal as "to cultivate the collective imagination" towards imaging a better world.

Environmentalist Rob Hopkins says "we believe that this decline is first and foremost underpinned by the rise in trauma, stress, anxiety and depression which, neuroscientists have shown, cause a reduction in the hippocampus, the part of the brain most implicated in imagination." Wendy Suzuki agrees, writing in *Forbes* "long-term stress is literally killing the cells in your hippocampus that contribute to the deterioration of your memory. But it's also zapping your creativity".

The Imagination Sundial contains four main elements:

- **Space** … the mental and emotional space that expands our capacity to imagine. Our busy and stressful lives are riddled with fear and anxiety, which inhibits our potential for imagining. Space is about how we can slow down, feel safe, open up and connect with others and the natural world to rekindle this capacity. "Morning pages" is a practice recommended by Julia Cameron in *The Artist's Way* to help people with artist's block. It is an individual practice of continuous freefall writing of three sides of paper every morning, an unfiltered emptying of your mind, and appreciation of what is there.

- **Place** … the gathering points for collective imagining, designed for connection and creation, collaboration and chance encounter, encouraging diversity of people and ideas. In Portland, Oregon, Intersection Repair invites residents who live around a shared intersection to come together to imagine what they want their street to look like, then collectively paint the road surface. The results are truly beautiful and it starts to change the way people see the place. Communities start holding street parties, setting up mini-libraries and just generally gathering in the place they once ignored.

- **Practices** … that connect us and change our frame of possibility. Practices are the things we can do together that take us out of our rational thinking minds into something altogether different, breaking down our internal constraints and societal norms to open up a greater sense of what is possible. A good practice creates bridges between the real and imagined, the known and unknown. For example, "what if" questions are a simple way to open up a range of possibilities. They are sufficiently open-ended that they don't feel prescriptive while allowing people to shape their own creative responses.

• **Pacts** … of collaboration that catalyse imagination into action. Action drives belief, and belief inspires further action. It is an agreement that brings together people and organisations who together can make things work. In Italy, for example, Bologna's Civic Imagination Office works with communities across the city through six labs, using visioning tools and activities to come up with a diversity of ideas for the future of the city. When good ideas emerge, the municipality sits down with the community and creates a pact, bringing together the support the municipality can offer, and what the community can offer. In the past 5 years, over 500 pacts have been created.

A MORE INSPIRED APPROACH TO INNOVATION

Innovation demands human ingenuity. It is exciting, it is about people, about the future, with limitless possibilities.

It is an essential role of every business leader, every business function. Whilst innovation has long centred around the tangible, technical icon of the product, organisations have finally opened their minds to many more forms of innovation.

Innovation used to be associated with long, disciplined, stage-gated processes by which ideas were productised and taken to market. Today's innovators, in small and large businesses, get excited by design thinking and lean development. These are useful tools to create more insightful and faster solutions, but there is much more to innovation.

A more inspired approach to innovation has nine dimensions (see Figure 4.1):

- **Human-centred** rather than driven by products
- **Problem-solving** rather than limited by capability
- **Future shaping** rather than aligning with today
- **Whole business** rather than functionally isolated
- **Fast and experimental** rather than slow and perfect
- **Sustainable impact** rather than profit obsessed
- **Growth driving** rather than unaligned commercially
- **Portfolio building** rather than isolated innovations
- **Active adaptation** rather than launched and forgotten

Innovation is not like most other business functions and activities. There is no department or VP of innovation in most companies. There is rarely even an innovation strategy or budget. There are few standard templates, rules, processes, or consistent measures of success. In a sense, each act of innovation is a unique feat, a leap of imagination that can be neither predicted nor replicated. It is certainly not business as usual.

That's also the beauty. Innovation is pervasive, a challenge for every function and person across the business. It can have

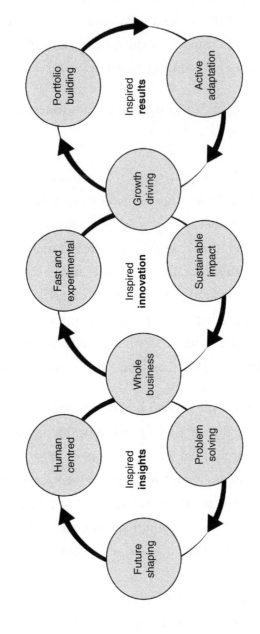

FIGURE 4.1 The nine dimensions of inspired innovation.

process, but it can also break all the rules, and sometimes needs to. By being rooted in every part of the business, and drawing on budgets from each, it can be a more collaborative, integrated and formidable approach.

Leaders are the ultimate innovators in companies, not necessarily entrepreneurs as in the founders of start-ups, but setting the agenda, ensuring that it has the resources and space to thrive, and that the business delivers today, but also creates a better tomorrow.

CODE 23: SEARCH FOR BETTER IDEAS
Innovation starts by finding the right question. Engage people in a bigger conversation, and then seek to address it in more enlightened ways.

When Canadian science graduate Christopher Charles visited Cambodia, he discovered that anaemia was a huge public health problem.

In the villages of Kandai province, instead of bright young children, Charles found many were small and weak with slow mental development. Women were suffering from tiredness and headaches, and were unable to work. Pregnant women faced serious complications before and after childbirth.He realised that anaemia was a big problem, with almost 50% of women and children suffering due to a deficiency of iron in their diets. Regular solutions, like iron supplements, were neither affordable nor available, and were distrusted by many people.

Charles had a novel idea. Inspired by previous research, which showed that cooking in cast iron pots increased the iron content of food, he decided to put a lump of iron into the cooking pot, made from melted-down metal. However, people rejected that too, not keen on a coarse lump of metal mixed into their food.

He searched deeper into local anthropology, and then hit upon the symbol of luck in Cambodian culture, the fish. He recast his iron in the shape of a fish, and called it the "Lucky Iron Fish", and designed it to release iron at the right concentration to provide the nutrients that so many women and children in the country were lacking.

Scientific analysis showed that, by using the iron fish each day, it provided 75% of an adult's daily recommended intake of iron. In practice, he found that within 12 months, around half of those using it were no longer anaemic and, after 3 years, the condition was largely eliminated.

WHERE DO GOOD IDEAS COME FROM?

The romance of the "eureka" moment, when amazingly smart individuals have sudden creative epiphanies, and jump out of their overflowing baths like Archimedes, is unrealistic.

In *Where Good Ideas Come From,* Stephen Johnson says that most new ideas emerge out of the fragments of others, a product of new environments which allow new possibilities. Indeed, most good ideas can actually be broken down into the useful remains of the failures of others.

Bill Gates tells how the origins of Microsoft lay, not in a flash of genius, but evolved from many hours with his friend, Paul Allen, tinkering with their high school's mainframe computers, a culture of change blowing through society, and a hunch that computers could be made much smaller and more connected.

Crisis, recessions, wars are often the birthplace of new ideas, as markets are shaken-up, consumers think differently, and there is an urgency to create something different, cheaper, faster, better. Microsoft's founding environment in 1975 was shaped by an economic downturn that put an end to years of post-war growth. Similarly, Disney in 1929, McDonalds in 1955, CNN in 1980, Airbnb in 2008, all emerged out of tough times.

Taking inspiration from Johnson, here are nine sources of better ideas:

- **Adjacent ideas.** Most innovations are derived from the fragments of what exists today, bringing together other ideas, new capabilities, or aspirations.

- **Evolving ideas.** Most new concepts tend to emerge slowly, gaining acceptance as they mature and their founders gain confidence in their evolving work.
- **Building ideas.** Ideas tend to build on each other like platforms, Apple's insight into computing led to the iPod, to iTunes, to iPhones, to AppStore.
- **Network ideas.** Exposing ideas to more people, enables them to spread faster, and for ideas to multiply in richness and rise in crowds.
- **Collaborative ideas.** Openness of ideas allows them to grow further and faster, rather than competition that restricts them and patents that hide them.
- **Random ideas.** Sometimes new possibilities emerge by chance, out of chaos or unintended actions driving lucky combinations or new insights.
- **Serendipitous ideas.** Ideas converge in a shared physical or intellectual space, bringing a diversity of people together and enabling creative collisions.
- **Unconventional ideas.** Errors can be surprisingly creative moments, because they challenge what we think is right, and show possibility beyond convention.
- **Recycled ideas.** Expatiation is when something developed for a specific purpose is eventually used in a completely different way.

Ideas are the currency of today's world. Where machines can outperform us at anything which we already know, we need ideas to move us forwards. In the business world, we codify ideas into intellectual properties – patents, designs, trademarks, and brands.

Ideas are packages of consciousness, of creativity, and of inspiration. As a result, they are not only the building blocks of the future, of innovations and progress, they also captivate us, they give us hope, they fuel our dreams and desires, we want them.

TROUBLEMAKERS AND RULEBREAKERS

"Rebels have a bad reputation", says Francesca Gino, a behavioural scientist. "Rebels are people who break rules that should be broken. They break rules that hold them and others back, and their way of rule breaking is constructive rather than destructive. It creates positive change."

Gino tells the story of the time when she was browsing the shelves at a bookstore when she came across an unusual-looking book in the cooking section: *Never Trust a Skinny Italian Chef* by Massimo Bottura. The recipes in it were playful, quirky and improbable. Snails were paired with coffee sauce, veal tongue with charcoal powder. Francesca, who is Italian, says remixing classic recipes like this is a kind of heresy in Italian cooking. "We really cherish the old way," she says. But this chef, one of the most influential in the world, couldn't resist circling back to one, big question: Why do we have to follow these rules?

> We think of them as troublemakers, outcasts, contrarians: those colleagues, friends, and family members who complicate seemingly straightforward decisions, create chaos, and disagree when everyone else is in agreement. But in truth, rebels are also those among us who change the world for the better with their unconventional outlooks. Instead of clinging to what is safe and familiar, and falling back on routines and tradition, rebels defy the status quo. They are masters of innovation and reinvention, and they have a lot to teach us.

Gino argues that the future belongs to the rebel. Curiosity and insistence on questioning the status quo are among the qualities she believes separate good leaders from great ones, and the people who can't wait to get to work from the ones who count the minutes until they can leave. These qualities are part of an instinct to rebel against what feels comfortable. Adopting them she says is the key to "creativity, productivity, and making work suck less".

START BY ASKING BETTER QUESTIONS

Start by asking Why … then Why, Why, Why, Why, Why, Why.

The "seven Whys" is an incredibly simple technique when talking to somebody and seeking to understand their real problem.

As you learn more, keep asking "Why?" again, each time delving deeper into the real drivers of a problem. If you can get to the bottom of a problem, then of course, you have a better opportunity to solve it.

"The important and difficult job is never to find the right answers, it is to find the right question. For there are few things as useless, if not dangerous, as the right answer to the wrong question" said business guru Peter Drucker.

Drucker's insight has long been an inspiration for Hal Gregersen who is based at the MIT Sloan School of Management. He believes that the best starting point for innovation is to ask powerful provocative questions. The most innovative leaders question the world constantly, provoking others to think openly and differently.

Key to this is asking the right questions, or "catalytic questions" as he calls them – What if?, Why not? – questions that break down the limits of people's current thinking, allow them to challenge more of the conventions, see things from different perspectives, and accelerate their better thinking.

Gregerson uses his distinctive "Question Burst" methodology as an alternative to more conventional brainstorming-type approaches. His methodology seeks to explore the question through rapid collaboration, rather than jumping to the answer. This allows people to concentrate on the problem, rather than jumping too quickly to possible answers that might be answering the wrong question.

He uses three steps in the process:

- **Explore the challenge:** Select a challenge you care deeply about. Invite a few people to help you consider that challenge from fresh angles. Ideally, choose people who have no direct experience with the problem and whose worldview is starkly different from yours. In two minutes, describe the challenge.
- **Expand the question:** Spend the next four minutes collectively generating as many questions as possible about the challenge. Don't answer any of the questions and don't explain why you're asking the questions. Go for at least 15–20 fast questions in four minutes. Write them down word for word.
- **Commit to the quest:** Consider the questions and select a few "catalytic" questions from the list, ones that hold the most potential for disrupting the status quo. Commit to pursuing at least one new pathway you've glimpsed, and use that as the foundation of the problem to solve.

As we progress through organisations to become business leaders, we shift from functional experts where we are expected to have all the answers, to a broader perspective where our most useful contributions are to ask better questions. At the same time, with years of experience we feel we know much more than many others, and can become closed and defensive, rather than good listeners. Former Uber CEO, Travis Kalanik was caught on video whilst taking a ride being challenged about the business by his driver who was unaware of his passenger's identity. Kalanik's defensive verbal attack on the driver went viral and resulted in him being fired.

CODE 24: EMBRACE A DESIGNER MINDSET
Design is about problem solving, by creating a better artefact, an experience, or even a transformation. It requires insight and perspective, engineering and craft.

David Kelley is like a mad scientist, brilliant and bustling, one of the most creative people you will ever meet. He is the designer behind many icons of the digital age, from the first mouse for Apple, to the thumbs up/thumbs down button on TiVo's remote control.

After an initial engineering career with Boeing and NCR, which he found stagnant and frustrating, he started to learn about the cross-functional power of design. In 1978, he co-founded the design firm that ultimately became IDEO, now recognised worldwide for its innovative approach to design, or more accurately, a design-driven approach to innovation.

Kelley also created the methodology for "human-centred design" which more recently became known as "design thinking". He founded the "d.school" at Stanford, the Hasso Plattner Institute of Design, where students from business, engineering, medicine, law, and other diverse disciplines learn to solve complex problems collaboratively and creatively.

Kelley argues that a "design mindset" seeks new ways to solve problems and create improved futures by combining analysis and imagination. It seeks to build ideas up, unlike critical thinking, which breaks them down.

DESIGN AS CREATIVE PROBLEM-SOLVING

Kelley calls it "the messy front-end" of any innovation project, finding the right problem to solve. That might require lots of going around in circles, as a team explores the problems, reflects on the challenge, asks more questions, takes different perspectives, and takes time to think. This matters.

Here are some of the principles which Kelley sees as key to great design:

- **Navigate ambiguity**: Getting to a new place means that you need to be comfortable working with ambiguity, paradoxes which are not yet resolved, and directions which remain unclear.

- **Learn from others**: Teams will always beat the lone genius. Hard work and big brains are no match for creative diversity. This requires openness to learning, connecting, improving.
- **Experiment rapidly**: Ideas thrive on momentum, a rapid process of trying and testing multiple ideas, encouraging learning and also unlearning, keeping moving to stretch and shape ideas, and sustain a feeling of progress.
- **Build and craft things intentionally:** The best way to engage somebody is to show them something. It might be a picture, diagram, prototype. This gives people something to play off, to challenge and improve.
- **Communicate deliberately:** Focus on the users, not the decision-makers. Show what the future will be like for them, and use storytelling, anecdotes of real people, to make it more real and human.

Asking the right question, defining the right problem, will make all the difference later. Whilst we can embrace all sorts of fast, experimental and iterative approaches to innovation, if we start with the wrong problem, we're unlikely to create the best solution. Kelley calls it a state of not knowing: "Wallowing in that state of not knowing is not easy, but it's necessary," he says.

HUMAN-CENTRED THINKING

"Design thinking" is a problem-solving methodology. It typically starts by spending time with users, people whose problem you are solving, to find out what their current everyday experiences are, and to use those to find insights into what the real underlying challenges are and how they might be addressed.

Importantly, it is not just about the "design stages" of product development (initial sketches, graphic design, prototyping, etc.) but a more holistic approach that is built on deep insight, and where creativity lies as much in interpreting the problem as in finding solutions.

The key phases are:

- **Understand**: make sense of the problem, and explore it more deeply
- **Empathise**: gain a deeper understanding of the user's needs and aspirations
- **Define**: bring together analysis to agree the user's need to be addressed
- **Ideate**: create a wide range of possible ideas that could evolve into solutions
- **Prototype**: develop some of the ideas, making them more tangible
- **Test**: evaluate the concepts, gaining user feedback, and explore how to improve

Importantly this is not a linear process, but may require multiple iterations, particularly from test back to ideate to improve the ideas, but also back to define in order to better shape the questions. At the same time, it is important to use the pressure of time to drive creativity and the search for the best outcome.

Christoph Meinel and Larry Leifer of the HPI-Stanford Design Thinking Program laid out four principles for the successful implementation of design thinking:

- **The human rule**, which states that all design activity is ultimately social in nature, and any social innovation will bring us back to the "human-centric point of view".
- **The ambiguity rule**, in which design thinkers must preserve ambiguity by experimenting at the limits of their knowledge and ability, enabling the freedom to see things differently.
- **The redesign rule**, where all design is redesign; this comes as a result of changing technology and social circumstances but previously solved, unchanged human needs.
- **The tangibility rule**, the concept that making ideas tangible always facilitates communication and allows designers to treat prototypes as "communication media".

Whilst the process is usually considered as an iterative process up until the point of development, it is equally useful to consider iterating ideas and solutions once they are in the market, practical and commercial. This is even more important when the "design" is not simply a product, but an entire experience, a system, or business model.

DESIGN IS FUNCTION AND FORM

One basic principle of good design is that form follows function.

In 1896, Boston architect Louis Sullivan used the phrase when describing his vision for the functioning of a modern city. He said that it needed a new form of building, one which would become the "modern structural steel skyscraper." He argued that a tall building's exterior design (form) should reflect the activities (functions) that take place inside its walls.

Years later his protégé Frank Lloyd Wright went further, arguing that in great design "function and form become one".

In today's world of business, anything can be designed – a customer experience or business model, a website or a loyalty scheme, an organisation structure or purpose statement – always following the principle of function and then form.

Alex Osterwalder and Yves Pigneur even call themselves infor-mation designers, seeking templated structures that can help businesspeople to think and express their ideas rigorously and clearly.

One of the best ways to translate function into form is by seek-ing simplicity. Simplicity when achieved can seem easy, clear and even beautiful. John Maeda, former President of the Rhode

Island School of Design, wrote a great book called *The Laws of Simplicity*. He says that simplicity is achieved in 10 ways:

- **Reduce.** The simplest way to achieve simplicity is through thoughtful reduction.
- **Organise.** Organisation makes a system of many appear fewer.
- **Time.** Savings in time feel like simplicity.
- **Learn.** Knowledge makes everything simpler.
- **Differences.** Simplicity and complexity need each other.
- **Context.** What lies in the periphery of simplicity is definitely not peripheral.
- **Emotion.** More emotions are better than fewer.
- **Trust.** In simplicity we trust.
- **Failure.** Some things can never be made simple.
- **The One.** Simplicity is about subtracting the obvious, adding the meaningful.

Furniture designer Charles Eames said, "Design is an expression of a purpose, and it may later be judged as art". Design depends largely on constraints, the problem to be solved and, in business, solved in a way that can be practical and profitable. He then considered the difference between art and design: "Art can have no other reason for existing other than to be viewed or otherwise experienced. Design requires a function. If the design is visually striking, then it may also be considered art," he added.

Maeda says "The best designers in the world all squint when they look at something. They squint to see the forest from the trees – to find the right balance. Squint at the world. You will see more, by seeing less."

CODE 25: CREATE UNUSUAL CONNECTIONS

Concept fusions take multiple ideas – often nature or science, other sectors or markets, modular or decoupled – and connect them in novel ways.

Tinker Hatfield joined Nike in 1981, having started out as a pole-vaulter. Then having trained as an architect, he rapidly became Nike's lead shoe designer. He realised that his architectural skills could be applied to shoes, and is credited with designing the "cross-trainer" as a multi-sport shoe when he realised people at his Oregon gym brought various shoes with them for different activities.

He first made a name for himself, working alongside basketball legend Michael Jordan to create the Air Jordan boots that set Nike on a path to global brand success. In 1987, Hatfield designed the Nike Air Max running shoe. Inspired by visiting the Centre Georges Pompidou, he famously included a window in the shoe's midsole to show the air cushion.

At 67, he is now Nike's Vice President for Design and Special Projects, and oversees Nike's Innovation Kitchen. A profile of Hatfield in *1 Granary* magazine, said "to make an impact, whether it's in science, poetry or design, you need out of the box thinking. Unexpected ideas. The type of epiphanies that extend beyond the traditional confinement of your field. People who can produce them are rare, but once they find their creative outlet, true magic happens."

CREATIVE FUSIONS

Out of all the creative techniques which you will come across, the one that I have found the most powerful is the ability to connect two unconnected ideas. Like the Medicis of years gone by, it is about bringing unfamiliar ideas, situations, talents, challenges, and solutions together. I am also driven by the ancient Chinese wisdom of yin and yang, the opposing forces which always seek each other, and when they come together, they form something of beauty and harmony.

In *The Ascent of Man*, Jacob Bronowski claims that "a genius is a person who has two great ideas" and the ability to get them to fit together. Consider Ravi Shanker, bringing together the music of India and Europe, Paul Klee, combining the influences of cubism and primitive art, or Salvador Dali, combining scientific perspective with random visualisation.

One of the easiest ways to think more creatively in business is to apply existing ideas from outside your market. Look at what is happening in other sectors, in other countries, in other companies, and creatively explore how you can apply these to your business. The great thing about these ideas is that they are already tested, they can be produced, and people buy them, albeit in a different context. The challenge, therefore, is to find the relevant "parallels" and to apply the lessons in new and relevant ways.

The simplest but most provocative questions are ones like "How could we create the iPhone of our industry?" which encourages people to think of the whole business model by which devices and content, distributors and customers work together and make money. It might actually deliver an idea for digitalising the basic products into components, renegotiating relationships with suppliers for exclusive content, and letting customers select and combine them like iTunes, or it might be about creating the most aesthetically pleasing.

Fusion might also be about more radical crossovers. Whilst it is many years since I studied particle physics, I still use some of the simple ideas in my innovation projects with clients. Understanding atomic structures is a model for thinking differently about how products and services work together. Applying the characteristics of astrophysics gives me a categorisation tool for managing portfolios. Or I might apply my love of running. Imagine applying the discipline of track athletics to the entertainment industry, to create more drama in games and shows, or seeking to replicate the breakthrough of Nike's Air sole to new types of bottles for chilled beer.

The most creative people in your business don't have that talent by birth but through different experiences. We sometimes call them border-crossers, people who bring with them insights and expertise from completely different fields. The musician who works in the design team might seem an oddball, but could be the source of most creativity. The astrophysicist in your creativity workshop might seem like she has her head in the clouds, but is probably capable of some of the best cross-over thinking and most distinctive ideas.

INSPIRED BY NATURE

The Mercedes-Benz Vision AVTR was launched at the 2020 Consumer Electronics Show, as a futuristic concept for mobility. Its radical appearance, like a translucent liquid blurring into its environment, was described as "a new interaction between human, machine and nature" by fusing its exterior, interior and user experience. Its four-wheel drive, allowing each wheel to work independently allows a crab like motion, including sideways, powered by graphene-based organic fuel cells, eliminating all metals and carbon impacts.

James Cameron, the director of Avatar, the movie which explores how humans would coexist alongside other natural and mixed life forms, said, "When I look at this beautiful car, I see the physical manifestation of the velocity of an emotional, spiritual idea".

Biomimicry is the imitation of animals and plants, the models and systems of nature, to inspire new ways to solve complex human problems.

An early example was the study of birds to enable human flight. Although never successful in creating a "flying machine", Leonardo da Vinci, who trained as an anatomist was fascinated by the flight of birds, inspiring his designs for mechanical flight. Centuries later, the Wright Brothers succeeded in human flight, apparently inspired by racing pigeons.

Otto Schmitt developed the concept of "biomimetics" in the 1950s, studying the nerves in squid to engineer a device that replicated the biological system of nerve propagation. A decade later, Jack Steele coined the term "bionics" as "the science of systems which have some function copied from nature".

Examples of innovations in today's world inspired by nature include:

- **Bullet Train** inspired by the kingfisher: the world's fastest train enabled by a nose cone that imitates the bird's long beak, reducing noise and increasing speed.

- **Gecko climbing shoes** inspired by geckos: mimic the tiny hairs on a geckos toes which allows it to climb up vertical surface, creating an adhesive force.
- **Cylus backpacks** inspired by armadillos: the rigid yet flexible structure takes its cues from the scaled mammal using a series of recycled rubber inner tubes.
- **Mariek Ratsma shoes** inspired by bird skulls: copying the hollow and exceptionally light bone structure to create strong, lightweight shoes.
- **Kau prosthetics inspired** by tentacles: a highly flexible and controllable replacement arm using a curling motion at its tip to grip objects.

"When we look at what is truly sustainable, the only real model that has worked over long periods of time is the natural world," says James Cameron.

INSPIRED BY PARALLEL MARKETS

Lewis Hamilton's Mercedes Formula One car has a steering wheel more like a games console.

It might look like an Xbox controller on steroids, but it is designed like this for a reason: all the critical controls need to be within reach of Hamilton's thumbs so he doesn't have to move his hand from the custom grips while taking a corner.

Those at the bottom of the wheel are for when he's on a straight. However, it is not just the layout, materials are made as light and thin as possible, helping to reduce the overall weight of the car.

To manufacture, the wheel costs around $50 000.

On a similar theme, McDonalds has reengineered its Drive-Thru concept with the help of F1 motor racing teams who design the pit-stop environments and processes for absolute speed. Every hundredth of a second whilst changing tyres and refuelling can make the difference between winning or losing a race. McDonalds even takes its Drive-Thru service staff to live F1 events so that they can witness the spectacle of the pit-stop crew.

Learning directly from other markets – retail from transport, finance from healthcare, fashion from entertainment – has the advantage that many of the ideas are already proven to work in other environments and are familiar to consumers. Whilst it might be a radical innovation in your own sector, you can embrace it with more confidence and speed.

Here are some examples of innovations inspired by other sectors:

- **Yo Sushi! bars** inspired by baggage systems: the winding airport systems were the inspiration for delivering food on a table-top carousel.

- **Dyson vacuum cleaners** inspired by sawmills: Dyson took inspiration from a sawmill for his cyclone system of collecting dust without needing a bag.
- **McLaren baby strollers** inspired by aircraft wheels: the hydraulic landing gear of aircraft was the inspiration for the foldable mechanism.
- **Philips light bulbs** inspired by mobile phones: "pay as you go" payment models inspired Philips to offer LED light bulbs, charging only when used.
- **Hilti power tools** inspired by car leasing: the manufacturer was inspired by the car-leasing model to offer tools, service and repairs, for one monthly fee.

"Parallel" markets are typically contexts which have some similarity to your own – maybe dealing with long queues, or needing to personalise service – where you need a fresh solution. It might even be from your own sector, but a solution found in different geographies or different parts of the market. There is nothing wrong with "copying" an idea, provided it isn't illegal, although it may require some adapting before applying it.

> **CODE 26: DEVELOP NEW BUSINESS MODELS**
> Whilst products and services are quickly copied, business models are much harder to imitate, from platforms and exchanges to subscriptions and giving it away free.

Business model innovation is the architectural secret behind many of the most innovative start-ups of the last decade.

Way back in 1959, Xerox created breakthrough copying machines, but they were too expensive for many companies to buy. Their advance was not the machine, but the way people paid for it – leasing the product, then paying per copy for its use, with the price descending over time.

Gillette similarly innovated their business model, selling low-priced razors to fit regular high-priced blades. Fifty years later Nespresso adopted the same model.

How can you reach new audiences, changing the payment model, adding new services, using your assets in different ways, maybe licensing the manufacturing to partners, or sales to franchisees?

Business model innovation reconfigures the architecture of your business, transforms your proposition, and can massively boost your performance. Technology companies in particular, from Airbnb to Boeing, Coursera to Deliveroo, have thrived by thinking beyond the product and fundamentally reinventing the way in which they do business.

INNOVATING THE WHOLE BUSINESS

In *Ten Types of Innovation* Larry Keeley defines the most important types of innovation found across any business. Many organisations don't just innovate in one area, but combine many of the types together.

- **Profit model**: how you make money (e.g. Fortnite)
- **Network**: how you connect with others to create value (e.g. Huawei)
- **Structure**: how to organise and align your talent and assets (e.g. Netflix)
- **Process**: how you use signature or superior methods to do your work (e.g. Inditex)
- **Product**: how you develop distinguishing features and functionality (e.g. Corning)
- **Product system**: how you create complementary products and services (e.g. Apple)
- **Service**: how you support and amplify the value of your offerings (e.g. Zappos)
- **Channel**: how you deliver your offerings to customers and users (e.g. 3DHubs)
- **Brand**: how you represent your offerings and business (e.g. Burberry)

- **Customer experience**: how you foster compelling interactions (e.g. Peloton).

Which ones matter most? Keeley analysed the innovation activities of over 1000 large companies over a 10-year period. He found, perhaps not surprisingly, that almost 90% of all time and resource went into product innovation. However, when he evaluated the business impact, measured by economic value, he found that the innovations that made the most difference were network, then profit model, then customer engagement.

We waste too much time and resource focused on product innovations that deliver solutions that are largely incremental, quickly copied and offer little financial return. We spend far too little on what makes a difference, innovating how the business works.

DEFINING THE BUSINESS MODEL

Business models explain how organisations work – how they create value for customers, and in doing so, how they create value for all other stakeholders. They can map the current business, or explore options for the future.

The approach originates from mapping "value networks" in the 1990s, understanding the systems across business and its partners through which value (both financial and non-financial) is created and exchanged – by whom, how, and for whom. I remember working with Pugh Roberts to create a multi-million dollar dynamic model for Mastercard which showed varying any one driver – such as interest rates, or branding – affected everything else. And thereby being able to test new ideas and optimise the model.

Business models represent the dynamic system through which a business creates and captures value, and determine how this can be changed or optimised. They are a configuration of the building blocks of business and their creative reconfiguration can be a significant innovation.

Business models became fundamental to business strategy, driven by them, but also driving their content. Hambrick and Fredrickson's Strategy Diamond is all about aligning the organisation, achieving an economic logic between strategic choices. It helps to align the business, matching the right strategies for outside and inside, using the proposition as the fulcrum, and profitability as the measure of success.

Business models can often appear very mechanical, lacking emotion and easy to imitate. In 2001, Patrick Staehler, seeking to explain the new breed of digital businesses, created a business model "map" driven by the value proposition, enabled by the value architecture, creating economic value and sustained by cultural values. The last point here is most interesting, in that it captured the distinctive personality of a business, its leadership styles and ways of doing business. This is much harder to copy and also sustains the other aspects.

INNOVATING THE BUSINESS MODEL

New business models are the most effective way to transform organisations, to innovate the whole way in which the business works. Inspired by a new generation of businesses – Airbnb to Uber, Dollar Shave Club to Netflix – we see dramatically new business models in every market, particularly driven by collaborative ecosystems, data engines, network effects, and new payment models.

Airbnb makes money by helping you to make money out of your spare room, connecting host and guest, then taking a small fee from each. Nespresso makes great coffee, selling discounted machines, and then getting you to sign up to an everlasting and incredibly profitable direct revenue stream of coffee pods.

What if your business started leasing rather than selling, became part of the sharing economy? What if you facilitated an exchange between buyers and sellers and took a cut? How about moving to a subscription model, or a freemium model, or a referral model, or an advertising model?

We used to think that a business simply made things and sold them. Now it is much more complicated. Or rather, there are many more innovative ways to achieve success. Some have been around forever, like franchising and licensing, luxury or discounter, family or not-for-profit, barter or pay-per-use models, whilst others have been enabled through digital platforms.

There is an infinite number of potential business models which you could creatively develop; however, some of the most common formats, applicable to almost every type of business, include:

- **Advertising-based models.** Services are free to users, whilst advertisers pay to engage with the audience attracted, e.g. Google, Facebook.
- **Razor-and-blades models.** The facilitating item, like a razor, is sold cheaply, then accessories, like blades, at a premium, e.g. HP, Nespresso.
- **Added-value models.** The facilitating item, like an iPad, is sold at a premium, then accessories, like apps, sold cheaply, e.g. Apple.
- **One-for-one models.** The company donates a product to a charity, or person in need, for every product sold, e.g. Toms, Warby Parker.
- **Cashflow models.** High volumes are generated at low margins, payments received quickly from customers, paid slowly to suppliers, e.g. Amazon, Dell.

- **Platform-based models.** These bring buyers and suppliers together, typically charging both of them to connect and transact, e.g. Airbnb, Uber.
- **Subscription-based models**. These charge a regular, e.g. monthy, fee for unlimited use of a product or service, e.g. Netflix, Zipcar.
- **Freemium models**. These encourage trial or a basic level of usage free, but charge for additional or premium options, e.g. Spotify, Fortnite.
- **Direct to consumer models**. Products which in the past would have been sold through intermediaries, are sold direct, e.g. Allbirds, Casper.

Alex Osterwalder's "Business Model Canvas" emerged as the most common template on which to map a business model. He popularised the approach so much that his supersized canvas now features in workshops throughout the world, always with an array of multi-coloured sticky notes as teams debate the best combination of solutions for each box. Whilst the canvas lacks the sophistication of value driver analysis and dynamic modelling, it is about testing hypotheses in each aspect and how they could work together, and in that respect works as a thinking model.

Business models have become a practical tool for rethinking the whole business, seeing the connections and then innovating the business. In fact they offer a great platform to facilitate new strategy and innovation thinking.

CODE 27: EXPERIMENT WITH SPEED AND AGILITY
Insight and imagination, experiment and evolve, marginal gains and big bets, speed and scale. These entrepreneurial mantras replace the linear processes of old.

Halo Top was founded by former lawyer Justin Woolverton in 2011 and within 5 years became America's top selling ice-cream, creating revenues of $350 million.

The brand's origins lie in Woolverton's late-night kitchen experiments, seeking indulgence without guilt the next morning. His experiments typically involved throwing random healthy foods together. Any dairy, any fruit, any juice, vegetables too. He tried many different concoctions, eventually resolving on a recipe so good he believed he could sell it. He sought out a local kitchen with an industrial food mixer, and evolved the recipes further, testing them on friends. More changes. More testing. Eventually he was ready.

Halo Top is distinctive for its pint-sized tubs emblazoned with its calorie count, normally something which competitors try to hide away. 280 calories for a pint of fabulous-tasting ice cream proved irresistible to many. Within six months his brand was hitting Los Angeles stores, funded entirely by his own credit card debt. Soon retailers like Whole Foods joined the party, and within three years he had over 20 flavours, selling 30 million tubs through 34 000 stores. Woolverton, no longer working in law, continued to experiment in his kitchen, evolving the recipe as he learnt what worked, tripling his revenues in the next two years, and then selling the business, reportedly for more the $2 billion in 2019.

FAST EXPERIMENTS

As a physicist I had to learn to be creative. Whilst quantum mechanics and particle physics might seem logical and mathematical pursuits, the heart of scientific progress is the ability to imagine, to create a hypothesis, which you can then go on to test and validate. Einstein was a terrible mathematician, spending his days walking in the Swiss mountains imagining new connections in his mind – time and distance, energy and mass – but then relying upon his wife, a trained mathematician to evolve his ideas into numbers and formulae.

Imagination enables us to leap forwards. Similarly, every innovation starts with a hypothesis – typically in the form of an insight, and then an idea – perhaps shaped through understanding customers more deeply, and applying design thinking.

The concept of "lean development" started with Silicon Valley entrepreneurs Steve Blank and Eric Ries in 2000, and was captured in Reis's 2011 book *The Lean Start-Up*, which has largely transformed innovation, not just for entrepreneurs but for large companies too. GE for example, took his process and created an organisation framework called Fast Works for rapid and agile innovation.

Blank wrote an article, *Why the Lean Start-Up Changes Everything*, saying that it's "turning the conventional wisdom about entrepreneurship on its head. New ventures of all kinds are attempting to improve their chances of success by following its principles of failing fast and continually learning. And despite the methodology's name, in the long term some of its biggest payoffs may be gained by the *large* companies that embrace it."

The idea is to quickly iterate solutions, with the belief that it is better to start with an imperfect solution then make it better, than to spend a long time perfecting the wrong solution. This is achieved by getting an initial idea out quickly, a prototype if you like, known as a "minimum value product" (MVP), and then learning from customers how to improve it. This creates a "build, measure, learn" loop that iterates over time.

In technology, this is often known as an "agile" approach. Many developers have come together to define how the approach is different in their *Manifesto for Agile Software Development*, which says the agile approach achieves:

- Individuals and interactions over processes and tools
- Working software over comprehensive documentation
- Customer collaboration over contract negotiation
- Responding to change over following a plan

Many innovators see a business plan as their "enemy" in that it rigidly assumes a solution and its likely impact, before any experimentation has even begun. Similarly, techniques such as Kaizen and Six Sigma are often at odds with today's fast and fluid approach in that they seek efficiency through documentation, standardisation and optimisation. An echo of the "fixed mindset" in a "growth mindset" world.

SCALE AND MULTIPLY

"Starting up is easy, scaling up is harder", is a common refrain as small companies find it hard to move beyond initial audiences, resources and applications. The same applies to products launched by large companies who want to move from niche to mainstream.

"Blitzscaling" is a technique for igniting and managing "dizzying growth" as championed by LinkedIn founder Reid Hoffman.

It prioritizes speed over efficiency in an environment of uncertainty and allows a business to shift from "start-up" to "scaleup" at a furious pace, one that seeks to capture the imagination of the market, building on word of mouth and group behaviour.

I first came across the term when discussing innovative growth strategies with Richard Branson. In consumer-based markets, he argued, particularly technology ones where new ideas can spread quickly, it is better to expand rapidly, even if initially unprofitably, to become the de facto standard or at least the definitive brand of the sector.

Some companies scale incredibly fast. At its peak, PayPal grew 10% per day. That means for a while, every week, PayPal doubled its user base. After one month of such growth, your customer base would have increased by a factor of 16.

Hoffman defines four factors that enable companies to scale at lightning speed:

- **Network effects.** |The best networks become more attractive to others with every additional participant, because of the multiplied connections.
- **Available market.** Start-ups grow in a niche, but then need to reach out to additional audiences as they "cross the chasm" to find a larger market

- **Fast channels.** Your distribution partners or platforms need to be able to cope with the rapid expansion, most easily online.
- **Good margins.** This allows you to invest in sales incentives, including discounts, but still have sufficient profit to sustain investment in growth.

Exponential effects become particularly important at this time, not just in order to grow through networks of consumers, enabled by social media, partner networks and word of mouth, but also in the ability to scale your business model. Salim Ismael's *Exponential Organisations* is a particularly useful guide to this. Examples of ways to build more scalability into your business include:

- **Fast staff**: having a flexible employee base, treated responsibly, enabling you to add people rapidly on demand, for specific tasks, to support sales and delivery.
- **Fast culture**: building an autonomous culture that enables fast and distributed working, where people are empowered to make decisions locally.
- **Fast partners**: focusing on a small number of critical assets and activities yourself, and then working with outsourced partners to provide or achieve everything else.
- **Fast insights**: using data and algorithms to spot patterns in emergent behaviour, and learn rapidly where to focus on how to adapt value propositions and price.

The shift from start-up to scale-up is when a small business starts to need more structure, and a different cultural, strategic, operational, financial and leadership approaches. While Steve Jobs likened working at a start-up to "being a pirate", he said working for a scale-up was like "joining the Navy". Hoffman describes the phases as:

- **Family stage**, e.g. one to nine employees: the CEO is often a product specialist, personally drives growth and is involved in almost every decision.
- **Tribe stage**, e.g. 10s of employees: the CEO begins to delegate, hire key employees and manage the people who are driving growth.
- **Village stage**, e.g. 100s of employees: the CEO focuses on creating a growth-oriented culture and developing the leadership skills of the executive team.
- **City stage**, e.g. 1000s of employees: the CEO transitions to a high-level position that focuses on organisation direction and coordination through teams.

The challenges involved in getting a business started, finding a successful customer proposition and business model, and then scaling it up, can take time, but also extreme energy and perseverance. Few leaders have the fitness or resilience for such journeys. Amazon's Jeff Bezos has an antidote, it's called "Day 1".

"IT'S ALWAYS DAY 1"

Amazon is a relentless innovator, aided in part by its private ownership which shields it from the distractions of the short-term demands of public reporting and activist investors. Innovation is also driven by the unquenching desire of Jeff Bezos and his team to do better, to do more for customers.

Bezos says that it typically requires 50 big ideas to launch every successful new business. It's therefore important to actively weed out the less likely ideas in order to focus resources on winners.

Amazon's "fast and agile" approach uses many of the principles which we have explored, but also a number of innovative techniques, for example:

- **Pizza teams:** Keep teams small so that they are intimate, fast and efficient; never have teams larger than would require an order of two pizzas.
- **Embrace failure**: Not everything works, and Amazon has a mantra of "think big, test small, fail fast and learn always", even for projects like Amazon Fire.
- **PR and FAQs**: At the start of any project, teams imagine potential press releases and FAQs for a new concept, to test its logic and customer-centricity.

Each year Bezos writes a letter to his shareholders. He talks about Amazon's latest adventures, innovations and performance, and also offers insights and ideas for every business to learn from his experiences. However, one theme he comes back to every year, is the idea of "Day 1".

If you go to Amazon headquarters in Seattle, you will find a building named "Day 1" where Bezos's office is located. When he moved buildings, he took the name with him. Outside there is a sign which says, "There's so much stuff that has yet to be invented. There's so much new that's going to happen."

"Day 1" is when everything seems possible. Dreams have no limits. Confidence and energy are high, as are anticipation and optimism. No obstacle can get in your way. But then complexity starts to creep in. Your inbox grows full, your schedule becomes choked by meetings, more people bring more complexity, and the organisation slows down, becomes more rigid, more risk averse.

Bezos was recently asked in a staff meeting what Day 2 looks like. His reply was instant. "Day 2 is stasis. Followed by irrelevance. Followed by excruciating, painful decline. Followed by death. And that is why it is always Day 1."

> ## CODE 28: DREAM CRAZY
> In a technological world, it is our creativity – audacious ideas, counter intuition, beautiful designs, and novel fusions – that inspire love, desire and progress.

Ideas are not in themselves innovations, but innovations need big ideas – big frames for thinking, to explore more possibilities, and develop more ideas.

Purpose gives organisations a bigger frame for innovation, to innovate within *why* they exist, rather than being limited by *what* they do. Limits are useful too. Constraints drive creative intensity, be it time limits like IDEO's one week of design thinking, or limits such as the need to meet specific customer needs or reduce specific environmental impacts.

Perhaps the most useful, and one of the simplest techniques I have ever found for stretching possibilities comes from Alphabet. In a world where most businesses would be quite happy to settle for five–10% growth, it asks – as we saw in Code 2 – "Why go for 10% better, when you could go for 10 times better?"

THE MOONSHOT FACTORY

Ten years ago, Astro Teller was asked by Google founders Larry Page and Sergey Brin to build a "moonshot factory". They called it "Google X", and eventually simply "X" as part of Alphabet.

Astro (his real name is Eric, but his friends thought his spiky hair reminded them of astroturf) was born in Cambridge, England then grew up just outside Chicago, Illinois. He had great pedigree; his grandparents include French economist and mathematician Gérard Debreu and Hungarian-born American theoretical physicist Edward Teller.

Teller followed a similar path, studying computer science at Stanford, and then gaining a PhD in AI. He wrote a novel, *Exegesis*, when he was 27 about an AI program that develops consciousness and begins to correspond with its creator. His early career saw him co-found BodyMedia, a maker of wearable devices that measure sleep, perspiration and calories burned.

At X, he became known as "Captain of Moonshots", leader of crazy ideas.

In 2010, he was asked to create "something far beyond an innovation lab". Ideas were initially fuzzy, but X knew they wanted to create an organisation that could invent and launch breakthrough technologies that would make the world a radically better place.

They also recognised that X could play an important role in Google's future development, reaching beyond its core business and beating what many called the innovator's dilemma, to create the future business whilst still focused on today's.

10X BETTER, NOT JUST 10%

Teller set about creating an organisation of diverse, creative people and encouraged weird, extreme thinking. He says "humanity is choosing to keep much of its potential off the table, underemployed, and underutilised. Many people go to work at jobs that aren't designed to be fulfilling, and many more don't get the chance to contribute at all."

The "10x not 10%" mantra emerged as a symbol of ambition, to stretch people's thinking. Asked by me how it works, Teller asked me to imagine two teams of people seeking to improve the fuel performance of a car. If we assume that this is currently 50 mpg, one team would seek to improve it 10% to 55 mpg, which would reflect fairly normal progress. The other team would have a 10x goal, seeking a solution that would deliver 500 mpg. This team would have to think more radically, change perspective, solve the problem in a new way. And even if they failed (sort of) by reaching, say, 200 mpg, it would be real progress.

"Most organisations are forced to focus on their own profitability and short-term goals at the expense of everything else, leaving the status quo intact, or at best only making the world incrementally better. Yet the massive problems facing us this century need the widest array of minds, the wildest imaginations, and enormous commitments of time, resources, and attention."

Teller hopes that X will prove that "good for the world" can be financially rewarding, so that more organisations will be inspired to operate in a similar way. He says, "What I've come to realise is that our main cultural battle is against fear and the strong gravitational pull toward conventional ways of thinking and behaving. All of us have been conditioned for years not to fail, not to be vulnerable, and to minimise risk."

CREATING THE FUTURE AT X

When they started, Teller says X wanted to focus on big problems, often the most significant social and environmental challenges, using breakthrough technologies to solve those problems in radically new ways.

Projects have ranged from Google's self-driving car which has now evolved into a separate business; Waymo, developing software for driverless cars; Glass which is AR-based glasses for use in industrial environments; Loon, bringing universal internet access through flying balloons and is now a separate business; and Dandelion which sells geothermal energy direct to consumers. And many more successes, and some failures.

Teller describes seven big lessons from X:

- **Don't think you can predict the future.** Few people are better than random at knowing which ideas will succeed in the long run. Instead, try audacious things and decide quickly when you're wrong. Most ideas will demand many iterations.
- **Take a long-term view.** Work on hard problems with a 5–10 year horizon. This gives space to explore and experiment and learn more deeply. Taking the long view also enables you to think through the implications not just the applications.
- **Find space for weirdos.** Willy Wonka had to build a chocolate factory to house the Oompa Loompas because they struggled to survive in the real world. Most innovators and dreamers are too disruptive for most organisations.
- **Dream like a child, test like a grown-up.** Be optimistic. People enjoy ridiculously hard problems, and the possibility of magical solutions. Indeed a 10x goal can sometimes be easier than a 10% goal, because you have more mental freedom to explore solutions.
- **Seek extraordinary results.** Most X projects don't have quantified goals, but most people like some kind of plan and measure. Teams are asked to drive many experiments and come back when they've found something that makes everyone say "holy s**t."

- **Be passionately dispassionate.** Inventing the future requires the ability to ruthlessly let go of ideas that aren't good enough, and move on to better projects. Some ideas could change the world, but if they are never going to be commercially possible, then move on.
- **Create fearless teams.** The lone inventor having a eureka moment is a myth; innovation comes from great teams. This doesn't mean innovation by committee or consensus. X has incredibly diverse teams – rocket scientists and concert pianists, physicists and artists.

SUMMARY: HOW WILL YOU RECODE YOUR INNOVATION?

5 questions to reflect on:

- Find your ingenuity … What would make your innovations more ingenious?
- Designer mindset … How can you get deeper insight into function and form?
- Customer agendas … What are the significant shifts in your consumers' minds?
- Faster experiments … How could you solve problems better and faster together?
- Moonshot thinking … What are the "10x not 10%" goals for your business?

5 leaders to inspire you (more at businessrecoded.com):

- James Watt, Brewdog … Scotland's punk brewer, crowdfunding his innovations
- Rene Renzepi, Noma … the world's top chef, foraging for local ingredients
- Devi Shetty, Narayana Health … doctor to Mother Teresa, caring for India's poor
- Katrina Lake, Stitch Fix … reinventing shopping with an intelligent monthly "fix"
- Jensen Huang, Nvidea … the world's most successful CEO, and the power of AI

5 books to go deeper:

- *Out of Our Minds* by Ken Robinson
- *Creativity Inc* by Ed Catmull
- *Questions and the Answers* by Hal Gregersen
- *Change by Design* by Tim Brown
- *10 Types of Innovation* by Larry Keeley

5 places to explore further:

- Strategyzer
- Board of Innovation
- Idea to Value
- Disruptor League
- The Lean Startup

UBUNTU

Recode your organisation

HOW CAN THE BEST TEAMS ACHIEVE MORE TOGETHER?

From passive hierarchies to dynamic ecosystems

Ubuntu *comes from Xhosa and Zulu languages, referring to the essential human virtues, compassion and humanity. It was a favourite word of South Africa's Nelson Mandela who reminded people of the power of togetherness, how together they can achieve more.*

Consider the changing nature of work and organisations:

- Organisations in which employees perceive meaning at work are 21% more profitable. However, only 13% of employees worldwide feel engaged.
- The ideal team size is between four and nine, with an optimal 4.6 people. Such teams bring diversity but can also make fast decisions and get things done.
- Around 30% of useful collaborations typically come from only 4% of employees. Women are 66% more likely to initiate collaboration.
- Companies where women are at least 15% of senior managers have more than 50% higher profitability than those with less than 10%.
- Companies in the top quartile for racial and ethnic diversity were 35% more likely to have financial returns above national industry medians.
- Migrants make up just 3.4% of the world's population, but they contribute nearly 10% of global GDP. 51% of CEOs of billion-dollar unicorns are migrants.
- 75% of millennials want to work from home or from another location where they feel more productive.
- Of the children entering primary school today, 65% will end up working in job categories that do not yet exist.

How will you work better?

CODE 29: DO HUMAN, INSPIRING WORK
Human skills will grow in value – complex problem-solving and creativity, emotional intelligence and partnership building. Let machines do the simple, repetitive tasks.

When it comes to grocery stores, there's nothing quite like Trader Joe's, which has amassed a cult following across America. Every time I walk into a store, my eyes light up with the colourful interiors, handwritten notices, quirky stories behind the foods, genuine interest of the staff, most dressed in outlandish styles, and their eagerness to help. I always emerge with a smile.

Joe Coulombe was the original Trader Joe, and having started out as Pronto Market convenience stores in 1958, created his own stores. Joe did things differently, and his stores reflected his love of Hawaiian beach culture with walls decked with cedar planks and staff dressed in cool Hawaiian shirts. Most importantly, he started putting innovative, hard-to-find, great-tasting foods in the "Trader Joe's" name.

Value mattered to Joe. And the premium, exotic specialities he brought together were complimented by his low-priced own-label ranges which combined quality and quirkiness. In 1979, Joe sold his brand to Theo Albrecht, better known for his low-priced Aldi food stores in Europe. Aldi and Joe both believed in keeping things simple. No discounts, points cards, or members clubs. With a limited range, the stores drive a better supply deal in return for bigger volumes, and can be more responsive to market trends.

Storytelling is everywhere at Trader Joe's, from the handwritten signage and rustic displays, to the free coffee and sampling, the radio ads and chatty check-out dudes. Whilst most competitors focus on automation and speed, this store is real and human, worth coming just to chill out. Even if you never get to visit a store, sign up to the Fearless Flyer online. With off-beat stories and cartoon humour, unusual recipes and showcased products, it's an intriguing read.

RISE OF THE SUPERHUMANS

The world often seems to be working against humanity. We build walls across the borders of America, fence people in who seek to migrate in search of a better life to Europe, apply deep surveillance policies in China, prefer to be an isolated island than a connected continent in UK, automate our factories and workplaces for speed and efficiency, prefer to date online rather than in reality, and to chat with social media friends rather than in local communities.

At work, we are told that machines, from AI to robotics, will affect at least 30% of the current activities of at least 70% of job roles. It is the most repetitive tasks that are likely to be automated, robots on production lines, chatbots instead of call centres. Knowledge-based jobs from accountants to lawyers, air traffic controllers to investment bankers are likely to be some of the most disrupted.

When Elon Musk declared that "in the future robots will be able to do everything better than us, I mean all of us", few experts disagreed. However, more recently he has shared a more thoughtful view, saying that "automation is not the future, human augmentation is."

Augmented humanity can be a key driver of the future work, enhancing what we can do:

- **Assisted humanity**: The interface between people and machines is evolving rapidly from keyboard to voice, to eyes and brains. Digital assistants like Alexa and Siri are already common on our phones and in our homes, and will increasingly navigate us through unattended stores. Everyone at work will have their own assistant.

- **Intelligent humanity**: As interfaces change, machines learn more about our thought processes and behaviours, using algorithms to predict what we need and to enhance our knowledge. They will help us to solve complex problems, consider more options and risks, and make smarter decisions.
- **Connected humanity**: Collaborative working becomes easier and continuous whether we are together or apart; distributed working at home or around the world is no impediment to working together, as knowledge flows seamlessly, and individual tasks are joined up intelligently.

Virtual reality tools like Google Glass augment how we work, for example engineers being able to read instruction guides through the lenses of their eyewear whilst simultaneously working on machines, or surgeons being able to operate whilst also getting realtime diagnostic data on the patient's organs and vital statistics.

At the same time this augmentation can be physical too. In Odense, at the SDU's Athletics Exploratorium, I came across engineers simulating the use of exoskeletons to help dockyard workers carry loads which would have previously required cranes, craftsmen to have tools connected to their bodies.

Technology won't replace us, but it could make us "superhuman".

THE FUTURE OF WORK

By 2025 the majority of workers will be freelance individuals working around the world, independent of distance or background. They will apply their human, emotional, and creative skills to solve ever-more complex problems. They have the hunger to keep learning throughout their lives, the agility to keep adapting and updating their skills, and the open-mindedness to see things differently.

Modern and high-tech working environments are enhanced by a community feeling with shared facilities and resources. Many of the workers are not even employed by the companies, instead they are happier to remain freelance "gig-workers" working on projects that require specialist inputs. New ideas, new skills, new innovations and new opportunities swirl around in the creative atmosphere, and new partnerships often emerge out of the fusion. This is the new world of work. No jobs for life. Few permanent roles. Fluid job descriptions. Multiple jobs at the same time. And companies working together.

Some of the jobs of the future will be highly technical, whilst others will be much more human. In exploring the jobs of the future, Ben Pring from Cognizant explores 4Es to consider the skills required:

- **Eternal skills:** Some human skills have existed since our very beginning. No matter how brilliant our technologies become, these human skills, along with many others, will be of value through eternity.

- **Enduring skills:** The ability to sell has always been important. Other such enduring abilities – being empathetic, trusting, helping, imagining, creating, striving – will always be needed. Such skills will be central to jobs of the future.
- **Emerging skills:** New skills for the future relate to the complexity, density and speed of work. The skill to use a 315mb Excel spreadsheet, or to navigate a drone virtual cockpit. These will enhance our ability to utilise new machines.
- **Eroding skills:** Many skills that used to be special are now normal –to manage a social media platform, to product a fantastic presentation – whilst others are redundant like photocopying, or replaced like data entry.

However, the World Economic Forum suggests that more jobs will be created than lost, 133 million created and 75 million lost over the five years to 2025, as we see a huge evolution in the workplace of what people do, as well as how they do it. Top emerging jobs will include:

- Data analysts and scientists
- AI and machine-learning specialists
- Software and application developers
- Sales and marketing professionals
- Digital transformations specialists

Beyond technology, data and AI, many new roles will also emerge in the broader aspects of engineering and sustainable development. The increasing number of elderly people will drive a boom in care work, and many more creative roles will emerge through relentless innovation and more human pursuits, like sport and entertainment.

Completely new jobs in specific industries will emerge such as:

- Flying car developers
- Virtual identity defenders
- Tidewater architects
- Smart home designers
- Joy adjutants

Analysis by BCG in 2020 shows that 95% of most at-risk workers could find good quality, higher paid jobs, if they are prepared to make the transition. This shift also offers the opportunity to close the wage gap, with 74% of women and 53% of men likely to find higher paid roles. It suggests that around 70% of those affected will need to make a significant shift in job, requiring a huge skills revolution.

At the same time, it is not just about refitting people for new jobs. The "dandelion principle", embraced by organisations like SAP, starts by hiring great people with a diversity of backgrounds and skills to create a richer talent base. It then seeks to build jobs around people, rather than people around jobs, in a more symbiotic way.

MORE HUMAN, MORE CREATIVE, MORE FEMALE

As machines take on our more physical skills, the opportunity is for people to be liberated from the drudgery of repetitive tasks to add more human, creative and emotional value. Imagination will drive progress, whilst machines sustain efficiency.

Human skills matter not only within the workplace, but also in engaging with consumers. In a world of automated interfaces, brands will differentiate on their ability to be more intuitive, empathetic and caring. The roles of people, assistants in stores, nurses in hospitals, teachers in classrooms, will be to add value with premium levels of service.

Creative skills are not only in demand in the areas of communication, marketing and innovation, but also in rethinking how organisations can better work, how business models can be transformed, and how machines themselves can be deployed in better ways.

Typically these "softer" skills are what we could call more "female" attributes. Of course, that is to stereotype genders, but it certainly requires more empathy than apathy, intuition than evidence, influence than instruction, care than control. At the same time it requires men to adopt these behaviours too, and in general to embrace inequalities and diversity.

BCG's 2020 research suggests that analytical and critical thinking skills will be crucial to the future of the work, alongside more emotional intelligence and social influence. Learning and creative capabilities will be the most significant growth areas for development in the coming years. They identified these priorities as:

- Analytical thinking and innovation
- Active learning and learning strategies
- Creativity, originality and initiative
- Technology design and programming
- Critical thinking and analysis
- Complex problem-solving
- Leadership and social influence
- Emotional intelligence
- Reasoning, problem-solving and ideation
- Systems analysis and evaluation

Meta skills, rather than technical or specialist skills which we may have trained for or focused on in the past, will become more significant. These are the more enduring skills which allow us to evolve and adapt to relentless change. Sense-making, learning to learn, coping with uncertainty and change.

Sometimes this will require us to unlearn first, to let go of old assumptions and prejudices, and open our minds to new possibilities and perspectives.

In *The 100 Year Life*, Lynda Gratton recognises that, as life expectancy moves beyond 100, most of us will work for longer and transition more often, with around seven different phases in our career journeys – not just new jobs, but entirely new vocations.

CODE 30: WORK AS A LIVING ORGANISATION
In nature, few complex systems are organised through hierarchies. We need to develop businesses as living, adaptive, "collectively conscious" organisations.

Qingdao is the home of Haier, the world's leading home appliances business. Over the years, the company's CEO Zhang Ruimin has become an innovator, not only of washing machines and refrigerators, but of organisations and entrepreneurship too.

Once a devotee of the Six Sigma approach, Zhang has developed his own management ideology: *rendanheyi*. By dividing a company up into micro-enterprises on an open platform, and dismantling the traditional "empire" management system, *rendanheyi* creates "zero distance" between the employee and the needs of the customer.

At the heart of *rendanheyi* is the cultivation of entrepreneurship – by removing the costly level of middle management (Zhang famously eliminated the positions of 10 000 employees), you encourage innovation, flexibility and risk-taking.

THE QUANTUM MECHANICS OF BUSINESS

On meeting, we quickly found a common background, having both studied physics, and specifically quantum mechanics. I was curious about how he had embraced the ideas of physical science into his vision of how Haier should work as an organisation. We quickly got into a passionate and somewhat technical discussion about atomic structure and wave theory. Whilst I'm not sure atomic physics would be many business people's ideal topic, I was intrigued. Zhang said:

> When I first studied physics, I was amazed by the perpetual motion of subatomic particles. Electrons and protons coexist in a dynamic equilibrium, created by their equal and opposite charges. This sustains a continual existence, it enables atoms to come together in many different formats as molecules, each with their own unique properties, and within these atomic structures [are] huge amounts of energy.

The application to business becomes clear, and also many of the founding ideas behind why and how he has developed his *rendanheyi* model of entrepreneurial businesses.

"Applying this idea from physics to business," he says "small teams of people with different backgrounds, skills, and ideas, can coexist incredibly effectively. It is the ability to create small diverse teams where ideas and actions are equally dynamic, that enables a business to sustain over time. They become self-organising and mutually enabling. Ideas, innovation and implementation are continuous. And they can easily link with other teams, like atoms coming together as molecules, for collaborative projects and to create new solutions."

As a result, he challenges the old supremacy of shareholders in the value equation, putting a premium on employees and the value created by them and for them. However, at the same time he recognises the need to empower employees to be more customer intimate. As a result, the rate of growth has risen from eight to 30% in recent years.

"People are not a means to an end, but an end in themselves. We took away all of our middle management. Now things are working much better. Zero signature, zero approval. Now we have only one supervisor, which is the customer."

Haier's evolution has been rapid and relentless, as Zhang has driven the company from an old refrigerator factory – where indiscipline and poor quality was so rife that he took to shock tactics, taking a sledgehammer to some of the products to demonstrate that such mediocrity was no longer acceptable – to a pioneer of digital tech.

In the 1990s, Haier focused on the Chinese market, building a portfolio of high-quality standardised products. The 2000s were about internationalisation, reaching across the world, and then adding more localisation and customisation. The 2010s were all about digitalisation, embracing the power of automation and data, to the point where Haier is now one of the world's leading producers of "smart" products, embedded with IoT (internet of things) and connected intelligently.

However, the implications are profound. Today, Haier is not motivated by seeking to create the best product. With a brand purpose that seeks to make people's lives better, it looks beyond products to services, to how it can do more to help people live their everyday lives, with a focus on the intelligent home. Zhang describes how he sees the future:

In a digital world of globalization, connectivity and person-alization, there is no such thing as a perfect product. People will buy scenarios, or concepts, where the products might be free and act as enablers for services. Haier's products embrace IoT to ensure that they connect with other devices, with other partners in our ecosystems, and with people and their homes. In the future, maybe the product will be free, and people will pay for services – from food delivery, to home entertainment, security or maintenance.

ORGANISATIONS AS LIVING ORGANISMS

The way we manage organisations seems increasingly out of date.

Most employees are disengaged. Too often work is associated with dread and drudgery, rather than passion or purpose.

Leaders complain that their organisations are too slow, siloed and bureaucratic for today's world. Behind the façade and bravado, many business leaders are deeply frustrated by the endless power games and politics of corporate life.

Frédéric Laloux offers an alternative. In his book *Reinventing Organizations*, he uses the metaphor of an organisation as a living system, with radically streamlined structures that facilitate active involvement and self-management.

He envisions a new organisational model, which is self-managed, built around a "wholeness" approach to life and work, and guided by an "evolutionary purpose".

Wholeness means that people strive to be themselves, rather than putting on a mask when they go to work. This, he argues,

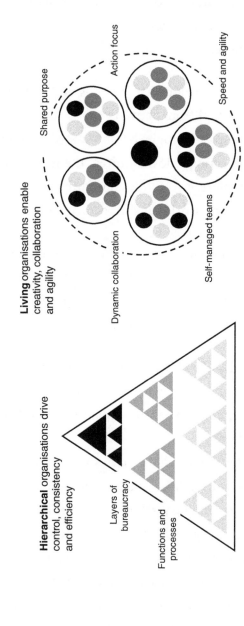

Hierarchical organisations drive
control, consistency
and efficiency

Layers of
bureaucracy

Functions and
processes

Living organisations enable
creativity, collaboration
and agility

Shared purpose

Action focus

Speed and agility

Dynamic collaboration

Self-managed teams

FIGURE 5.1   The living organisation.

can only be achieved when they let go of the idea of "work–life balance" which encourages a compromise. By aligning personal and organisational purpose and passions, you have less stress, and contribute more.

Evolutionary purpose means that meaning and direction of the business is not defined from above but drawn from what feels right amongst people. It might be articulated in a manifesto which defines the actions most admired, the new projects that receive the most interest. And it is constantly evolving, as both the culture inside, and world outside, evolve too.

Laloux describes humanity as evolving in stages. Inspired by the philosopher Ken Wilber, he describes five stages of human consciousness, with associated colours, and proposes that organizations evolve according to these same stages. They are:

- **Impulsive (red).** Characterised by establishing and enforcing authority through power, e.g. mafia, street gangs. For business, this is reflected in the functional boundaries and top-down authority.
- **Conformist (amber).** The group shapes its own beliefs and value. Self-discipline, shame and guilt are used to enforce them, e.g. military, religion. For business, this means replicable processes and defined organizations.
- **Achievement (orange).** The world is seen as a machine, seeking scientifically to predict, control and deliver, e.g. banking, MBA programmes. For business, this means innovation, analytics and metrics, and accountability

- **Pluralistic (green).** Characterised by a sense of inclusion, to treat all people as equal, more like a family, e.g. non-profits. For business, this means a values-driven culture, empowerment and shared value.
- **Evolutionary (teal).** The world is seen as neither fixed nor machine, but a place where everyone is called by an inner purpose to contribute, e.g. holocracy. For business, this means self-management and wholeness.

Most organisations today are "orange", still driven by analysis and metrics, driving profitability and growth. Examples of "green" organisations include Apple, Ben & Jerry's, and Starbucks. Examples of "teal" organisations might be Patagonia, Buurtzorg and Morning Star.

THE END OF HIERARCHY

What replaces the old hierarchies of organisations?

Henry Ford built his organisation for stability, efficiency and standardisation. Clearly defined processes and controls ensured that it worked like a machine, no space for deviance or change. Some decades later, Kaori Ishikawa went further to systemise the approach with total quality management, seen as the secret of Japan's industrial success in the late twentieth century. Efficiency was the goal, not creativity.

However, today's world requires a different approach. Business needs to be fast and adaptive to a world of change. Technology has transformed the roles of people inside organisations, automating processes, adding intelligent systems, and digital interfaces. The value of organisations lies in their ideas, reputation and reach. Organisations embrace the connectedness of the outside world, technology enabling knowledge sharing, fast decision-making, and collaborative working.

Flat organisations became fast and agile, putting customers at their heart. Yet this is all structural, and did not in itself create difference. In a world where businesses could essentially do anything, they have become more purposeful, and also more distinctive in their character and beliefs.

Expert teams don't need the old controls. Empowered and enabled, they become more self-managing, and teams collectively work together towards a higher purpose and strategic framework that guides but doesn't prescribe. As a result, the business develops a human-like consciousness. It resembles a complex adaptive system, where there is a wholeness built on multiple non-linear connections, combining progress with agility.

Buurtzorg, like Haier, is a great example of self-managing teams. The Dutch healthcare business provides home support to elderly people. It recognised that local teams, which acted largely autonomously, had a much great commitment to their work than if they were managed centrally using standard efficiency metrics.

Haufe Group is an innovative media and software business in Freiburg, in the heart of Germany's Black Forest. As an organisation they have long put people first, sharing in the development of strategy, and the rewards of success. When it came to appointing a new CEO, the company realised that this couldn't just be imposed on such a democratic structure, and so now holds elections to find who amongst peers will be the leader.

If, as Peter Drucker said, "the purpose of an organisation is to enable ordinary human beings to do extraordinary things", then organisations must evolve to make this possible.

CODE 31: COLLABORATE IN FAST PROJECTS
Projects will dominate organisation work, replacing the old structures and job roles. They include labs and incubators, bringing focus, collaboration, change and speed.

We're starting a new project. It's so secret, I can't tell you what it is, or who you will work for. But what I can tell you is if you choose to accept this role, you're going to work harder than you ever have in your entire life. You're going to have to give up nights and weekends probably for a couple years as we make this product.

Scott Forstall sent that email as he started his role as head of Apple's iPhone software division. Since its debut in 2007, the iPhone has become both a cultural and economic phenomenon, replacing Blackberry and Nokia as the world's most ubiquitous smartphone and transforming the entire market.

Soon after the first iPod was released in 2002, Steve Jobs began thinking about an Apple phone and in 2005 initiated a number of phone-related projects, including the doomed partnership with Motorola. The iPhone's ideation phase was kept low profile, with a limited investment and small teams. Many companies launch a full-scale project for every idea they generate, mostly ending up in wasted resources.

While many in Apple were enthused about a phone, Jobs was sceptical. As the project sponsor he was a powerful source of inspiration, a fierce curator of good ideas, but not afraid to reject less good ones. When he did give the green light to "Project Purple", in November 2004, he was fully engaged, dedicating around 40% of his personal time to supervise and lead the teams.

The Purple team was one of the most talented in tech history. Whilst they had never made a phone before, they were the best engineers, the best programmers, and the best designers around. And were sworn to secrecy for two and a half years. Whilst the final product might look beautifully simple, it was excruciating work. Jobs wanted to see a demo of everything. Designers would often create mock-ups of a single design element, like a button, 50 times before it met his exacting standards.

Jobs famously launched the revolutionary phone on 29 June, 2007 at Macworld. The final months had been frantic, with everyone 100% focused as the team raced to meet the fixed launch date.

Apple spent $150m developing the iPhone, according to some estimates, a smart investment given its subsequent impact on the market. It transformed Apple's business.

1.4 million iPhones were sold in 2007, rising to 201 million by 2016, and more than a billion by 2020. iPhones account for 69% of Apple's total revenue, with an estimated margin over 50%, generating more than $54 billion in profits.

TEAMS BEAT INDIVIDUALS

At design firm IDEO they have a poster that dominates their workplace: "Enlightened trial and error succeeds over the planning of the lone genius".

There are two messages. Firstly that teams are more experimental, their diversity bringing more ideas and options to explore. Second, that however smart an individual might believe they are, they are unlikely to go as far or as fast as the team.

In my experience, it is often the team leader who thinks they know better and seeks to dominate the team. But it might equally be a technologist who is convinced that they know what customers want better than customers, or another person driven by their own perspective and passion.

Project teams need the uniqueness and expertise brought by individuals, but combined with the power of teamwork. The same tension exists at the business level. Many organisations feel they can or should do everything themselves, rather than working collaboratively with partner organisations.

It takes a more enlightened business to know what it is best at, and then to bring together others to do other tasks. Look, for example, at Nespresso's business model. They know that their authority and expertise lie in coffee, and in brand and marketing. Everything else, from making their coffee machines to managing their call centres, they leave to others.

FROM FUNCTIONS TO PROJECTS

"Projects not functions define today's organisation," says Antonio Nieto-Rodriguez from GSK. "In the past 90% of our jobs were functional roles, regular and managing, while 10% were working on projects. Today 90% of most jobs are project-based, about change and innovation, and very little of it maintaining the status quo."

Long gone, in most organisations, are the fixed offices with big desks to support executive egos. Gone, too, are the more open workspace cubicles, where people still liked to claim their domains, a sense of home at work. In a paperless world of clouds and laptops, desks are really not necessary. Also gone are the job descriptions which so many employees used in order to be clear on their tasks, and then refusing to go further.

Today everyone is part of a talent pool, and needs to have the flexibility to team and reteam with different leaders, different colleagues, different projects, as required.

Consulting firms have long worked in this way and offer a useful model to learn from. I spent almost 10 years in such an environment, and over that time worked on around 100 different projects, many in different teams, for different clients, with different leaders. Stability came in the form that I belonged to a certain skill group, with a notional leader, largely concerned with recruitment and thought leadership. My performance was based on a formula of how I spent my time and contributed to sales and delivery, plus my broader contribution to the organisation. It was an incredibly fluid structure, responsive to clients, but also flexible personally, in where I chose to live and how I chose to allocate my time.

FAST AND COLLABORATIVE PROJECTS

Project teams are most likely to bring together a diversity of talent, from different functions and organisations, employees and external talent. This is most obvious in areas like marketing, where creative agencies will work with their clients as joint teams, but equally in technological developments where expertise naturally resides outside.

Projects give an organisation more agility, to flex their size as their workload demands, to tap into skills as needed, and accelerate progress. They can embrace the same fast and lean principles as applied specifically to innovation – starting with a "minimum viable project" then testing and learning, stretching ideas but also eliminating bad ones quickly, working in parallel where possible, testing and learning to evolve once implemented.

Projects typically need dedicated team spaces to work, people to lead, processes to operate, metrics to evaluate, and incentives to reward. Most organisations already have innovation spaces, which range from creative kitchens and idea labs, through to incubators that accelerate new businesses, and venture arms to host independent start-ups.

Daimler's Lab1886, Disney's ID8 Studios, Nestlé's HENRi lab, IKEA's Future Home incubator, Nike's Explore Team, Shell's TechWork Labs. Whatever the form of these different environments, they all seek to create protected and dedicated spaces where ideas can emerge, and new projects and new businesses can flourish.

CODE 32: ALIGN INDIVIDUALS AND ORGANISATIONS
We need to align ourselves and our work much better, recognising the power of individuals and teams, and how diversity comes in many different forms.

Kendra Scott designed her first jewellery collection from a spare bedroom in her home in 2002, with $500 in cash, never dreamin that it would become a $1 billion business. But today her business is a thriving, making affordable modern jewellery with natural gemstones, is part-owned by Warren Buffett, and has over 100 stores.

90% of her 2000 employees are women, many of whom are mothers. And nursing rooms are commonplace at her offices and distribution centre in Austin, Texas. Kendra Scott Kids provides a children's playroom whilst shopping mums browse the store or make their own jewellery at the Color Bar, and once a year Camp Kendra is a day out for all employees' kids.

"If we can support our staff, these women, at this very special time in their lives, we'll have an employee who is incredibly loyal to our brand," says Scott. "We believe in their future." She has also created a Women's Entrepreneurial Leadership Program in partnership with the University of Texas which features workshops on starting and leading a business, through to advocating for equal pay. "We want women to thrive in our business, and every business," she says.

INDIVIDUALS AND ORGANISATIONS

Finding the right fit between people and business is not easy. It used to be driven by the business telling people to fit into specific roles and work hard. Today it is different.

"Purpose" starts with the individual, not the company, and increasingly people will seek out companies with values and behaviours that resonate, an alignment of personal and professional "Why". Organisations accept that people will move between companies over time, even encouraging this in some companies as a mark of progress, as they further their careers, guided by their "Why" more than their "What".

Kathleen Hogan, Chief People Officer at Microsoft, has developed a 5Ps system to see a better alignment between individuals and the organisation. She wanted to create "an every day, every employee experience." For people to think in a new way, become more inclusive and open-minded and connect with each other and the customer more empathetically, "there must be work conditions and experiences that facilitate a focus on and desire for growth and change every day," she says.

Microsoft's 5Ps are similar to Maslow's hierarchy of needs. By fulfilling the basic needs of an employee first, starting with pay, you can then explore the higher level "self-actualization" needs:

- **Pay.** "When it comes to work, human behaviour is multi-motivated, but pay is a foundational need." Microsoft seeks to ensure that salaries are fair, market-driven reflects contribution, and incentivises progress.

- **Perks.** Benefits start from protections such as health and pensions, to broader aspects for new parents and family life. It sees these benefits as more important than pay in motivating and retaining people.

- **People.** Microsoft seeks to develop a culture that is people centric, it encourages people "to grow and be your authentic self, to experience joy and inspiration, with a sense of inclusion and belonging (and fun!)"

- **Pride.** Doing more for people with differences, taking responsibility for the social impact of products, and care for local communities, "building a deep sense of belonging and pride in our company".

- **Purpose.** Understanding how people's everyday work makes a real difference to customers and society, in Microsoft's case by "empowering every person and organization on the planet".

Hogan says that it is the combination of these 5Ps, delivered and seen together, that is "where the magic happens". She says, "if you can bring these layers together, with a sense that the culture allows you to be your authentic self and you love the people you work with, being proud to tell others where you work because the company takes its stand on important issues and then, ultimately, feeling a sense of purpose, you have a universal experience."

Microsoft's new culture aims to create a strong customer focus, genuine diversity and inclusion, and "one" Microsoft. This intentionally applied purpose seeks to keep everyone focused on being better. For example, weekly leadership meetings start with a different leader sharing their "Research of the Amazing", a story about an individual, team or group in their organisation who has made a real difference as nurtured by the "growth mindset".

I witnessed this culture myself recently at a Microsoft event in Los Angeles. CEO Nadella kicked off with his rallying call for progress, some customer insights followed, showcasing new products. But then a number of employees came to their stage, and simply told their personal stories, some triumphing over adversity, some very normal but real. Hogan says, "coming back to that purpose and why this work matters, that is key to propelling you forward in your journey".

INCLUSION DRIVES COGNITIVE DIVERSITY

Diversity comes in many different forms, both the obvious – gender, race, age, disability, nationality, sexual orientation, education or religion – and the more hidden differences – how we think, behave and connect.

Diversity brings new perspectives, new skills and new ideas. Younger people learning from older, and old from young. Female attributes are more attuned to building empathy, creativity and relationships. Diversity brings tolerance, cultural understanding, language skills, technological literacy and much more. Whilst diversity is about opening up, inclusion is about connecting these talents.

Organisations with a healthy gender balance are likely to outperform others by 15%, whilst a good ethnic mix can deliver 35% better results, says research by McKinsey.

The power of connections lies in their quality not their quantity. As Erica Dhawan says "We too easily measure success in the digital world through the number of connections we have on LinkedIn, or Facebook likes, or Twitter followers. Connectional intelligence is about making the quality connections that translate into outcomes."

There is a "talent surplus" within most organisations, a pool of knowledge and capability that is available yet rarely fully exploited. Leaders need to harness the 5Cs of connectional intelligence: curiosity, combination, community, courage, and combustion.

CODE 33: CREATE ENERGY AND RHYTHM
Organisations thrive on progress. Continual learning, whether in the form of new insights or new education, enables people and business to adapt and grow, and to build rhythm and energy.

Sebastian Coe was always going to be more than a great athlete. I remember the summer of 1979, when as an impressionable 12 year old, I watched him smash three world records in 41 days. One of them, his 800 m time, would stand unbroken for two decades. He went on to become the only double Olympic champion over 1500 m, and continued to break records.

On retiring he started a second career as a politician, becoming an MP and then chief of staff for his party leader. He thrived in business too, building a successful sports management agency which he sold to Chime. Then he took on the huge task of organising the Olympic Games, London 2012, perhaps the most successful games in history. And now he is president of World Athletics, seeking new innovations to take his sport forwards.

I asked him how he managed to sustain a sequence of so many successes, in very different fields and roles. He said the secret was really in momentum. The ability to keep things moving, to use the experiences and successes in one field to drive into the next.

Momentum, he said, was particularly important as an athlete. Building fitness over many years of training, enhancing it through sustained periods of intense quality, and then mentally sharpening through a series of performances, are what most prepares an athlete to deliver their best on a given day. He has used this same approach throughout his life, sometimes in more intellectual or organisational ways, to ensure that he can deliver his best performance, and for his teams and organisations to do likewise.

He also says that he continues to be a student of sport, work and life. Constantly open to new ideas and approaches, constantly seeking to learn from others. I suspect one of the great benefits of his journey is the rich diversity of experiences he has had. His late father, who also became his coach, often talked about the value of a polymath, a renaissance man, a concept which Coe has demonstrated.

LEARNING AS YOUR ADVANTAGE

In today's world of relentless change, continuous learning becomes your advantage.

Being able to make sense of change, to learn from others, to embrace new ideas and theories, to take learning from failures, to decode the secrets of success in any given field, and then being able to constantly evolve and enhance what you know. This becomes your way to keep a step ahead of others. Learning creates energy and sustains progress.

Where markets evolve rapidly, consumer aspirations continue to evolve, and products are redundant before they are even launched. It is not easy to keep pace. Learning from your own business, but also from the world around you – customers and competitors, colleagues and peers, academics and advisors, and mavericks too.

Algorithms can learn in milliseconds, machine learning is able to interpret patterns and respond instantly. Humans take years, often decades, to see the broader trends that are unfolding. However fast-moving markets, connected systems, and disruptive technologies mean that we need to learn faster, to anticipate and respond to change.

Tuning into this hyperactive environment, organisations must combine machine and human learning, combine insight and foresight, new knowledge and capability.

Peter Senge's 1990 book *The Fifth Discipline* popularised the concept of learning organisations. He described them as "organisations where people continually expand their capacity to create the results they truly desire, where new and expansive patterns of thinking are nurtured, where collective aspiration is set free, and where people are continually learning to see the whole together".

Senge believed that only those that are flexible, adaptive and productive will excel, and that this required learning at all levels. He said real learning gets to the heart of what it is to be human,

the ability to reinvent ourselves, both individually and organisationally. This can only be achieved, he said, when we survive,
or adapt, but also enhance our capacity to achieve more.

A "learning advantage" can be embraced in a number of ways,
at increasing pace:

- **Continuous improvement:** traditionally seeks to drive gradual change, improving quality and efficiency, using Kaizen
  and Six Sigma
- **Learning loops**: a "test and learn" method that captures
  insight, as in "lean" development, then seeks to respond or
  adapt appropriately.
- **Sense and respond:** more digitally, more agile, iterative
  loop-based learning, for example co-creating new solutions
  rapidly with customers.
- **Self-tuning**: sensors and AI, bringing together huge amounts
  of data in realtime, enabling continuous learning and adap-
  tion.

As digital interfaces have enabled the learning to be more
rapid and intelligent, the organisation learns to respond
almost instantly to changes in the market, adapting with it.
The data-driven approach becomes quite logical; therefore
it is important to enhance the learning with more intuitive
and imaginative approaches too. Significant insights, such as

megatrends, provide learning through which the organisation can leap forward in more profound ways.

ENERGISING PEOPLE

Do you feel energised around some people and drained around others? Psychologists have shown that "relational energy" can affect attitudes, motivations and physical health.

Interacting with some people can increase our enthusiasm, stamina and effectiveness, but spending time with others can have the opposite effect.

Research by the University of Michigan found that "energy givers" are authentic, upbeat and supportive. They relate to others with empathy, are reliable, dependable and optimistic. They look for solutions instead of dwelling on problems. They are team players, the first to acknowledge others and help others flourish.

By contrast, "energy takers" are self-centred and diminish others. They lack empathy and their interactions are superficial. They spend their time talking about themselves and are intent on getting their own way. They focus on the negative, constantly demanding more, complaining about problems, and being quick to criticise others when things go wrong.

Here are seven ways in which I have found that people become more energised:

- **Align people.** Recruit and retain people who have a passion for organising purpose, whilst also connecting everyday tasks with this collective cause.
- **Engage people.** Understand what inspires people, share a positive vision, make them feel involved and see relevance, share progress and achievement.
- **Enable people.** Focus on others rather than yourself, how you can support people to perform their best, coaching, delegating and making everyone smarter.
- **Enrich people.** Stretch people in areas of natural strength, to unlock their potential, to do more of the work they love and to develop their best selves.
- **Liberate people.** Remove the blockers and dissipators of energy, whether personal blockers like self-confidence, or environmental blockers like processes.
- **Protect people.** People need pressure, but also breaks from the relentless pursuit of more. Help them learn from failures and shield them from distractions.
- **Amplify people.** Connect people to build collective energy, using positive influencers to motivate others and amplify the strength of teams.

It's amazing how small acts of leadership can make such a difference. I remember working late one night many years ago to finish a task. The office was otherwise empty, and most lights switched off. The CEO walked along the corridor on his way home. Seeing me, he walked in and spent two minutes asking what I was doing. At the end of he explained how my work might be really useful in the weeks ahead. He thanked me and he was off. I was energised. I never met him again, but I still remember that moment.

THE RHYTHM OF PROGRESS

Organisation rhythm drives pace, encourages alignment and sustains performance. It creates a cultural heartbeat in the organisation which keeps things moving and pressure sustained. It is useful to distinguish the concepts:

- **Pace** is the speed of moving forwards.
- **Rhythm** is the regularity of repeated patterns.
- **Momentum** is the ability to sustain progress.

Strategic rhythm is driven by markets, planning and budgets. Operating rhythm is sustained by metrics, reporting and incentives. Team rhythm is driven by projects, meetings and workstyle. Personal rhythm is driven by priorities, interactions and lifestyle.

In most organisations the rhythm is most influenced by a schedule of budgets and reporting. One-year plans and quarterly reviews drive analysis and discussion, as well as pressure to perform. Such review dates are scheduled years and months in advance and so become the immovable pillars of progress, and decision-making. No faster, no slower.

The problem is that the performance-driven cycle is not a particularly energising one. Its requirements are time intensive and largely seen as a burden by most leaders and their people. Also, the rhythm is a largely artificial one, having little relevance to the rhythms of the outside world, to markets and customers. And usually they are the same as those of competitors.

As a result, new products are released at the same time of year, new fashion ranges each "season", tech shows like CES each spring – to fit the cycle of investor reporting, industry shows and media reviews. Imagine, then, if you created a different rhythm. A faster one, or a more dynamic one. Some innovative companies work on a nine-month cycle, and so internally it feels like they keep gaining on competitors. Others develop micro and macro cycles of activities and reviews.

Pace and pressure become psychological drivers, creating urgency to complete tasks, focusing minds and driving creativity. More relaxed, recovery periods are useful too.

CODE 34: BE AN EXTREME TEAM
The All Blacks are the all-conquering team from a small island, who lock together in their Maori haka before going to work. What can we learn from such teams?

Richie McCaw, the former captain of New Zealand's "All Blacks", is regarded by many as one of the greatest rugby players of all time.

His teams won a remarkable 89% of their 110 matches in which he was their leader, including two World Cups. He even played through one cup final with a broken foot, knowing that he was a key component of the team. Whilst he recognises that the team is always more than any individual, he also believes that a leader defines a team, bringing together and creating great individuals.

After lifting the World Cup in 2015, McCaw said, "We come from a small Pacific island, a nation of only 4.5 million, but with a winning mindset. At the start of each game, when we lock together in our traditional Maori haka, we know that we are invincible".

CREATE YOUR "KAPA O PANGO"

The All Blacks have a bold and unwavering ambition to win, working on a four-year cycle with a common team, and setting mini goals along the way to retain sharpness and evaluate progress. They search out the best players who bring each technical specialism, but equally who will work best together, whilst also retaining a search for new talent and skills.

Being part of the team is everything, with a sacred induction, and commitment to the higher purpose.

As a team they constantly evaluate, challenge and stretch, themselves. They search the world of sport and beyond for new ideas, ways to improve physiological fitness, mental agility or technical skills. Like most sports, whilst they have a coach to guide them and captain to lead them out, their approach once in the game is that every one of them is a leader, all equal, all responsible, and all heroes when they win.

In his book *Legacy*, James Kerr describes some of the All Blacks' team beliefs:

- "A collection of talented individuals without personal discipline will ultimately and inevitably fail."
- "A sense of inclusion means individuals are more willing to give themselves to a common cause."
- "The first stage of learning is silence, the second stage is listening."
- "High-performing teams promote a culture of honesty, authenticity and safe conflict."

- "If we're going to lead a life, if we're going to lead anything, we should surely know where we are going, and why."
- "Be more concerned with your character than your reputation or talent, because your character is what you really are, while your reputation is merely what others think you are."

Richie McCaw talks about some of the distinctive beliefs which the team has embraced. These include many concepts from Maori culture, such as the "Kapa o Pango," which is the name of the haka, the traditional dance performed by the team before every match, and reflects the diversity of the nation's Polynesian origins. Such rituals become important in bonding the team, but also in creating its identity to others.

Another Maori concept is *whanau* which means "follow the spearhead" and is inspired by a flock of birds flying in formation which is typically 70% more efficient than flying solo. And finally *whakapapa*, which means "leave a great legacy", or translated more directly, "plant trees you'll never see by being a good ancestor".

THE TEAM ALWAYS WINS

Netflix has built a culture of "freedom and responsibility" which has helped it to dare to innovate more radically and transform an industry. Pixar's teams work together in wooden huts as an individual but collective workspace, embracing an openness of debate to turn initially mediocre ideas into billion-dollar hits.

Teams are where innovative ideas are most often conceived, futures shaped, projects implemented, and where employees experience most of their work. But it's also where the biggest problems can arise in limiting the effectiveness of organisations.

Alphabet recently set about investigating what makes a great team, in what they called Project Aristotle, a tribute to Aristotle's statement, "the whole is greater than the sum of its parts".

Effective teams, they concluded, have a high degree of inter-dependence, more than just a group working on a project, or functionally aligned. They have a distinctive identity and loyalty to each other. They plan work, solve problems, make decisions, and review together, and know that they need one another to achieve success.

Alphabet found that what really mattered was less about who is on the team, and more about how the team worked together. In order of importance, they found that effective teams are:

- **Safe.** This relates to people's perceptions of the heightened risks of taking part, or reduced risks of acting together, determined by their confidence in each other.

- **Dependable.** Participants trust each other to embrace their individual responsibilities, and deliver work of quality and on time.
- **Structured.** There are clear goals, with clear responsibilities of each participant, and an agreed way of working together.
- **Meaningful.** The team has its own sense of purpose, which is relevant to the organisation, but also to the values and ambitions of the team
- **Impactful.** Each participant's contribution is seen as important, whilst the real measure of impact is what the team can achieve together.

Each Whole Foods store manager can act largely autonomously, aligned by clear metrics but responsive to local communities and the passions of their local team. Zappos, the online fashion retailer, also now part of Amazon, embraces "weirdness and fun" as the ingredients to sustain their team success.

FEARLESS AND FEARSOME

Amy Edmondson's book *The Fearless Organisation* focuses on Alphabet's top priority, that teams need to have psychological safety, and how teams create safe spaces in organisations for people to be open, creative and grow.

Organisations can easily become paralysed by fear, which reduces people to conformity, to easy compromises, to incremental developments and mediocre performance. Leaders are responsible for creating such cultures of fear, and are equally responsible for creating an environment where people can be fearless, or even together, fearsome.

Psychological safety is created through three factors:

- **Positive tension.** It's not about always agreeing, about being nice for the sake of harmony, or constant praise. Creating an environment where tensions are constructive not destructive requires trust, allowing and respecting people for talking openly, with different perspectives and conflicting opinions.
- **Complimentary styles.** Team members will have different styles of behaviour, some extroverts and others introverts, some visionary and others pragmatic, some starters and other finishers. The team values these styles as complementary and equally important.
- **Collective attitude.** Whilst trust is important between participants, the key aspect of safety is that it is valued by each person as important to the group's ability to function well. Whilst team members are individually different, they acknowledge they are much less without the whole.

Extreme teams, like the All Blacks, take these traits to the limit. They seek great individuals who are prepared to work collectively, with commitment and courage. They seek more diversity, bringing together differences of capability and opinion. They thrive on dynamic conversations that can embrace extreme ideas. And they have a profound belief that together they can achieve amazing results.

CODE 35: BUILD A BUTTERFLY BUSINESS
Butterflies are incredible creatures – small bodies with huge wingspans, fast and agile, and having distant impacts – a great metaphor for today's business ecosystems.

ARM Holdings started out as a joint venture between Apple, a small British company called Acorn Computers, and VLSI Technology, seeking to build more affordable semiconductors.

160 billion chips later, ARM is now owned by Softbank and its Vision Fund, and employs 6000 people in 45 countries. It provides the technology for the vast majority of the world's smartphones and tablets, and a multitude of other connected devices.

Whilst Intel used to be the undisputed leader of the market, it ran into problems a decade ago as its sophisticated, but standardised, products couldn't meet the exacting needs of a fast-changing market. Every device manufacturer wanted something different, and quickly. ARM realised that device manufacturers wanted much more availability of custom solutions, responsive to a market that was growing exponentially.

ARM chose a radical business model: not to make any products. Instead, it focused on design. And then built an ecosystem of over 1000 business partners around the world who could manufacture its licensed designs fast and responsively to meet the diverse needs of customers and their ever-changing products. ARM's ecosystem strategy fundamentally differentiated it from Intel, with significantly greater revenues and profitability.

Softbank's Masayoshi Son acquired ARM for $32 billion in 2016, believing that as the demand for connected technologies continues to multiply, ARM's ecosystem will enable it "one day to become larger, and more valuable than Google".

ECOSYSTEMS BEAT EGOSYSTEMS

In the past, value was created inside the business, today it is created outside.

Alibaba and Tencent are great examples of companies building a complex network of partner companies, suppliers and outsourcers, complementors and connectors, distributors and communities. Together they create an ecosystem.

For any primary company, the initial question is what to do ourselves, and what others can do better or cheaper for us. Whilst this used to be a question of core competences, they were the strengths that made a company great in the past, and not necessarily those which will give it greatest leverage and value in the future. Instead, organisations need to think what will be core to the future, what assets will be most valuable, and what it can leave to partners to do for it better.

Ecosystems are about coexistence, and how together in the natural environment or in the business world, multiple partners can live and achieve more together.

In nature we are familiar with the complex systems by which plants and animals, landscapes and weather, connect to each other in a bubble of life. Ecosystems, like any network, are all about their connectedness, how to contribute to better innovation and shared developments, and as a value exchange with mutual benefits. Of all the factors, ecosystems bring agility to deliver today and create tomorrow.

Whilst organisations used to take pride in their independence, in their size and power, organisations today realise that they can achieve more together, that size is irrelevant, and success is much more about finding the right partners, who can contribute towards richer solutions, more agile structures and extended reach.

Similarly, they realise that the hierarchies which ensured control and consistency within large organisations, that pandered to the egos of leaders and owners, are not necessary in a networked world.

The essential characteristics of business ecosystems are:

- **Combination:** built around groups of multiple, diverse organisations without common ownership, with mutual interests and ambitions
- **Mutuality:** shared commitment to success, often aligned by purpose and strategy, and may use a common brand across all partners
- **Collaboration:** dynamic network of shifting, semi-permanent relationships, linked by flows of data, services and finance
- **Diversity:** combine aspects of competition and collaboration, particularly when they are complementary in what they do or offer
- **Evolution:** partners in the ecosystem evolving as they redefine their capabilities and relations to others over time

Jack Ma started out in 1995 by creating China Pages, an online directory for overseas customers, but found little traction. He then realised that it would be much more powerful to create a network of these businesses, so they could trade with each other and beyond.

Alibaba initially emerged as an ecosystem of small Chinese business, which then later connected them to consumers. It developed an ecosystem model. The strategic imperative was to make sure that the platform provided all the resources, or access to the resources, that any business would need. The emerging technology of algorithms and machine learning, together with the decreasing cost of computing power, made this possible. Former strategy director Ming Zeng says they developed a formula:

Network Coordination + Data Intelligence = Smart Business.

Smart Business became the title of Zeng's book in which he puts forward four steps as the basis for creating a smart business: creating datafication processes to enrich the pool of data which the business uses to become smarter; using software to automate workflows; developing standards and interfaces to enable realtime data flow and coordination; and applying machine-learning algorithms to generate business decisions.

PLATFORMS TRANSFORM MARKETS

Platform-based ecosystems dominate the world's markets. Eight of the world's 10 most valuable companies are platforms, including Amazon and Apple, Facebook and Google.

"Platforms" bring buyers and sellers together, using a common meeting place. They are value exchanges, or matchmakers, providing the conditions for people to make new connections. Whilst most of the interactions are virtual, exploiting network effects, many of their products and services can be physical.

You could argue that platforms are nothing new. Grain exchanges in Ancient Greece, medieval fairs, stock exchanges. However, technology has made today's platforms much more dynamic, powerful and valuable. Alex Moazed in *Modern Monopolies* says "platforms don't own the means of production, they create the means of connection."

Platforms have redefined markets by creating new business models and new categories, from ride-sharing to co-working. They enable huge numbers of small players to access markets which they would never normally have the resources to access. Imagine a street artist able to sell her quirky art across the world using Etsy. Or a homeowner being able to make money from a spare bedroom using Airbnb. Or an entrepreneur being able to find start-up investment, crowdsourced by Indigogo. At the same time, platforms allow consumers to access a more interesting, eclectic world.

The "platform economy" has become synonymous with:

- the digital economy, enabling anyone to access anything
- the on-demand economy, to access anything at any time

- the sharing economy, to use assets and resources more collaboratively
- the gig economy, to work for yourself on many short-term projects.

In *Platform Revolution*, Marshall van Alstyne says "no matter who you are or what you do for a living, it's highly likely that platforms have already changed your life as an employee, a business leader, a professional, a consumer, or a citizen – and are poised to produce even greater changes in your daily life in the years to come".

Ping An is a great example of taking the ecosystem model further. Starting out as an insurance company, founded in 1990, it is now publicly owned, and used this financial underpinning to support its growth into many other sectors. A little like Warren Buffett's Berkshire Hathaway, it has built on its financial powerhouse, but in its case by using new technology platform thinking. With a market value of over $200 billion, it is already one of the world's top 10 largest companies.

Good Doctor is Ping An's digital healthcare business, established in 2015, and now the world's largest healthcare platform with 300 million users. It describes its service model as "internet + AI + physicians" in the form of an online app, through which a patient will initially evaluate their health or specific condition using an AI-enabled diagnostic. If required, they will then be connected by video call, typically within an hour, to a real doctor, most likely one of 10 000 employed by Ping An sitting in its service hubs.

The doctor can then refer their patient for further diagnosis, treatment or medication. This is when the ecosystem of partners becomes invaluable, with a nationwide network of clinicians, hospitals and pharmacies, and even a home delivery service for prescriptions. The platform also offers wellbeing advice for health and wellbeing, for example, supporting new mothers and elderly people. A monthly subscription embraces an insurance fee to cover some costs, whilst a premium service called Private Doctor offers additional services and all-inclusive fees.

THE "BUTTERFLY" BUSINESS

A butterfly business is a relatively small business with a big imagination, which succeeds by orchestrating the ecosystem, bringing together a distinctive network of partners, often enhanced by a powerful and engaging brand reputation.

The butterfly can achieve dreams whilst staying small and highly agile, using its partners with complimentary skills, shared risk and reward, to add reach and richness, to have more influence and impact. Indeed, you could add many other examples, from

Airbnb to Uber, of asset-light companies succeeding through ecosystems.

What makes butterfly businesses special is when they go beyond the conventional thinking of ecosystems.

The butterfly business, which could be a start-up or an established corporation, comes together with its partners not simply in pursuit of financial gain, but with a shared purpose. An inspiring collective ambition, by which all the partners together can contribute towards a bigger goal and potentially a better world.

A strong common purpose creates shared direction, and an aligned culture.

The butterfly business operates closely with its partners with agile sharing of resources. It delivers a better experience for consumers, working together to design and develop innovative solution-based experiences, and then delivers them in a seamless, more personal, more responsive manner.

A butterfly with richer purpose has more positive impact, financially and beyond. It brings together a system-based approach to resources that deliver zero net waste. Or even better, achieve positive net impact. Indeed, an ecosystem is far more likely to achieve net zero, or even better, net positive impact, by working together.

Of course there is also "the butterfly effect", as famously coined 50 years ago by Edward Lorenz, a nature-loving meteorology professor at MIT.

Whilst seeking to simulate weather patterns, using a computer model based on 12 environmental variables, Lorenz entered some numbers. He realised that the smallest of differences in numbers, going down too many decimal places, could make a huge difference to the weather prediction.

Likewise, the business leader of the butterfly business can make huge differences to the positive experiences of consumers, to the mutual success of each partner, and to the continued evolution of the ecosystem.

SUMMARY: HOW WILL YOU RECODE YOUR ORGANISATION?

5 questions to reflect on:

- Fast work … What would change the pace and rhythm of your organisation?
- Pizza teams … How could you engage people in smaller, better teams?

- People and perks … What would better align people with your organisation?
- Extreme teams … How could you create safer but stronger teamwork?
- Build a butterfly … How to reinvent yourself as a "butterfly" business?

5 leaders to inspire you (more at businessrecoded.com):

- Reed Hastings, Netflix … people working together as a dream team
- Zhang Ruimin, Haier … creating a *rendanheyi* entrepreneurial organisation
- Cristina Junqeura, Nubank … leading equality and diversity in Brazil
- Jos de Blok, Buurtzorg … self-managed patient-centric Dutch healthcare
- Ari Weinzweig, Zingerman's … creating a passion for gourmet food

5 books to go deeper:

- *Reinventing Organisations* by Frederic Laloux
- *Humanocracy* by Gary Hamel
- *The Project Revolution* by Antonio Nieto-Rodriguez
- *Legacy* by James Kerr
- *The Fearless Organisation* by Amy Edmondson

5 places to explore further:

- TLNT
- Corporate Rebels
- Talent Culture
- Fistful of Talent
- Reinventing Organisations

SYZYGY

Recode your transformation

WHAT DOES IT TAKE TO TRANSFORM YOUR BUSINESS EFFECTIVELY?

From incremental change to sustained transformation

Syzygy has its origins in the Greek word suzugia, *meaning yoked or paired, and became popular in eighteenth-century Latin and English. More generally it means a conjunction or alignment. Synergy is a more modern word derived from it.*

Consider how these organisations have reinvented themselves:

- Berkshire Hathaway started as a merger of the Berkshire Spinning Association and Hathaway textile mill. Warren Buffett transformed it into an investment powerhouse.
- Domino's Pizza stands out amongst today's fast food retailers, reinventing itself to offer a digitally centric brand experience that people will pay more for.
- National Geographical grew famous through print. Then it started exploring more instant and immersive media, becoming the most popular brand on Instagram.
- Nintendo was founded in 1889 by Fusajiro Yamauchi as a playing card company, but was transformed by his grandson Hiroshi into a digital gaming empire.
- Shell was a London shop specialising in exotic shells from Asia before becoming the world's largest oil company, and now seeks to transform itself into clean energy.
- Western Union, once a network of early telegraph companies in the American outback, reinvented itself as the world's largest money transfer service.
- Wipro started in 1945 selling vegetable oil, before diversifying into other products. It is now one of the world's largest IT outsourcers and software engineers.
- American Express's Ken Chenault says, "successful transform demands unchanging change", requiring constant values but relentless reinvention.

How could you reinvent your business?

CODE 36: TRANSFORM YOUR BUSINESS
Few organisations can claim to effectively implement their strategies, far less to turn radical visions into practical actions that inspire people and transform performance.

Ørsted, the Danish energy company, is ranked as the world's most sustainable company, impressive given that 10 years ago 95% of its energy came from fossil fuels.

In 2012, then known as DONG (Danish Oil and Natural Gas), it found itself in a financial predicament as global overproduction sent gas prices plunging. The company's credit rating was downgraded to negative, raising the cost of its considerable debt.

The board hired a former leader of business transformation at Lego, Henrik Poulsen, as the new CEO. Whereas some leaders might have gone into crisis management mode, laying off workers until prices recovered, Poulsen recognised the moment as an opportunity for fundamental change.

"We saw the need to build an entirely new company," Poulsen says. "It had to be a radical transformation; we needed to build a new core business and find new areas of sustainable growth. We looked at the mandate to combat climate change, and we made the profound decision, to be one of the first to transform from black to green energy."

Poulsen emphasized both the short-term and long-term nature of the change. "We looked at the 12 different lines of business we were in and went through them asset by asset, to see where we saw competitive strength. Coal, oil and gas were rapidly eroding as businesses, so we decided to divest eight of our 12 divisions and use the proceeds to reduce our debt."

The business had also started looking beyond its core, and had invested in offshore wind power, but the technology was still too expensive, producing energy that was more than double the price of onshore wind. Under Poulsen, the company embarked on a systematic "cost-out" program to reduce the expense of every aspect of building and running offshore wind farms while achieving scale in this emerging market.

Poulsen renamed the company Ørsted, after the legendary Danish scientist Hans Christian Ørsted, who discovered the principles of electromagnetism. This helped infuse a sense of purpose into the organization that drove it to cut the cost of offshore wind power by 60% while building three major new ocean-based wind farms in the UK and acquiring a leading company in the US to pioneer North American offshore waters.

Previously 80% owned by the Danish government, Orsted's IPO in 2016 was one the year's largest. Net profits have surged more than $3 billion since 2013, and Orsted is now the world's largest offshore wind company, with a 30% share of a booming global market.

BUSINESS TRANSFORMATION

What motivates a business leader to embark on strategic transformation?

Sometimes it's a financial crisis, sometimes it's the threat from a disruptive competitor, sometimes growth stagnates as markets mature or decline, sometimes it's the opportunity to ride a new global megatrend, and sometimes it's the result of proactive strategic planning.

To better understand the dynamics of why and how transformation happens, Innosight's "Transformation 20" study evaluated the strategic change efforts of many companies, seeking to identify best practices across industries and geographies. The ranking is based on three factors: finding new growth (% of revenue beyond core), repositioning the core (giving the legacy business new life), and financial growth (revenue, profit and economic value over the transformation).

Innovation guru Scott Anthony describes the essence of this kind of transformation: "What businesses are doing here is fundamentally changing in form or substance. A piece, if not the essence, of the old remains, but what emerges is clearly different in material ways. It is a liquid becoming a gas. Lead turning into gold. A caterpillar becoming a butterfly."

Here are some examples of such transformations:

- **Adobe:** transformed from product to service, from document software into digital experiences, marketing, commerce platforms and analytics
- **Amazon:** transformed its own infrastructure into "Amazon Web Services" which enables other organisations to operate their online businesses.
- **DBS:** transformed itself from a regional bank to a global digital platform, a "27 000-person start-up" and crowned "Best Bank in the World".
- **Microsoft:** transformed from a business model based primarily on selling product licenses (IP), to a cloud-based platform-as-a-service business.
- **Netflix:** shifted from DVDs by mail into the leading streaming video content service and now a top original content provider.
- **Ping An:** transformed itself from insurance into a cloud tech business providing fintech and AI-based medical imaging and diagnostics.
- **Tencent:** transformed from a social and gaming business to a platform embracing entertainment, autonomous vehicle, cloud computing, and finance.

Transformation is about significant, lasting, non-reversible change to the way in which the company operates and creates value, typically where at least 25% of total revenues comes from new business units or business models. It can take time, 10 years as demonstrated by Orsted, but also sets the business on a new course for a better future.

Whilst digital technologies are a significant enabler of transformation, companies should beware of the term "digital transformation," which is often used to describe the automation of business functions, seeking more efficiency and speed, or broader applications of technology. Similarly, "culture change" is not the same as business transformation. In both cases it is only transformative if it is accompanying by a more holistic reinvention of the business, including its strategy and business models, propositions and performance.

PIVOT TO A NEW SPACE

The destination of any transformation might be quite different from how it was initially envisioned. Many projects, and even businesses, find that they reach a point where they need to significantly change direction, based on what they have learnt. This is a "pivot", and has been a feature of many start-up journeys in recent years:

- **Instagram** initially known as Burbn started out as an online discussion forum developed by Kevin Systrom whilst learning how to program, but now has 1 billion users sharing their images and videos.

- **Slack** started as a game called Glitch, developed by Stewart Butterfield after he sold Flickr. The game didn't take off, but its platform evolved to become Slack, a place for collaborative working.
- **Twitter** was previously known as Odeo, a podcasting platform before podcasts took off. Jack Dorsey decided to shift to microblogging as he called, it, rebranding it as Twitter, and turning it into a leader in short posts and status updates.
- **YouTube** originated as a dating site, encouraging people to upload videos of themselves. Few people embraced the concept, but when the site opened up to anyone who wanted to share a video, over 2 billion people signed up.

For larger organisations, they need to learn to pivot as part of their evolution, and as a sequence of transformations.

As they ride the "S curves" of market change, they accelerate as new ideas take off, but then slow as ideas mature. Eventually, without change, the old business declines, as the market moves in new directions, and a new S curve takes off. The challenge of transformation is to ride the S Curves, jumping to the new curve whilst still thriving on the old curve, transforming before you need to.

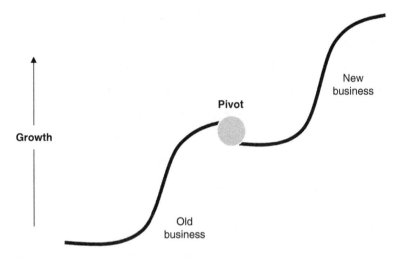

FIGURE 6.1 Pivoting in the S curves of market change.

EVOLVE TO REVOLVE

Transformation does not have to be a sudden shift from one state to another, and can be more evolutionary. Indeed, a persistent, focused approach to incremental change, not simply on efficiency but on improved competitive performance, can sometimes have just as much transformational impact.

I first learnt about "marginal gains" whilst watching cycling. Dave Brailsford was the new performance director of Team GB, who in recent years have come to dominate the sport. Marginal gains was said to be his secret to superior performance.

Brailsford and his coaches began by making small adjustments you might expect from a professional cycling team. They redesigned the bike seats to make them more comfortable and rubbed alcohol on the tires for a better grip. They asked riders to wear electrically heated overshorts to maintain ideal muscle temperature while riding and used biofeedback sensors to monitor how each athlete responded to a particular workout. The team tested various fabrics in a wind tunnel and had their outdoor riders switch to indoor racing suits, which proved to be lighter and more aerodynamic.

Then they went further. They tested different types of massage gels to see which one led to the fastest muscle recovery. They hired a surgeon to teach each rider the best way to wash their hands to reduce the chances of catching a cold. They determined the type of pillow and mattress that led to the best night's sleep for each rider. They even painted the inside of the team truck white, which helped them spot little bits of dust that would normally slip by unnoticed but could degrade the performance of the finely tuned bikes.

"1%" became the team mantra and led to phenomenal success, including six Tour de France victories in seven years, and multiple Olympic gold medals. Whilst some have become concerned that the search for an edge can take sports to blurred ethical practices, Brailsford has always maintained that every gain was scientific and legal.

Indeed, in 2018, Brailsford was the technical mastermind behind Eliud Kipchoge's first sub two-hour marathon, focusing on every marginal gain from the surface and camber of the road, to the weather temperature and humidity, pace making and shoe design.

From cycling to marathon running, cyber security to car manufacturing, organisations have found that 1% improvement can make a big difference. Lots of small changes can add up to more than one big change. Concentrate on making many 1% improvements and you'll find the compound effect is huge, without putting all your eggs in one basket of transformational change.

CODE 37: EXPLOIT THE CORE, EXPLORE THE EDGE
Transformation has a dual focus – improving today and innovating tomorrow – reinventing the business so that it can do both, to become an ambidextrous organisation.

I spent much of 1999 working with Philips. I remember it well, largely because of the regular short flight from London to Eindhoven. Even the earliest flight, often delayed by fog, meant that I rarely arrived at the head office before 11:00 because of the time difference. In Holland, lunch is at 11:30, and always a cheese roll and carton of milk. They grow tall on their dairy intake. As we ate, change was always the topic of conversation.

Philips was founded back in 1891 by Gerard Philips who bought an empty factory in Eindhoven, where the company started the production of carbon-filament lamps.

Over the next century the company started to extend into other electronics businesses such as vacuum tubes, electric shavers, radios (and even a radio station). Televisions followed, which evolved into a battle of formats for video cassettes and laser discs. Toothbrushes too. Throughout this time, the core lighting business had continued, evolving from filament bulbs into new formats such as LEDs, supported by its semiconductor business.

In the early 2000s, Philips symbolically shifted its head offices from Eindhoven to Amsterdam, and started to acquire a number of healthcare companies, from diagnostic scanners to surgical devices. Its core started to shift away from electronics. In 2018, it formally divested its lighting business, which was renamed as Signify, although continuing to use the Philips brand on its products under license. Healthcare became the new core business.

TRANSFORM FOR TODAY AND TOMORROW

How can you create the future, whilst at the same time deliver today?

Change unlocks new opportunities to create new markets. It is the moment when a business typically needs to protect and improve its current activities, but also seize the opportunities of tomorrow, to explore and create new businesses.

Business needs to be ambidextrous; it needs to think and work in the short- and long-term simultaneously. And, like the Roman god Janus, with his with two sets of eyes, focus on what lies behind and on what lies ahead at the same time.

Short-term sales earn the cash, but also the permission, to create a better future. However, this is not a sequential challenge, nor a parallel challenge. The organisation shouldn't delay tomorrow in order to win today or work separately on both.

The trick is to ensure that today leads to tomorrow, short-term actions lead to long-term progress. Too many leaders become obsessed by the short-term and lose sight of the bigger goals. Of course, a heads-down focus on grinding out results looks good, often subservient to the perceived impatience of investment analysts. But this misses the point. Investors are most interested in future success, today is just a guide to it.

DUAL TRANSFORMATION

Scott Anthony, in his book *Dual Transformation*, describes this shift as three components.

- **Transformation A:** repositioning and improving the core business to maximise resilience (e.g. Adobe moving from packaged software to SaaS).

- **Transformation B:** creating a new growth engine (e.g. Amazon adding cloud computing services, and streaming content on top of ecommerce).
- **Capabilities C:** the best way to share assets and resources, brand and scale, and managing the interface between the core and the new.

Transformation A involves accepting changed circumstances, devising new metrics, and bringing in fresh talent experienced in emerging work environments. Transformation B requires understanding of future opportunities, changing consumers, and value patterns. This helps develop new business models through iterative experimentation and willingness to pivot. This may involve acquiring other companies and forging new partnerships, depending on expectations of impact periods.

Anthony likens the capability link to an airlock in a spaceship or submarine. This team includes savvy veterans and diplomatic managers, but the business leader will need to drive hard decisions on which core skills are relevant during transformation, and arbitrate during the inevitable arguments and turf wars. Tough calls will need to be made regarding speed of operation, pricing options, and the assessment of some of the inevitable failures along the way. Other challenges in dual transformation are balancing attention and assets, and protecting traditional income streams while also growing new sources in a slow and experimental manner.

SHIFTING THE CORE

As businesses evolve, their centre of gravity moves.

We see this in the evolution of IBM, which grew famous as the innovator of mainframe computers. As the market shifted, driven by technological evolution, from mainframe to desktop to laptop, IBM found many more competitors.

For some time it moved with the trend, developing its own desktops and laptops, whilst also exploring new business areas, particularly in services like consulting. Eventually, it recognised that its strength was no longer in making any type of computers, but in the advice it could offer, and shifted to become a consulting business at its core.

The shift in the core can be seen in three stages:

- **Focus on the core.** Clearly define your core business, strengthen it and seek to drive growth through it in existing and new markets.
- **Beyond the core.** Extend into adjacent markets, that can leverage off the core like IBM into services, with their own revenue streams.
- **Redefine the core.** As markets evolve, the old core business may start to decline, before which is the time to shift to consolidate the new core.

Whilst this shift might seem a fundamental transformation of the business, as we saw with Philips, it might simply be about following the same purpose, but interpreting how to deliver on that purpose in new and evolving ways. The shift might equally be represented by a more intangible asset, such as brand or capability, which can be deployed with partners in new industries, as in the shift of Ping An.

CODE 38: START OUTSIDE IN, AND INSIDE OUT

Should you start with the customer or the culture, with the need or the dream? It's both, but the catalyst and focus of change should be outside not inside.

DBS is regarded by many as the world's most innovative bank. The Singapore-based bank seeks to deliver a new kind of banking experience that is so simple, seamless and invisible, that customers have more time to spend on the things they care about.

CEO Piyush Gupta calls it "the invisible bank," where financial transactions are embedded deep within the activities of everyday life – from travel to shopping, eating to entertainment. No longer do people need to think of banking as a separate activity, it is part of everything.

Whilst much of DBS's transformation from a very average regional bank to a global leader, has been about digital technologies, Gupta says that it is not about the technology.

"If we just tried to apply technology to the existing banking model, we would just end up being an efficient bank" he says, which he sees as ok, but not exactly ambitious. What he really wanted to do was transform the concept of banking so that it can make people's lives better.

Every child in Singapore, for example, now wears a DBS fitness band, which is supplied free of charge by schools. The device enables kids to gamify their fitness, comparing how many steps they have made each day, to improve health. However. it also has a GPS whereabouts app, so parents know where their kids are, for safety. And an electronic payment app for school travel and meals.

To achieve this transformation, Gupta realised that he had to create a customer-centric business first, before he could digitalise it. This required a fundamental change in culture and processes, products and services, Over three years he worked tirelessly to get people to see what they did from a customer perspective, using high energy "hackathons" in the business, to engage people and generate new ideas.

Only when he was satisfied that the business had a new mindset, and had at least started on a transformation to true customer-centricity, did he begin to explore the potential of new technologies to facilitate and accelerate the transformation.

"This is not putting customers at the centre of banking," he says "but about embedding banking into people's everyday lives".

OUTSIDE IN

In my book *Customer Genius*, I describe the transformational journey to become a customer-centric business. From a vision about making life better, to deep insights about what matters most to your customers, through problem-solving and value propositions, customer experiences and relationships, I defined a business built around people, not around products.

Transforming your business from the outside in starts with:

- Customers: who do you want to serve, why and how?
- Insight: what do they really want, and what matters most?
- Experience: how to develop solutions to deliver the benefits?
- Engagement: why they will be attracted to the proposition?
- Delivery: how to deliver it, in a distinctive, profitable way?

Customer-centric businesses thrive on a passion for service, to "go the extra mile" for their customers, to build retention and loyalty as a more certain future streams of profits. It is a simple, human, motivating way to think about why you are in business.

Most companies have been trying to develop a "customer-centric" culture for at least 25 years. Being in tune with the customer enables companies to be more responsive to markets, to retain customers through better service, to differentiate from competitors, but also be more aligned with the changing outside world.

INSIDE OUT

But then I hit an ideological barrier. An alternative perspective is that business should change from the "inside out". Shouldn't you start with the values and virtues of your organisation, and then make them strong and attractive? "Steve Jobs never asked customers what they wanted, and customers don't really know anyway," they would say. Or to quote Richard Branson "employees come first, customers come second".

Transforming your business from the inside out starts with:

- People: what do we do, what are we motivated by?
- Capability: what are our skills, our distinctive strengths?
- Products: which products to develop, quality and cost?
- Process: how to deliver it in a fast and efficient way?
- Sales: how many can we sell, to ensure our profitability?

There is logic in this approach too. Whilst the old adage that a business should "focus on your core competences" is outdated – maybe true in a steady-state world, but not one of relentless changing opportunities and partnerships – the real strength of thinking inside out is to build on your culture. If organisations are defined by people, then cultures, and the beliefs and behaviours which they drive, are sources of strength and differentiation.

You could say that this is semantics, but for many leaders it can be confusing. "Inside out" is guided by doing what you do better, the more efficient use of resources and new applications of capabilities. "Outside in" is driven by doing what customers want, innovation and agility in response to change.

I remember this "outside in vs. inside out" debate as I discussed growth strategy with an executive team of a Silicon Valley company. They were a technology company, in fact almost every person was a trained software engineer. To them the most important document was the "product roadmap". This guided their progress through subsequent releases of products, as their products got better – in their case, faster, smaller, cheaper.

I questioned whether this is what customers really wanted. Shouldn't we be guided by what matters most to customers, and when they want it, and how we can enhance the product through additional products, services, and experiences? Yes maybe. But the product, to them, was king. It took at least 18 months of culture change before I eventually got them to begrudgingly respect the "customer roadmap".

TRANSFORMING WITH PURPOSE

The answer, as in the story of DBS's transformation, is of course that you need both. The best starting place actually is neither outside nor inside, but with your purpose. Why do you exist? What is the contribution which you seek to make to the world, to society, to people?

A purpose is ultimately an "outside in" statement. It is based on what you enable people to do, rather than what you do. However a purpose is "inside out" in the sense that it becomes the guiding principle of the whole business, its culture, its strategic choices, and motivation for why we come to work each morning.

Transformation goes beyond what do customers want, or what capabilities do we have. It needs to start at a higher level. You might not currently have the right customers, or even be in the right market. As Steve Jobs said, they might not be able to articulate what they want, although I suggest he was actually bringing a customer mindset into play for them.

In a world where you can do anything, be guided by your purpose. Create a business that succeeds by doing more for the world, bringing together the inspiration of the outside, and imagination of the inside.

CODE 39: ENGAGE PEOPLE IN CHANGE
How to engage people in an emotional journey of resistance and renewal. From business case to project plans, quick wins and symbols of change, it is not easy.

Reshma Saujani is on a mission to get more girls to embrace technology. She is a lawyer by training, the first Indian American woman to run for US Congress, and the founder of Girls Who Code, a non-profit organisation which seeks to close the gender gap in technology, specifically by promoting coding to young women.

Girls who Code has camps set up across the US, and has helped over 100 000 girls to have a lot of fun learning programming languages, being inspired by stories of how technologies are able to do phenomenal good, and developing an enthusiasm for them as part of their future careers.

Saujani says that the traditional image of a programmer as "a boy in a hoodie in a basement" needs to change, and that girls need encouragement to act bravely, to be unafraid of technology. Her analysis shows that in 1995 only 37% of computer scientists in the US were female, which has fallen to 24% over the last two decades. Participants in Girls Who Code's camps are 15 times more likely to choose to major in

IT fields compared to the national rates, she calculates. "We're building the largest pipeline of future female engineers in the United States," she says.

BOILING FROGS AND BURNING PLATFORMS

"The most emotionally wrenching and terrifying aspect" of any major organisational change is getting people to realise that change is essential, "building the extreme intensity that people have to feel if they are to step into the void," says Noel Tichy, author of *Control Your Destiny or Someone Else Will*, the story of GE's transformational journey over recent decades.

Everybody likes the status quo – it is familiar, comfortable, and we find a way to succeed within it. But then change comes along and pulls the rug from under our feet, threatening our jobs, projects, bonuses and careers. We don't like change.

Making the case is much easier when there is a crisis. But then it's often too late.

As Charles Handy loved to say, a frog that jumps into a bucket of boiling water will jump out, but a frog that sits in cold water that is gradually heated to boiling point, will not sense the danger, until it is too late. There are plenty of organisations, many executives, who are happy to sit tight and hope things don't get too "hot", at least not before they move on to their next job.

Change therefore needs proactive leadership. Leaders must inspire people to take the brave step into the unknown, to define an inspiring vision, and to guide them on the journey. Managers need to coordinate and control what can often be an incredibly complicated process of transitioning a multi-billion dollar enterprise from one state into another.

Some call it the "burning platform", a term that was based on the Piper Alpha oil rig disaster of 1988. Crisis gives us a good reason and excuse to change. Many changes, however, need to create their platform, or at least articulate it.

One simple, but effective, way to think of making the case for change is in the following formula, demonstrating what is required to overcome people's natural resistance:

Change will happen if A x B x C > D

where

A = an inspiring vision of the what the future will be like

B = the reasons why the current approach cannot continue as it is

C = the first practical steps towards the future

D = people's resistance to change, and preference to stay as they are

The case for change should be made simply and definitively. The vision should be engaging personally, so that people can quickly recognise the benefits to themselves. The reasons why today is not sustainable might be financial, or logical – a declining share, rising cost-base, new competitors – and how if extrapolated, it would severely restrict the business's future.

I also find that a "size of prize" estimate of the potential financial benefit achievable from the change can focus minds, even if it is simple a rough magnitude of scale, based on some very broad assumptions.

John Kotter, in *Leading Change,* has some even more direct tactics for overcoming the resistance of people to change, including cleaning up the balance sheet to take a significant loss in the next quarter; moving the head office to disrupt old habits and symbolise a new start; telling business units they have 24 months to become number one or two in their market or face closure; toughening up the performance targets of senior managers to provoke "honest" discussions.

CHANGE AS AN EMOTIONAL ROLLERCOASTER

The change curve, developed by Elisabeth Kubler-Ross in the 1960s, is simple yet explains so much about how we respond to change in life and at work (see Figure 6.2).

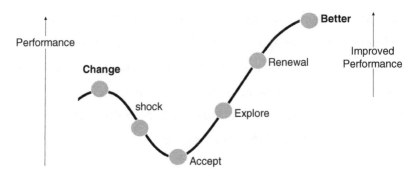

FIGURE 6.2 The emotional change curve.

Originally developed to explain the grieving process, it is equally useful when people are faced with any form of change. A new project at work, a change at home, a new tool to get used to. People don't really like change. It takes us a while to let go of the old ways and recognise that change is not so bad, and actually it could be quite good.

There are three essential phases, as individuals come to terms with change:

- **Shock and denial.** The initial surprise of any change, good and bad, is to lose focus, slow down as we consider its implications, performance dips. We fear the unknown, we like what we know, and we seek more information. Denial often follows, we cope by reverting to what we know and avoid thinking about the new. Communication is key in this phase, with reassurance and support, but also giving people time.

- **Anger and depression.** We start to address the implications of change, often with initially negative feelings at the loss of the old known ways, seeking to blame others, often the organisation. Anger leads to self-doubt and anxiety. Engagement matters most here, often as a shared experience, seeking to get people through this trough, to a point where they are ready to explore the future.
- **Acceptance and renewal.** Optimism dawns, and we start to explore the possibilities of the change, recognising that it is inevitable, and so working with it not against it. People support each other, and there is now a desire to get through the change, and established in the new approach. Working with people to design this new state helps them feel part of the new order, and more acceptant of it.

The challenge is to recognise how people will inevitably feel at each of the stages, and help them through it. Whilst they need a little time to take in new ideas, to make sense of them, the key challenge for business leaders, is to accelerate people through the trough and into the upturn, where they start thinking more positively and embracing the new possibilities.

Any form of change programme is ultimately about going from an old state to a new state, one in which they ultimately feel more positive, and performance individually and collectively improves. At the same time, as change become more frequent, even continuous, the change curve still applies. The new challenge for leaders is to avoid people feeling change fatigue, and instead stay positive on the journey.

LEADING THE CHANGE

Change management is the collective approach to guiding individuals and organisations through change, and a component of broader business transformation which would also involve strategy, processes, technology and much more.

From creating a sense of urgency, to building support across the organisation, forming a plan and enlisting resources, removing barriers and generating short-term wins, to sustaining and instituting change as the new normal, leadership of change is a significant task. Indeed, as change persists, it becomes a full-time tasks for many leaders.

There are four important phases to lead organisations through:

- **Engaging in change.** All stakeholders need to understand and hopefully support the change – why it is needed, what it will involve and how it will happen.
- **Preparing for change.** Mapping out a programme of change horizons – how will we move from to the new world in practical steps, with what actions and resources required when?

- **Delivering the change.** Making the change happen comes down to people and effective management, sustaining the momentum to overcome resistance.
- **Making change stick.** The change must be seen through to completion, sustaining commitment for it, as it rapidly becomes the new "business as usual".

The changed organisation is a compelling place to work. It creates a fresh start, to build a new reputation in the outside world, to drive innovation and new levels of service, to change the opinions of analysts and investors, and to shine as a business leader.

However it should never really feel complete. Instead it should be alive, agile, anticipating the next move forwards.

> ## CODE 40: BUILD ROCKET SHIPS TO THE FUTURE
> Driving transformation is not easy as part of everyday business. Organisations therefore develop a range of alternative routes to creating more radical change, faster.

Spot is a dog-like robot that can climb stairs and run across rough terrains, has 360 vision, can carry 40 kg loads, and endure temperatures of -20^0C. Handle is a robotic arm that can move boxes in a warehouse or guide surgical instruments within operations. Atlas is the world's most dynamic humanoid robot, it can run and jump and has 28 hydraulic joints.

Boston Dynamics began as a spin-off from MIT, where they developed the first robots that ran and moved like animals. The lab combines the principles of dynamic control and balance with sophisticated mechanical designs, cutting-edge electronics and intelligent software to explore how robotics can transform the worlds of healthcare to manufacturing.

The Chinese Academy of Sciences (CAS) in Beijing acts as the national scientific think tank that provides advice to Chinese businesses, large and small, and the government, specifically on using technologies to develop the economy and social improvement. It is the largest research organisation in the world, with over 60 000 researchers working in 114 institutes across China. Based on the total number of research papers published in Nature and its affiliate network, CAS ranked #1 among the world's leading research organisations.

Silicon Valley's PARC is an open innovation company that has been at the heart of some of the most important technological breakthroughs. It brings together scientists, engineers and designers focused on specific future themes. Creativity and science are core to PARC's mission to reduce the time and risk of innovation. Teams assemble and grow organically, combining expertise and capabilities to work with start-ups and corporates.

INNOVATION LABS

Innovation labs have evolved from the Skunk Works which Lockheed Martin started decades ago. Moving from insular research and development roles of the past, like the secretive projects of Xerox PARC or Bell Labs, to a more open structure, with two roles:

- **Develop innovative concepts** and business models without the distractions, demands and expectations, and internal obstacles of most organisations – to create significant new opportunities for existing business.
- **Develop new ventures** that require collaborative working and investments with external partners – be that other companies, new start-ups, and specialists – and may even lead to a new business.

An innovation lab is typically an open, collaborative space where people from different departments with outside partners, tech experts, designers and academics seeking to emulate the culture, speed, tech integration and disruptiveness of a start-up, in order to develop new products, services, experiences and business models that take advantage of new business strategies and advances in technology.

Innovation labs may be run in-house, or by independent companies, or venture capital funds who want to ensure that their investments are spent effectively. In-house labs run by corporates may want to bring start-ups into their fold providing resources or investment, with a motivation to learn from their specialist expertise, to share in their entrepreneurial culture, or to have first option on the outcomes.

INCUBATORS AND ACCELERATORS

There are many different types of innovation labs – often known as incubators or accelerators. Incubators give birth to new start-ups and nurture their early stage development whilst accelerators enhance the ability of start-ups to scale-up into more significant business, by adding more corporate structure, collaboration and more.

Of course, many companies also develop innovation labs as vanity projects – colourful bean bags, lots of white boards, bikes hanging from the ceiling, a few robots sliding around, table football in the corner, you get the idea – but innovation labs can play an important role in driving more radical ideas, new cultures and future growth.

The dedicated focus of an innovation lab has significant commercial benefits:

- Faster development of new products and new business models that solve core customer needs and drive new revenue streams.

- Protect against the threat of disruption from competitors, especially start-ups using new digital approaches.
- Be a working lab to collaborate with customers to address specific challenges and develop more customised solutions.
- Demonstrate products and capabilities to current and future customers, and business partners.

Culturally, being separate from the main business has additional benefits:

- Explore the potential of new technologies separately from current solutions, enabling more creative applications.
- Build multiple innovation centres dedicated to important new categories, geographies and technologies.
- Create a collaborative working space closer to industry innovators, and new technology centres.
- Shift the company culture towards greater innovation, technological integration, and collaboration internally and externally.

BUILD YOUR OWN ROCKET SHIP

The origins of today's Mercedes Benz go back to Gottlieb Daimler, who started out in a Stuttgart garage in 1886. Today, Daimler's Lab1886 continues the tradition of innovation. It is a network-based initiative, where the German car maker explores new business models, through to new engine mechanics, fuel concepts and interior designs.

"Today, we are facing a lot of mega-trends like digitalisation and globalisation," says the lab's director Susanne Hahn. "All these technological and social regulatory movements will change the automotive industry over the next 10 years significantly. We already have, within the Lab1886, a rich portfolio of concepts ready for the future."

The incubator works along the four pillars: connected, autonomous, shared and service, and electric drive. The lab has locations in the US, China and Germany, defining its goal as "to move faster from an idea to a product or business model".

Any of Daimler's 300 000 employees can submit an idea, and then work on it full-time in the lab if successful. Employees can submit ideas based on any of the themes to the company's internal crowdsourcing platform, with the best forwarded to the company's "shark tank" panel of experts, and then to the incubation phase. Teams are also given coaching, co-working space, and funding to develop prototypes and pilots.

Projects are eventually either transferred into the appropriate line of business or spun off into new companies. Hahn says that the original ideator also has the potential to become the CEO of the new company.

Car2Go, a peer-to-peer car sharing platform, is one graduate of Lab1886, spun out as a separate company with 2.5 million customers. Other projects include a travel optimization app called Moovel, and external partnerships, such as a collaboration with start-up Volocopter, to explore the world of urban air taxis and vertical take-off vehicles.

CODE 41: CREATE A CIRCULAR ECOSYSTEM
Dematerialisation enables the trade-off between business and the environment to become transformational as the circular economy becomes a positive force.

The curse of plastic is everywhere – in our overflowing bins, along beaches, and in trees. Retailers across the world have recognised the problem, charging for plastic bags in some countries, making plastics a criminal offence in others. Humans have produced more than 8.3 billion tonnes of plastic since the 1950s, according to the UN, most of which ends up in landfills and could take centuries to decompose.

Ecovative, believes it can massively help the world reduce its plastic waste by using an alternative material, mycelium, created from the root structure of mushrooms.

The New York biotech company grows mycelium into specific shapes and sizes by taking organic plant waste and inoculating it with mycelium. After the mycelium grows through and around the agricultural materials, it binds them together, providing a natural alternative to packaging materials. The process takes around a week, with minimal water and electricity consumed to make the parts.

Beyond packaging materials, Ecovative sees application in fashion with vegan leather, plant-based meats, construction where it is strong and has excellent insulating properties, and in healthcare to build new organs. At the end of the material's useful life, you can break it up and dig it back into the Earth, even your own garden, a nutrient not a pollutant.

"My dream is to one day grow a lung and seed it with lung cells and use the mycelium to create the capillary network and use the human cells to create the actual lung," says founder Eben Bayer.

DOUGHNUT ECONOMICS

"Humanity's 21st century challenge is to meet the needs of all within the means of the planet," says economist Kate Raworth. "In other words, to ensure that no one falls short on life's essentials (from food and housing to healthcare and political voice), while ensuring that collectively we do not overshoot our pressure on Earth's life-supporting systems, on which we fundamentally depend – such as a stable climate, fertile soils, and a protective ozone layer."

She illustrates the challenge as a doughnut, with social and planetary boundaries.

The doughtnut's outer boundary reflects our environmental limits (air pollution, biodiversity loss, land conversion, etc.), beyond which lies ecological degradation and potential tipping points in Earth's systems. The doughnut's inner boundary reflects our social limits (health, education, justice, equality, etc), reflecting the agreed minimum social standards in the UN's Sustainable Development Goals.

Between social and planetary boundaries lies an "environmentally safe and socially just space" in which humanity can thrive.

In 2018, Raworth applied the model to 150 countries in a study for the G20. Her findings were provocative, saying, "The doughnut challenge turns all countries – including every member of the G20 – into 'developing countries' because no country in the world can say that it is even close to meeting the needs of all of its people within the means of the planet."

In fact, Vietnam was identified as the country closest to the "safe and just space". Some countries like India act within environmental limits but fall short socially. Industrialising nations like China are rapidly crossing environmental limits, while high-income nations like the US massively overshoot both boundaries.

In 2020, Amsterdam became the first city to embrace the doughnut model as a framework for its future development.

CIRCULAR DESIGN

A decade ago, former long-distance yachtswoman Ellen MacArthur launched a foundation to promote a "circular economy." This sought to create a new economic model for businesses, which eliminated waste and replenished natural resources. Promoting a "closed loop" system, it encouraged reuse, sharing, repair and recycling as ways in which an organisation ultimately has a "zero impact" on its world.

Nike sees sustainable innovation as a design challenge – not just of its shoes and clothing, but of its entire business ecosystem – from the dyes to the colour of its fabrics, to the production systems of its shoes and the fair wage of workers in its factories.

John Hoke, Nike's Chief Design Officer says "One of the most powerful things design can do for Nike, athletes and, frankly, the world, is play a role in creating a better future by making better choices that holistically and thoughtfully think through the complete design."

by considering everything around the design solution – how we source, how we make, how the product is used, how it's returned, how it's ultimately reimagined. As designers, we are wired to be problem solvers. We get to think about designing ideas that have the highest performance impact possible. While simultaneously having the lowest environmental footprint or impact.

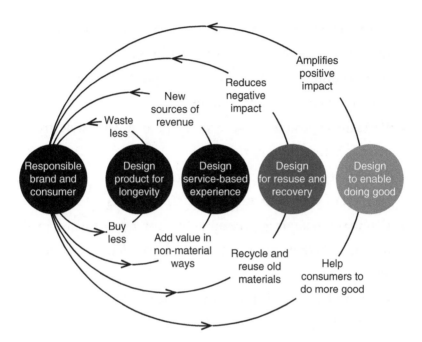

FIGURE 6.3 Creating a circular economy.

Nike recently partnered with many other companies and academics to create "10 Principles of Circular Design" as a process to rethink products, how they are made and sold:

- **Materials:** selecting low impact materials that use pre- and post-consumer recycled feedstock.
- **Cyclability:** designing with the end in mind; thinking through how a product will be recycled at the end of the use phase.
- **Waste avoidance:** minimizing or eliminating waste in the product-creation process, and beyond.
- **Disassembly:** products that can easily be taken apart and recognizing the value of each component.

- **Green chemistry:** chemical products and processes that reduce or eliminate the use of hazardous substances.
- **Refurbishment:** prolong the use of a product through repair of component parts or materials.
- **Versatility:** products that easily adapt to growth, style, trend, gender, activity and purpose.
- **Durability:** products made strongly by construction details, method of make and durable material choices.
- **Circular packaging:** packaging that is purposeful and made of materials that can be repurposed, recycled or biodegradable.
- **New models:** establishing new service and business models to extend the product life cycle.

Over the years, Nike's view to solving problems that embraces sustainability has broadened dramatically, not just to reduce waste but to improve products. One of the most significant was the development of "Flyknit" which ended the process of cutting pieces of fabric for shoe uppers, and instead knitted them to the perfect shape. This massively improved the fit and performance of the shoe for consumers too. Recently they developed "Flyleather" which takes recycled natural leather fibres, and turns them into high performance leather, with all the qualities of old, plus more.

NET POSITIVE IMPACT

Many companies embraced the challenge of MacArthur's "zero impact" circular economic model. Of the many impacts of industrialisation, carbon emissions have perhaps been one of the most damaging. "Offsetting" became a popular action, companies paying to plant new trees which capture the carbon, as a way to neutralise their impact, or reduce their guilt, of carbon-emitting factories and travel.

Ant Financial, for example, created an audacious loyalty program for its Chinese consumers, enabling them to collect offset points from any kind of purchases they made, equivalent to their environmental impact. The points allowed people to plant trees in "Ant Forest", supported by a gamified app which enables you to choose where you want your tree and to watch as it grows, and the huge forest across Chinese wasteland is thriving.

However, creating zero impact seems like only a start. Some organisations, most recently Microsoft, have set a target for "negative carbon" by which they capture more carbon than is emitted. Datacentres, for example, use huge amounts of energy, so by building solar and wind farms, they can power their facilities and contribute renewable energy to local communities, thereby offsetting more that they use.

LanzaTech, based in Chicago, is looking beyond trees to capture carbon. The biotech start-up has developed a way to turn emissions into ethanol, a renewable fuel. Instead of letting carbon emissions bellow out of the factory, they are piped into a bioreactor and fermented, as in beer making, into ethanol. The process uses a natural gas-eating bacteria developed specifically for fermentation. One steel mill can recyle enough carbon to create 9 million gallons of ethanol, which has been demonstrated by Virgin Atlantic as an effective aircraft fuel. Similar initiatives include Braskem turning city waste into biofuels in Brazil.

We are now at the point where businesses are not simply creating zero waste, but can create a "net positive impact".

The impacts are environmental, but also social. A business can give more to the world, in its total balance sheet of resources and effects, than it takes. It can do this, not by just thinking of creating more efficient processes, which seek to reduce waste in a similar way to reducing costs, but by increasing the upside. Creating products and services that embrace a sustainable benefit, and through the purchase and application by millions of customers, can multiply the positive impact many times.

Additionally, by thinking at an ecosystem level, to work with the many different partners involved in the creation and distribution of their solutions, businesses have more opportunities to ensure that the net zero, or net positive, impact is multiplied.

CODE 42: HAVE THE STRATEGIC AGILITY TO NEVER STOP
Change in the outside world is fast and relentless, and so too should it be inside. Strategic agility has become an essential characteristic of every business, and its leaders.

Li and Fung is a fabulous business, founded in Guangzhou in 1906 as an exporter of Chinese porcelain and silk. For much of the twentieth century it focused on low-cost manufacturing of textiles. That was until salary levels grew, and places like Indonesia were able to achieve much lower cost bases. The business reinvented itself as a virtual resource network, helping brands to find the right partners for the business, in terms of expertise, quality, and price.

Walk into a Li and Fung office in Sao Paulo or Istanbul, Barcelona or Toronto – or any one of their 300 offices in over 50 countries – and the small team of sourcing experts will help you find the best designers, manufacturers and distributors for your brand. Around 40% of the world's textiles, and many other consumer products, touch the Hong Kong-based company's networks. If you need finance, they'll find you an investor, and if you need merchandising, processing or customer service, they can find the right partner for that too.

THE NEVER-ENDING JOURNEY

Markets accelerate, change is constant, therefore transformation becomes continuous. Businesses and their leaders need to be adept at being "transformational".

This starts with continuous sensemaking of the external environment, foresight to find new opportunities and spot emerging risks, developing meta skills for people to keep relearning, ecosystems to provide a broader range of capability sources and agility to adapt. Above all these is having purpose, a "north star" to follow, as markets and business evolve.

Consider the transformational timelines of Amazon and Alibaba, shown in Table 6.1, as examples of the practical evolution of thinking that creates revolution in markets.

Amazon and Alibaba have both progressed through a belief in the disruptive power of digital technologies and data analytics.

Amazon's approach has been driven more by customers, developing a deep understanding of customer needs and driving organic growth by delivering a better experience, and the "flywheel" effects of this as a repeated cycle.

TABLE 6.1 Transformational timelines of Amazon and Alibaba.

	Amazon	Alibaba
	"to be Earth's most customer-centric company"	"to make it easy to do business anywhere"
1994	Amazon founded by Jeff Bezos as "the world's largest online bookstore"	
1997	Amazon IPO results in an initial valuation of $300m	
1998	Expands into consumer products, including CDs and DVDs, "the everything store"	
1999	1-Click patented as fast and simple online ordering process	Alibaba founded by Jack Ma and 17 others as China's first online B2B marketplace
2000	Partners with Toys"R"Us in exclusive deal to sell toys and games online	
2001	Amazon Marketplace for third-party sellers, as more choice for consumers	
2002	Super Saver shipping makes buying easier for customers	
2003	CDNow acquired, an online music store	Taobao Marketplace created, a B2C and C2C online marketplace

(continued)

TABLE 6.1 Continued

	Amazon	Alibaba
	"to be Earth's most customer-centric company"	"to make it easy to do business anywhere"
2004	Joyo acquired, largest Chinese online bookstore, to help entry into China	Alipay, online payment system launched. AliWangwang, instant messaging launched
2005	Amazon Prime, a customer membership programme, with free shipping	Yahoo! invests $1bn for 40% stake in Alibaba (worth $10bn at later IPO).
2006	Amazon Web Services, enabling other companies to use Amazon infrastructure	Koubei acquired, China's largest online classified listings business
2007	Amazon Kindle and Amazon Music launched, selling digital content	Alisoft, internet-based software company. Alimama, online advertising exchange
2008	Zappos acquired, online fashion retailer with exceptional service reputation	Taobao Mall online retail platform to complement Toabao C2C portal
2009		Net.cn acquired, a leading basic internet service provider in China
2010	Amazon Studios, creating TV series and movies delivered through Amazon Video	AliExpress, enabling Chinese companies to sell to international customers

Year	Amazon	Alibaba
2011	Amazon Appstore for Android, plus Yap acquired, voice-recognition technology	Taobao splits into Taobao Marketplace (C2C), TMall (B2C) and eTao (group buying)
2012	Kiva Systems acquired, warehouse robotics. Amazon Game Studios launched	Zhong An insurance co-founded with Tencent and Ping An
2013	Amazon Fire, tablet computer launched embracing Appstore and Kindle Store	Cainiao Smart Logistics Network launched with eight logistics companies
2014	Amazon Echo, voice command device, followed by Dot and Alexa	Alibaba IPO results in an initial valuation of $25 billion. ChinaVision acquired
2015	Amazon Dash ordering buttons, Amazon Fresh groceries, and Prime Now deliveries	Ant Financial Services, embracing Alipay, plus loans, investments. AliMusic launched
2016	StoryWriter screenwriting app and Lumberyard for games developers	Alibaba Cloud, creating infrastructure for other companies to use. Alitrip travel
2017	Whole Foods Market acquired, with hundreds of stores, plus Souq.com	Hema physical store launched. Fliggy travel platform, including Marriott partnership
2018	Ring acquired, smart home security. Amazon reaches $1 trillion market cap	"Five New" ecosystem strategy includes manufacturing and energy. Market cap $500bn
2019	Amazon Go, automated physical grocery stores. Bezos wealth estimated $150m	Founder Jack Ma retires as chairman to focus on philanthropy. Ma wealth estimated $40m

Alibaba's approach is more driven by its dynamic market. It has been more visionary, as demonstrated by its recent "Five New" ecosystem strategy to develop an AI-enabled future of new retail, new finance, new manufacturing, new technology, and new energy.

Both seek cultural, structural and strategic agility to continually drive forwards.

STRATEGIC AGILITY

The agile business wins by focusing on the future, by making change normal.

By embracing experimentation and adaptation as part of normal business life, change becomes less daunting and invasive. Few strategies are set in stone, most organisational models are fluid, rules become principles, disruption is encouraged.

Traditional forms of stability, such as detailed strategy documents or job descriptions, are replaced by summaries that outline broader areas, define boundaries rather than details, and can be easily adapted over time.

The key attributes of strategic agility are to:

- **Focus on purpose**, rather than strategy … try putting your strategy on one piece of paper, use the power of three ideas, embrace frames not details.

- **Focus on customers**, rather than competitors ... be driven by insight not by being a little difference, solving problems not being cheaper, growth not share.
- **Focus on opportunity**, rather than capability ... driven by future not your past, what you could do not did do, then find partners to help you do it.
- **Focus on people**, rather than structures ... think about people and personalities, not job titles and status, and the power of small teams to achieve more.
- **Focus on outcomes**, rather than process ... give people space to solve problems in creative ways, seek better outcomes not compliance.

The agile business is fluid, which can be disorientating but also liberating.

Agile organisations are complex adaptive systems. Distributed organisations, network-based ecosystems, empowered and self-managed teams, mean that whilst small parts might be clear, they don't lead to an understanding of the whole. The benefits of the whole, are not achieved as before through standardisation and connectedness, but more through an inter-connected web of many personal relationships and projects.

Organisations from Alibaba to Baidu, Haier to Supercell, Wikipedia to Al Qaeda, are examples of organisations who have defied the desire for structure, and instead exist as many moving parts, almost feeling chaotic. Indeed agile organisations are often said to operate "on the edge of chaos".

EMOTIONAL AGILITY

Harvard psychologist Susan David's book *Emotional Agility* is about how to "get unstuck, embrace change, and thrive in world and life".

She says emotional agility is perhaps more important than IQ or EQ. She describes it as the process that enables us to "navigate life's twists and turns with self-acceptance, clear-sightedness, and an open mind".

Emotional agility is about tackling change, uncertainty and ambiguity directly with curiosity and courage. It requires you to stand back from yourself "to see yourself as a chessboard with many pieces, not just being one of them". It is about staying true to your aspirations and values, your own purpose, if you like. And staying resilient, to sustain energy and momentum as your adventure unfolds.

There are four dimensions, to build your emotional agility:

- **Face change.** Be open to experiencing your emotions without judgment, using them as data points without overly influencing you. In this way you are more in control of what affects you, more stable in the face of instability.

- **Step back.** Depersonalise you and your emotions. Rather than saying "I am sad", say "I'm noticing that I'm feeling sad", helping you to more logically understand the drivers of your emotions and what actions you can take.
- **Take control.** Use your values to shape your choices, attitudes and behaviours, which means firstly being clear on what you do value, your beliefs and priorities. In this way, you have a personal compass to navigate change.
- **Move forwards.** Change can come in the form of tweaks as well as leaps. Tweaks become habits, your new normals, which collectively progress and multiply over time. These are far more likely to endure than one-off dramatic changes.

Ultimately, it takes us back to the growth mindset to positively embrace change. You need the emotional strength to turn change into your advantage. From being buffeted by external forces, you develop the ability to embrace change as the most energised and enriching way to grow your business, but also to grow yourself.

SUMMARY: HOW WILL YOU RECODE YOUR TRANSFORMATION?

5 questions to reflect on:

- Transformational ... are you prepared to make significant change, continually?
- Ambidextrous ... do you balance exploiting your core and exploring your edge?

- Sustainable … how to become a circular business, with net positive impact?
- Strategic agility … are you building the desire, flexibility and energy to change rapidly?
- Emotional agility … have you the personal capacity to embrace ongoing change?

5 leaders to inspire you (more at businessrecoded.com):

- Jeff Bezos, Amazon … it's always "Day 1" in his world of relentless transformation
- Bob Iger, Disney … a ride of a lifetime, from Disney+ to superhero movies
- Jessica Tan, Ping An … transforming markets far beyond its insurance business
- Piyush Gupta, DBS … making "the world's most innovative bank" invisible
- Javier Guyeneche, EcoAlf … upcycling fashion with plastic bottles and fishing nets

5 books to go deeper:

- *Dual Transformation* by Scott Anthony
- *More from Less* by Andrew McAfee
- *Emotional Agility* by Susan David
- *Cradle to Cradle* by William McDonough
- *The Project Revolution* by Antonio Nieto-Rodriguez

5 places to explore further:

- Innosight
- Strategy Tools
- Brightline Initiative
- Forum for the Future
- Ellen Macarthur Foundation

AWESTRUCK

Recode Your Leadership

DO YOU HAVE THE COURAGE TO CREATE A BETTER FUTURE?

From good managers to extraordinary leaders

Awestruck means to be filled with awe and revealing it to others. Awe has its origins in Viking culture, and meant both fear and wonder. It is about being moved, inspired and driven by something so great and impressive that few have the courage to approach.

Consider these inspirations for business leaders:

- "Change will not come if we wait for somebody else, or some other time. We are the ones we've been waiting for. We are the change that we seek," said Barack Obama.
- "Leadership is lifting your vision to higher sights, raising your performance to a higher standard, building your personality beyond normal limitations," said Peter Drucker.
- "Don't be intimidated by what you don't know. That can be your greatest strength and ensure that you do things differently from everyone else," said Sara Blakely.
- "Great entrepreneurial DNA is comprised of leadership, technological vision, frugality, and the desire to succeed," said Steve Blank.
- "Courage is not the absence of fear, but the triumph over it. The brave man is not he who does not feel afraid, but he who conquers that fear," said Nelson Mandela.
- "People will forget what you said, people will forget what you did, but people will never forget how you made them feel," said Maya Angelou.
- "Your time is limited, so don't waste it living someone else's life … Have the courage to follow your heart and intuition," said Steve Jobs.
- "Never give up. Today is hard, tomorrow will be worse, but the day after tomorrow will be sunshine," said Jack Ma.

How will you lead the future?

CODE 43: STEP UP TO LEAD THE FUTURE
Leadership is about amplifying the potential of people, of organisations, of ideas and of brands. Visionary and servant, transactional and transforming, catalyst and coach.

What it Takes is the memoir of Steve Schwarzman, cofounder and CEO of Blackstone, one of the world's largest investment firms.

Schwarzman grew up in an entrepreneurial family selling curtains in Philadelphia. His father was content with owning one store, but Steve was not. He had more ambition. At high school he wanted to bring the best bands to play. At college he started a dance society to meet more girls. He joined Lehman as a trainee, where he learned about finance and discovered his real strength. In 1985 he co-founded Blackstone with friend Pete Peterson, and grew it to hold over $500 billion in assets under management.

He believes that leaders in today's complex and uncertain world need clarity of purpose, to dare to think big and realise the profound impact of AI, saying "It is just as easy to do something big as it is to do something small".

He believes that successful leaders must have the confidence and courage to act when the moment seems right. They accept risk when others are cautious and take action when everyone else is frozen, but they do so smartly. This trait is the mark of a leader. "To be successful you have to put yourself in situations you have no right being in. You shake your head at your stupidity, but eventually it gives you what you want."

WHAT IS LEADERSHIP?

3.5 billion people will make up the global workforce by 2030, around half of which are likely to be self-employed. If we assume that in organisations people typically work in teams of around 10 people, then there will be around 220 million leaders in organisations over the next decade, plus many more who lead in virtual and collaborative ways.

However, most surveys say that leaders are struggling. The majority of employees believe that they can do their jobs as well, or if not better, without their supervisors and managers (80% in one Gallup study). Only 15% of people feel truly engaged in their work, and many say that managers are one of their main reasons for leaving jobs.

"Managing," of course, is not the same thing as "leading". Managing is typically described as using controls to achieve a task. Leading is about influencing, motivating and enabling people to contribute, and achieve more. Managers do things right, leaders do the right things. Managers focus on methods to achieve efficiency, leaders focus on purpose to achieve effectiveness. Or managers have their heads down, leaders have their heads up.

Anyone in the organisation can be a leader. Not everyone in the business is a manager, although managers need to be leaders.

Not everyone is born a leader, but anyone can become one.

Leadership is your choice, not something which is given to you. Leadership is not a job title, a position of authority, or a magical gift. It starts with having confidence. Having a vision that you believe in. Having the courage to step forwards. Engaging other people. And yourself, being the change you want to see in others.

LEADERS SHAPE THE FUTURE

When writing *The Complete CEO*, I and my co-authors found that very few CEOs could actually define leadership. They were comfortable describing their positions in organisation hierarchies, and the defined responsibilities of their roles, but few were able to say what it meant "to lead". Eventually I got words about inspiration and influence, vision and direction, followership and alignment, but quite inconsistently.

Marissa Mayer, the previous CEO of Yahoo!, defines leadership as "helping believe in a better tomorrow, with a better outcome than you have today".

DDI's *Global Leadership Forecast* in 2018 said that only 42% of leaders felt that the overall quality of leadership inside their organisations was high, and only 14% of leaders felt they had a strong "bench" of next generation leaders ready to step up. Most sports teams have at least double their first team squad as reserves ready to step up if required. Another DDI report on leadership development in 2015 stated that 71% of organisations said their leaders are not ready to lead their organisations into the future.

Dave Ulrich sought to bring together all the best leadership theories, models and competencies in *The Leadership Code* and summarised leadership as five overarching roles:

- **Strategist:** leaders shape the future
- **Executor:** leaders make things happen
- **Talent manager:** leaders engage today's talent
- **Human capital developer:** leaders build the next generation
- **Personal proficiency:** leaders invest in their own development

I know Ulrich quite well. He even took off his tie and gave it to me whilst we were once on stage together in Istanbul. He is probably one of the most business-oriented leadership experts around, and much of his personal work is in connecting leaders to strategy, and their impact to value creation. Yet he says himself, too many leadership ideas and the development of leaders, are done in a vacuum, as a separate skill.

So whilst most leadership thinking tends to focus on the leadership role in the context of leading people, teams and organisation – which of course, matters – Ulrich rightly argues that the most important question a leader needs to answer is: "Where are we going?"

In today's world, organisations need leaders, more than ever, to look forwards.

Leaders don't have to be strategists in the traditional sense of spending many hours analysing markets, developing rigorous plans supported by lots of commentary and financial projections. The strategic contribution of a leaders needs to be context setting – defining a clear purpose, envisioning what the future will look like, stretching mindsets of what is possible, articulating the ambitions, the big choices, and horizons to aim for.

Business performance is the measure of how well leaders do this. Warren Buffett will of course remind us that a CEO of a public company is legally responsible to deliver a return to shareholders, but he would also agree that this is more an outcome. Value creation is the framework to engage all stakeholders in progress. The challenge for leaders is not to become obsessed by financials, but to define purpose and be the moral compass of the organisation, to achieve more, in a better way.

Leaders earn their power from how they inspire people with ideas, influence people about what's right, and the impact they have through their actions. This is quite different from the old power of leaders, which came through position, experience and expertise. Instead of leadership based on command and control, I see a leader as a:

- **Catalyst:** the leader stimulates and stretches the organisation, asking the important questions, adding energy and urgency, focusing on insights and goals.
- **Communicator:** the leader articulates purpose, vision and direction, listening and engaging with people, building empathy and trust, creating a better future together.
- **Connectors:** the leader connects ideas, people, activities and partners; encouraging learning and collaboration; facilitating new capacity for innovation.
- **Coaches:** the leader supports rather than commands; to think, act and deliver better; and encouraging the confidence to rise up.

I also love the definition of leaders as "amplifiers" – they amplify the potential of people. And equally of organisations and all their stakeholders. They open up new spaces to go for, and through inspiration and influence, they create a belief and confidence that it is attainable. Amplifying is about increasing the capacity to succeed, and therefore about transforming your potential, personally and organisationally.

LEADERS WITH PURPOSE

Danone has been transformed under Emmanuel Faber's leadership, with a new sense of purpose, a responsibility to all stakeholders and a B Corporation priority for sustainability. As a result, the "how" matters as much as the "what" in what the business does, but also how its leaders lead, saying that breakthrough results can only be achieved when people dare to express and demonstrate their leadership potential.

Danone describes its unique style of leadership using "CODES", the behaviours which bring its values and beliefs to life. These five behaviours shape everything in its culture, from recruitment to development, performance and rewards:

- **C ... Create a meaningful future.** Challenge the status quo and generate breakthrough ideas, every day can be a fresh adventure, full of new possibilities and real excitement, demanding a sense of purpose for yourself, team and colleagues.

- **O ... Open connections inside and out.** Open to new thinking and fresh perspective, developing networks inside and outside, interacting at all levels and building trust to understand all stakeholders, and design products of the future.
- **D ... Drive for sustainable results.** A culture of speed and agility, where individuals are free and express their talents, anticipating and driving progress in a way that sustains value creation for the business, consumers and the community.
- **E ... Empower yourself and diverse teams.** Leadership not micromanagement, releasing the power of the team with the right mix of support and freedom, enabling people to express their uniqueness and foster collective performance.
- **S ... Self-aware.** Being aware of your own strengths and development needs is essential to learn and grow, maintaining self-balance at work by recognising when to step back and when to reach out to others.

CODE 44: HAVE THE COURAGE TO DO MORE
The best leaders are sense makers and future shapers, stepping up to see the future and shape it in their vision, with the courage to lead beyond the knowns of today.

"The longest journey you will ever take," said Buddhist monk, Thich Nhat Hanh "is the 18 inches from your head to your heart."

Mary Barra is a courageous leader. Her predecessors as CEO of GM had failed to see a changing world, to transform the business and its products, even as the company's North American market share fell from 50% in the 1970s to around 15% by the turn of the century. As the market collapsed in 2008, GM declared bankruptcy.

Barra demonstrated the difference courage can make. Immediately after she took the top job, she testified before a hostile Senate investigating committee about deaths from failed ignition switches in Chevrolet Camaros. Rather than make excuses, Barra took responsibility for the problems and went further to attribute them to "GM's cultural problems".

She then set about transforming GM's archaic, finance-driven culture into a dynamic, accountable organisation focused on building quality vehicles for the future.

DARE TO BE MORE

When Apple looked to Einstein and Picasso, saying that "the people crazy enough to think they can change the world, are the ones who do", I would suggest that courage is their real asset.

Courage, according to my dictionary, is "the choice to confront agony, pain, danger, uncertainty" and includes moral courage, "the ability to act rightly in the face of popular opposition". Creating the future takes courage.

Courageous leadership is what every employee hopes for and what every company needs. A courageous leader guides their people, empowers them by example, gives everyone confidence to do their jobs to the best of their ability.

Do you dare to create the future? The answer might seem obvious, but it means letting go of today, of what has worked over time, and what may still be delivering fairly good results. Of course, there are ways to mitigate risks and to do both, but it is typically a leap forward.

Courageous leaders have a strong belief in themselves, and whilst the future may still seem uncertain, you need to believe in the choices you make. Yet if they succeed, they leave a legacy of progress, which is far more satisfying than just maintaining the status quo.

Courage comes in many forms. It starts from inside, asking yourself if you are courageous enough. It requires you to put yourself out there, to be comfortable with being uncomfortable, grasping difficult issues, confronting things directly, grasping the "elephant in the room", and seeking higher standards.

Whilst courage requires boldness and energy, it also demands empathy and humility. Listening carefully to others, revealing your vulnerabilities, saying you don't know if you don't, delegating and giving credit to others, standing behind people in moments of failure, admitting mistakes and changing direction when needed.

Consider the three types of courage required of leaders in the workplace:

- **"Courage to try"** … which is the courage to take the first step. If you are doing something for the first time, it takes courage. It requires energy to overcome inertia, bravery to beat shyness, guts to give it a go. You might fail, you might get it wrong, or you might do something completely incredible.
- **"Courage to trust"** … which is required to relinquish control. As a leader, you will need this courage in order to delegate to your employees, to give over control to staff, and to show your team that you trust them. It not only shows people that you trust them, but also that they can trust you not to micromanage their work.
- **"Courage to tell"** … which is needed to speak up, openly and with conviction, about your beliefs and ideas. It is about being assertive, confident, and caring. It's not about sitting there, biting your tongue, or agreeing to disagree, it's about speaking the truth, saying what needs to be said, stepping up.

Courageous leaders set the stage for others to follow, to accelerate progress.

VULNERABILITY AND CONFIDENCE

Courage is about leaders having the confidence to stand naked in front of their people, and to declare that they all need to do better, says Brené Brown in *Dare to Lead*.

Brown says that the biggest barrier to being a courageous leader is not fear. Everyone is afraid of change, complexity and uncertainty. The question is how we address fear – do we put up our shields in defence, or do we step forwards to tackle it?

She says that, for many leaders, their defensiveness limits their courage. They become more concerned about image than action, about being right, than making things better.

Brown describes four ways in which we can grow our courage:

- **Being vulnerable:** having the courage to take part even if we can't control the outcome, opening ourselves up to people, taking on difficult conversations.
- **Living values:** standing up for what we believe in, whether it be expressing a strong opinion on a controversial topic, or following through with actions.

- **Trusting people:** being the first to trust others, having the vulnerability and courage to have well-judged faith in people, and they will then reciprocate.
- **Rising up:** how we respond to fear or failure, when things don't go according to plan, using our "growth mindset" to rise up to do better.

Whilst you need to step up to look beyond, you need to step forwards to take action.

Yet the future fills many of us with trepidation. It's the unknown, and we don't like not knowing. 54% of CEOs said that the uncertainty was their single greatest obstacle to creating the future, in a recent survey by EY, while IBM found only 41% of organisations believed they had the leaders to execute business strategy in today's uncertain world.

We need to embrace uncertainty, and the opportunities it offers. We have grown to depend on precise knowledge, and detailed analytics based on the past. We prefer to make decisions based on certainty, to minimise risks and to maximise efficiency. When we are faced with incomplete information, high uncertainty and therefore much higher risk, it is easy to feel paralysed. What can you do?

- **Jump in.** Without embracing a challenge, you will never understand it, so better to start somewhere, to get started, to make sense of the situation. Actually the biggest part of making decisions, is understanding the problem.

- **Accept you don't know.** You're unlikely to have all the data, so start to explore the options and consequences of taking them, evaluate them the best you can within the context of what you are trying to achieve.
- **Make the best choice you can.** No decision will be perfect, because there are no right answers, and many decisions will have both upsides and downsides. 60% confidence that it is the right choice is good, 80% confidence is great.

The CEO Genome is a research project by Elena Botelho and Kim Powell, seeking to understand the common attributes of leaders. They found that much of what people assume to be the route to leadership is actually wrong in today's world.

Whilst we might think of leaders as the most ambitious in our team, over 70% of CEOs never had designs on the top job until much later in their careers. And whilst an elite education used to get you places, only 7% of leaders went to top-tier universities, 8% didn't seek any higher education at all.

Most leaders have had to overcome some form of adversity in their journey, which may not create a "perfect" resume, but does equip them better to lead in the real world. Adversity in upbringing, adversity in previous jobs, adversity in their personal life. These are the moments that flex our muscles, but more importantly our minds. They are the moments that give us hunger, and determination, and courage.

Leadership demands confidence and conviction. As a leader you suddenly have a constant stream of decisions coming at you, some strategic, many tactical. Whilst delegation is an essential tool, for many questions, the buck stops with you. You need to be decisive. You need to be reliable. You need to be adaptive. And you need to be bold.

Whilst many leaders can speak eloquently, can engage with their people, say all the right things about the need to focus on customers, to believe in people, and to drive profitable growth, the courageous leader is able to do much more. They have:

- Courage to inspire people to reach for new levels
- Courage to challenge the status quo
- Courage to take big decisions despite many unknowns
- Courage to innovate in areas or ways not done before
- Courage to act rapidly and decisively
- Courage to initiate difficult conversations
- Courage to take blame, to listen to everyone
- Courage to be open, honest and admit mistakes
- Courage to give credit where it is due

Leaders can always take the path of least resistance, they can maintain the status quo and not rock the boat, they can avoid addressing the real problems and instead seek temporary solutions, they can seek only small changes and avoid strategic risks, they can play politics and blame others, and seek to see out their term with the promise of a good pension. Or they can realise that in a world of relentless change, this will simply lead to quiet stagnation, to gradual decline, for themselves and their organisations.

CODE 45: DEVELOP YOUR OWN LEADERSHIP STYLE
There are many models of leadership – inspiring and humble, democrat or autocrat. Most important is to be yourself, to be your best yourself, and strive to be better.

Pablo Isla, CEO of Inditex, is the humble Spanish king of fast fashion. Like a sports coach he sees the power in his team, and his job is to make them the stars.

On first meeting, Isla might not strike you as one of the world's leading CEOs. He is quiet and unassuming, but as leader of Spanish fashion monolith, Inditex, that is his strength. During his 12 years at Inditex, with brands from Zara to Mango, he has increased enterprise value seven times over, engaged in global expansion at a rate of on average one new store opening a day, and has made Inditex Spain's most valuable company.

Isla's priorities have been about achieving greater integration and efficiency. Firstly, creating an omnichannel shopping experience, that combines the best of aspects of technology and stores. Secondly, an integrated supply chain, able to quickly react to changing fashion.

The single word which most employees use to describe his style is humble. He seeks to avoid any form of hierarchy, he hates meetings, and despises ego. Instead, he likes to make decisions informally as he walks around. He even avoids his own store openings, wanting the focus to be on the store and his teams.

"The strength of our company is the combination of everybody, much more than of any single person. We try to be a low-profile company, being humble, of course being very ambitious, but being humble," he told *Harvard Business Review.*

"The core shopper dreaming of a $50 pair of affordable but high-fashion high heels from Zara wants to hear about the new store in her neighbourhood, not about how in control some privileged executive is." Of all his staff, he highlights the role of front-line store managers who are empowered to make product selections and who he sees as the people who he is there to serve.

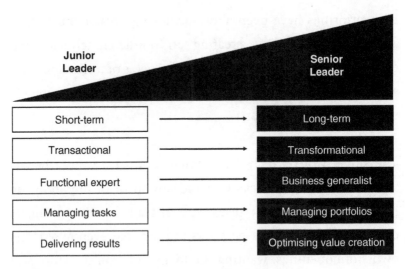

FIGURE 7.1 The changing perspectives of leadership.

HOW GREAT LEADERS GROW

As leaders progress in the organisation their roles changes, from technical to functional, tactical to strategic, management and leadership. With these role come changing perspectives and responsibilities:

- Short term to long term
- Transactional to transformational
- Functional expert to business generalist
- Managing tasks to managing porfolios
- Limited stakeholders to multiple stakeholders
- Getting the job done to optimising value creation

Whilst we might think of leadership as one approach, the styles of leadership are different as we progress in an organisation. The "six passages" concept of leadership was developed by Walter Mahler in the 1970s, based on leadership behaviours and successions in GE, and focuses on the "critical crossroads" that leaders face during their career.

Figure 7.2 shows the seven "levels" of leadership, the six "passages" or transitions from one stage to the next, and the change in skills and mindsets which the transition demands:

- **Leading self:** individual contributors, professional staff, driven by tasks and expertise, establishing credibility, delivering results.

  Transition 1: from skills to collaboration, from doing work to getting it done
- **Leading others:** leaders of small teams or projects, recruiting and developing, resolving conflicts, delegating, adapting to cultural differences.

  Transition 2: from personal to team agendas, from organising to coaching
- **Leading managers:** leaders integrate teams, managing trade-offs and politics, problem-solving, negotiating and risk taking, engaging people.

  Transition 3: from activities to functional strategies, from tasks to complexity

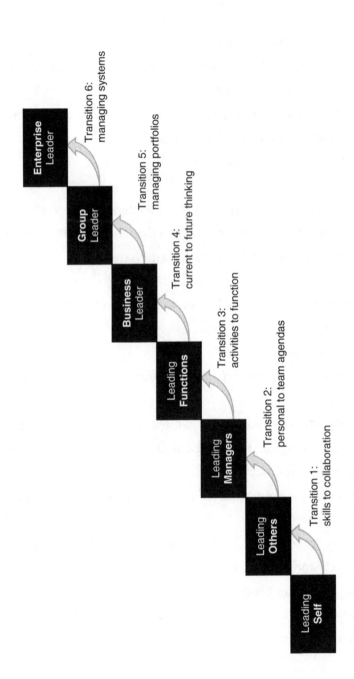

FIGURE 7.2 The seven levels of leadership.

- **Functional leaders:** aligning resources, developing leading practices, driving and implementing change and innovation, managing dispersed teams.

   Transition 4: from current to future thinking, from costs centres to profit centres

- **Business leaders:** developing vision, balancing short- and long-term, aligning with organisation, working across functions, exploring new business models.

   Transition 5: from managing business to a strategic portfolio of businesses

- **Group leaders:** managing performance across businesses, for today and tomorrow, catalysts of change and innovation, exploring new ventures and renewal.

   Transition 6: from internal to external stakeholders, managing whole systems

- **Enterprise leaders:** top executives, engage all stakeholders, set direction and build leadership team for today and future, shape culture and reputation.

In time, leaders assume greater responsibility, and leadership roles increase in their challenge, breadth and complexity. As leaders advance, they reallocate their focus to help others to perform effectively. They learn to value the work of leadership and believe that making time for others, planning, coordinating, and coaching are imperative in their new responsibility.

One way to consider the evolution is as a "T" shape, moving up the vertical when roles are largely built around function, to the horizontal where roles are much broader and cross-functional. As the leader moves from an area of expertise to general management, they shift from needing to have all the answers, to being able to ask the right questions.

Of course, many leadership attributes – such as accountability, engagement and delivery – are common at all stages although executed in different ways. Also, as organisations shift from tall hierarchies to flatter networks, then there are fewer stages of leadership, from seven to maybe only three.

WHAT'S YOUR BEST LEADERSHIP STYLE?

We all tend to have a preferred or "natural style" of leadership.

Leading in a way that feels right and natural to you is both easier for you, and more consistent and authentic for others. Whatever your style, people will engage with and trust you more, if they know that you are genuine.

At times though you may need to adapt your style, or embrace aspects of other styles for a specific purpose. Daniel Ek, CEO of Spotify, for example, found that he was too laid back for his teams when they were looking for direction and focus.

He worked on making the most of his own style, while strengthening aspects that met the needs of his teams.

There are many theoretical models of leadership to take ideas from.

Kurt Lewin classified leadership styles into autocratic, participative and laissez-faire. Tannenbaum and Schmidt saw leadership as a continuum of styles, ranging from autocratic to freed, but said that the best style at any time depended upon a variety of factors, such as the leader's personality and the situation they faced. Daniel Goleman, who coined the phrase "emotional intelligence", developed a framework of six different styles built on a leader's ability to emotionally engage with people in different ways – visionary, coaching, democratic, pacesetting, affiliative and commanding.

Here are some of the different approaches, grouped by their objectives:

Leading in an inspiring style … when you want to encourage people to work with you in creating a better future, providing energy and direction to move forwards:

- **Transformational** … *"Imagine if "*… opportunity to grow, yourself and business

- **Visionary** ... *"Come with me"* ... a new direction, empathetic, builds confidence
- **Pacesetting** ... *"We can do this"* ... driven to achieve, energising but exhausting

Leading in an nurturing style ... when you want to support people to be their best, although not necessarily about thinking about being creative or moving forwards:

- **Servant** ... *"Here for you"* ... secures resources so that people can act as see fit
- **Coaching** ... *"Try this"* ... empathy, supports individual needs, but less directive
- **Affiliative** ... *"People come first"* ... empathy, reassures and builds the team

Leading in an engaged style ... when you want to let people get on with their work, trusting that they have capabilities and desire to do the task:

- **Laissez-faire** ... *"Do what you think"* ... entrusting people to deliver, giving space
- **Transactional** ... *"You know what to do"* ... clear tasks, intervene if not delivered
- **Bureaucratic** ... *"Follow the process"* ... clearly defined technical steps to follow

Leading in a commanding style … when you want to be in charge and make the decisions, often when you believe people don't have the capabilities to decide:

- **Consultative** … *"Tell me what you think"* … you listen and then decide yourself
- **Persuasive** … *"This is what, and why"* … you decide then seek to persuade them
- **Autocratic** … *"Do what I tell you"* … demotivating but can work in a crisis

Knowing when and how to adapt your leadership style to different situations can have a huge impact on how your team will respond. For example, if you are trying to build capabilities within your team you may find that the coaching leadership style works best. If you have urgent deadlines, then pacesetting. If you need to be highly structured and compliant, then bureaucratic. If you want people to work together to create a better future for all, then transformational.

EVALUATING LEADERS

Korn Ferry, the search firm, developed a particularly useful assessment model for leadership development, in order to identify how ready and able individuals are to move to the next levels of leadership. They organise the qualities required in leaders into four distinct categories. Each dimension plays a distinct role in performance, engagement, potential, and personal career development:

- **Drivers and Traits**, which describe *who you are* ... drivers are the values and interests that motivate a person, traits are the natural tendencies of a person, influenced by personality and intelligence.
- **Experiences and Competencies**, which describe *what you do* ... experiences are projects or roles that can prepare a person for a future role, competencies are the observable skills and behaviours.

Most organisations regard an individual's "drive" as a key predictor of high potential, meaning their level of personal energy and engagement they have for their tasks. At the same time, people are more energised by roles that have a good fit with them. Leaders typically want to be leaders, they find the role of a leader interesting and the work of leading motivating. This is particularly tested as they have to allocate more time to leadership aspects of roles as they progress.

Traits also play a large role in how people develop, defining what is more natural for them and what is more of an effort. Traits endure over time and exert a strong influence on a person's outlook, attitudes and behaviours. Traditionally personality inventories, based on traits, have been the primary diagnostic tool for leaders.

Korn Ferry's leadership potential model embraces these factors, and evaluates how a person will progress through the different levels of leadership, and the transitions required:

- **Drivers**
  - Advancement drive: through collaboration, ambition, challenge.
  - Career planning: how narrowly or broadly focused are career goals.
  - Role preferences: achieving through others vs. through self.
- **Experience**
  - Core experience: what they've learned through day-to-day leadership.
  - Perspective: diversity of experience in many different areas.
  - Key challenges: their experience in addressing developmental challenges.
- **Awareness**
  - Self-awareness: of their strengths and development needs.
  - Situational self-awareness: how events impact their performance.
- **Learning agility**
  - Mental agility: to be inquisitive and mentally quick.
  - People agility: to read others and use this to enable change.

- Change agility: to explore new possibilities, take ideas from vision to reality.
- Results agility: to deliver outstanding results in new and tough situations.
- **Leadership traits**
  - Focus: the balance between details and the big picture.
  - Persistence: the passionate pursuit of personally valued long-term goals.
  - Tolerance of ambiguity: to deal with uncertainty or confusing situations.
  - Assertiveness: willingness to assume a leader role and comfortable with it.
  - Optimism: to have a positive outlook.
- **Capacity**
  - Problem-solving: spot trends and patterns and draw correct conclusions from confusing or ambiguous data.
- **Derailment risks**
  - Volatile: a risk toward being mercurial, erratic, or unpredictable.
  - Micromanaging: a risk toward controlling the work of direct reports.
  - Closed: a risk of being closed to alternative perspectives and opportunities.

Ultimately, your leadership is not measured by what you do, but by the impact you have. The way you can positively affect your people, the way in which they drive the activities of organisation, and what it achieves.

IE Business School, based in Madrid, is just down the road from the Santiago Bernebéu stadium, the home of Real Madrid, the Spanish football club who are Europe's all-time most successful soccer team.

I always take the business leaders who I teach at IE to the stadium as part of my programmes. We walk past the showcases of trophies, the photos of past successes, through the changing rooms, and out into the cauldron of competition where 80 000 fanatical spectators usually look down on the game.

I beckon them to sit down on the bench, the seats reserved for the coach and his staff, at the side of the pitch. For a few minutes they can be Zinadine Zidane, or whoever the coach is. He has spent hours on the training field with his players, sharpening fitness and skills, talking strategies and tactics, preparing for the competition. But once the match begins, his players are on their own. He entrusts all to his players. They now need to respond to whatever happens, to make their own decisions in the heat of competition. His own success is 100% entrusted in his team.

Whilst the coach can perfect his own leadership skills, how he uses them to influence others is what matters. His own success is entrusted in his people.

CODE 46: ACHIEVE YOUR PEAK PERFORMANCE
Embed the future in business as usual – make the processes of future shaping, business innovating and change making, the normal equilibrium of work.

Imagine that you are an Olympic athlete in the midst of competition. As you prepare for the greatest race of your life, you imagine the moments ahead, anticipate what might happen, consider alternative strategies. And maybe just dare to dream.

In reality, you need to be ready for anything. It's no use overthinking. You are in the best condition of your life, and you have run many races before. In reality you are simply consumed by the moment, at one with your body, focused on the race.

When you are at your peak, your body and mind flow in unison, you know what to do.

FINDING YOUR FUTURE FLOW

The psychologist Mihaly Csikszentmihalyi believes that peak performance comes from inside, and that people have the unique ability to create environments that facilitate the development of a state of mind which he calls "flow", or what some might call "in the zone".

Flow is the experience I get when I'm working intensely on a project, the challenge is significant, the team around me are great people, the timeframes are tight, and the ambition is very high. Once I am into the project, I find I can work at great pace, there is a stream of consciousness, ideas emerge rapidly.

Under the stress and stretch of high-octane situations, we can often do our best work. Csikszentmihalyi says, "the best moments usually occur when a person's body or mind is stretched to its limits in a voluntary effort to accomplish something difficult and worthwhile. Optimal experience is thus something we make happen."

It is a feeling of immersion, focus and concentration, removed from the repetition and distractions of everyday, you feel like you have more purpose, with heightened awareness of the situation and possibilities. Complexity seems less intimidating, and uncertainty less daunting. You are energised, you are empowered, you can achieve so much more.

Flow is achieved through an intensity of concentration and effort as you apply yourself to the task. You are energised by possibility, and released from the fear of failure. You rise above yourself, above the distractions of today. The experience of this flow is as good as the outcomes.

Five ways for business leaders to find their "flow" state every day are:

- **Select tasks** that are stimulating and engaging, they challenge you to the point of excitement. They are problems you would love to solve.
- **Assemble a great team**, people you love and trust, who you know that together you can do great things (or you, on occasions, you can also do this alone).
- **Define audacious goals** that go beyond the accepted norms, 10x not 10% targets, and also define a sense of what the rewards could be, personal or organisational.
- **Focus your mind**, a stream of consciousness towards the goal, eliminating the daily trivia, the distractions of the normal workspace.
- **Immerse yourself** in the moment, active not passive, thinking ideas, doing tasks, making progress, building momentum, going for the goal.

The "flow" state of mind becomes the everyday state of business leaders. It becomes normal. Every day, working towards the future, whilst also delivering today. Your mind working overtime, connecting ideas, searching for progress, focused on the actions which will create a better tomorrow. Indeed, you can only ever do things today, even if your mind is focused on a better future.

PLAYING TO YOUR STRENGTHS

We have grown used to exploring the "strengths and weaknesses" of human character, or in this case of leadership behaviour. The problem is that this kind of diagnostic encourages us to focus on our weaknesses, to make them better, to be "good enough" at everything.

An alternative is to focus on your strengths and how to make them better.

Yet few business leaders say they get to use their strengths in most of their work. The challenge in any team is to bring a diverse group of people together, where their combined strengths are irresistible. This means that, as long as all the important attributes are covered, then the team will be strong in all areas and amplify its impact far beyond that of any individual.

Psychologist Martin Seligman studied cultures around the world to understand what they regarded as "strengths" in their leaders. The research explored major religions and philosophical traditions and found that the same six virtues were shared in almost all cultures. Gallup's *StrengthFinder* assessment model is one of the most useful tools for exploring the practical component of these virtues as 24 character strengths:

- **Virtue of Wisdom.** The more curious and creative we become, the more we gain perspective, knowledge and wisdom. Component strengths are creativity, curiosity, open-mindedness, love of learning, and perspective.
- **Virtue of Courage.** The braver and more persistent we become, the more confident we feel, and more courageous we act. Component strengths are bravery, perseverance, honesty and vitality.
- **Virtue of Humanity.** The more we approach people with respect, appreciation, and interest, the more engaged they become. Component strengths are love, kindness and social intelligence.
- **Virtue of Justice.** The more responsible we are, embracing fairness and justice, the more stable community we can build for mutual benefit. Component strengths are teamwork, fairness and leadership.
- **Virtue of Temperance.** Being forgiving, humble, prudent, and in control of our behaviours, helps us to avoid being arrogant, selfish, and unbalanced. Component strengths are forgiveness, humility, prudence and self-control.
- **Virtue of Transcendence.** Never losing hope in humanity's potential, appreciating nature and people, enables us to connect with a higher purpose. Component strengths are appreciation of beauty, gratitude, hope, humour and spirituality.

Additional studies have shown that women typically score higher in interpersonal strengths, such as love and kindness, honesty and gratitude. Men tend to score higher on cognitive strengths, creativity and curiosity, hope and humour, but also highly on honesty. Whilst these differences are interesting, and largely conform to stereotypes suggesting that they might be shaped by culture, there are also many shared strengths.

Playing to your strengths not only enables you to perform better, and contribute more to a team, it can also result in feeling more engaged and confident, and enable you to progress faster.

THE LEADER'S PLASTIC BRAIN

We used to assume that we each have our established ways of thinking and behaving, and as we get older the capability of our brain to learn and adapt declines. Yet our brain can grow new neurons at any age. Each neuron can transmit up to 1000 nerve signals a second and make as many as 10 000 connections with other neurons. Our thoughts come from the chemical signals that pass across the synaptic gaps between neurons: the more connections we make, the more powerful and adaptive our brain can be.

Tara Swart is a neuroscientist, practising medical doctor, and executive coach, with a background in psychiatry. I first met her on stage in Bratislava, where we both were delivering our "Big Idea" for Europe. Her first book, *Neuroscience for Leadership*, was more of an academic text, while her new book, *The Source*, is more populist, and claims most of the things we want from life – health, happiness, wealth, love – are governed by our ability to think, feel and act. In other words, by our brain.

Keeping the brain fit through exercise, continual learning and rich experiences, enhances your mental agility. In the past, leaders relied more upon experience and procedure; in today's world, we need leaders who can make sense of new patterns, imagine new possibilities, thrive on diversity of thought and complexity of action. Leaders need to have a mind that is always ahead, seeing and anticipating what next.

"Think of the brain as the hardware of a computer," says Swart. "Your mind is the software. You're the coder who upgrades the software to transform the data (your thoughts). You also control the power supply that fuels the computer – the food and drink you consume, when and how to exercise and meditate, who to interact with .... You have the power to maintain or destroy your neural connections."

Mindful activities, such as yoga or meditation, reduce levels of cortisol and increase the fold of the outer cortex of the brain, allowing the prefrontal cortex to better regulate our emotional responses. Swart says just 12 minutes a day, most days of the week, will make a noticeable difference. New experiences such as travel, learning a skill, such as a foreign language, and meeting new people can stimulate the growth of new neurons.

There are some obvious ways to improve your brain function, such as drink more water, get more exercise, and don't read from electronic screens in the last hour before bed. Sleeping less than seven to eight hours a night isn't sustainable for most people, because that's how long it takes to clear out toxins. Sleeping on your left side helps the brain to flush out toxins more efficiently, and downing a spoonful of coconut oil before a big meeting boosts brain power for about 20 minutes.

CODE 47: BUILD ENDURANCE AND RESILIENCE
The journey ahead will have high and lows. Endurance demands physical fitness and emotional agility, but also taking moments to pause, and celebrate progress.

James Dyson took 15 years and 5127 attempts to perfect his bagless vacuum. When he succeeded, he created a revolution, but it required incredible persistence to get there. Perhaps his early life as a cross-country runner, training on the sand dunes of South Wales gave him the endurance to persist in his business life. Not only is the future difficult to create, but everything keeps changing on the journey towards it.

The mental toughness, the grit to persist, is not just about keeping going, but the resilience to overcome challenges and obstacles. Sometimes, just the sheer volume of information – emails, analyses, reports, ideas, articles, books, meetings – will become overbearing. As a leader it's easy to feel overloaded.

It's also easy to feel you need to know everything, which you don't, although you do need to prioritise what matters most. The biggest challenge for any visionary leader is not how to make ideas happen, but how to overcome all the people who say that they won't. Critics and pessimists can be frustrating, and a motivational drain.

There will also be moments of great success, people might even call you a hero. It will feel good, even to the humblest, and you will inevitably remind everyone that it was a team effort. Yet the euphoria can quickly disappear, with the next challenge.

Leaders need endurance, resilience, and gratitude, to cope with relentless change; to be able to change your own mind, to stay on the rollercoaster of progress, to keep teams engaged, and to thrive at both work and in your life.

THE ENDURANCE OF LEADERS

Endurance is as much about mind as muscle power.

Like an athlete – runner, cyclist, rower – there are many physiological elements at play, from core body temperature to oxygen intake, plus psychological factors, such as perceived effort and pain tolerance. Each of these factors is significant in the level of athletic performance humans which any person is capable of, especially when testing the perceived limits of performance, such as setting new world records.

Almost every athlete will attest to faster recovery if they jump into an ice bath after a competition. Yet studies show that this practice doesn't actually decrease inflammation levels, the thing the baths are intended to reduce. However, most physiologists will still say that if there's a method that helps you recover, even if it's purely psychological, then it is useful because sometimes belief is just as influential as science.

In *Endure*, Alex Hutchinson starts by retelling the race to break four minutes for one mile. For years, men across the globe had raced to within a second or two of the barrier, but never quite breaking the iconic time. When Britain's Roger Bannister finally ran 3.59.4 in 1954, Australian John Landy who had been trying to run the time for years, went on to improve Bannister's time by another second, only weeks later.

A number of important factors can help people, including business leaders, to endure more:

- **We always have a little more to give.** Watch how athletes pace themselves so that they always have one final effort at the end of a long distance event. And somehow an Olympic champion, despite a punishing race, can always rise to celebrate victory.

- **We can endure more than we think.** Athletes have a higher than normal pain tolerance enabling them to push harder. They learn to cope with this by training at a "threshold" pace, learning to sustain oxygen debt, despite its searing pain.

- **Fitness enables us to perform better.** Athletic performance greatly relies on oxygen intake, which is enhanced through heightened fitness. Business leaders also need oxygen, and the physical fitness to sustain leadership performance.

- **Fatigue reduces our performance.** Having a tired brain can affect how much we can endure physically. A tired brain is one that doesn't have a break, isn't refuelled, doesn't have variety, doesn't keep learning, doesn't get enough sleep.

- **Stress stops us performing.** Of the many factors, stress can be the killer. However, stress comes in two forms – stress from outside, e.g. timescales, and stress we put on ourselves. External stress can stimulate us, internal stress we can control.

Hutchinson's research led him to South Africa to work with Tim Noakes, the controversial sports scientist who first proposed the "central governor theory", which argues that the brain limits performance well before the body has reached its maximum output. He also explores the research of another pioneering scientist, Samuele Marcora, who has developed a series of brain-training exercises to push that governor.

He also recalls talking to Eliud Kipchoge just before he ran the world's first sub-two-hour marathon, when the Kenyan said he hadn't really changed anything in his training. What then, he asked, would make the difference? "My mind will be different," replied the runner. People he says, have a curiously elastic limit to what they can achieve, driven mainly by their mental toughness.

THE RESILIENCE OF LEADERS

Resilience is our ability to bounce back from adversity. It's what allows us to recover quickly from change or setbacks, trauma or failure, whether at work or in life. It is the ability to maintain a sense of purpose, a positive attitude, a belief in better, throughout times of challenge. Resilience sustains progress, whilst others might give up.

Psychology professor Angela Duckworth calls it grit. "Grit is passion and perseverance for long-term goals," she says. She compares it not to a marathon, but to a series of sprints combined with a boxing match. In business you are not just running but also getting hit along the way. As you seek to deliver on your strategy, to make new ideas happen, to transform the business, it's not just about coping with the time and effort. It's also about overcoming many challenges.

Grit keeps you moving forward through the sting of rejection, pain of failure, and struggle with adversity. "When things knock you down, you may want to stay down and give up, but grit won't let you quit," says Duckworth.

Most entrepreneurs have tremendous resilience, because they've had to fight for the business through some of the most difficult times. The search for seed funding when every venture capitalist dismissed them with a laugh or smile, the long days in a bedroom or garage trying to make the first prototype or win the first contract, the growing pains of scale-up as they have to adapt to survive and thrive. Letting go of control as investors take over, making you wealthy but taking away your baby. Most entrepreneurs know about grit.

But then so do corporate leaders. If not from starting up, then from surviving the challenges of internal politics, of learning how to engage and influence people in a positive way, of progressing as a star individual whilst keeping colleagues and teams on side. Of balancing personal ambition with collective progress. Resilience demands that we:

- **Have ambition.** Knowing what you truly want, and are prepared to work hard and persevere in order to achieve it. Vision isn't just a milestone, it becomes a pursuit. Whilst not everybody will know your ambition, you will, and it will keep you striving.
- **Have purpose.** This is why you want to achieve more, it's about what will be better when you achieve your ambition, not just for you, but your business, your family, your world. Purpose is how you contribute, what you fight for, why you get up in the morning.
- **Have passion.** You need to love it, to be great at it. Otherwise it's not worth the sacrifices, the long hours, and the pain. Aligning your purpose and ambition allows you to find love, for your work, your team, your business, and the world you seek to impact.
- **Have persistence.** You will sometimes fail. Few things change without challenges. Failure doesn't define you, it refines you. If you didn't fail, you wouldn't learn. There is always another way. Stay confident and stay strong.

Nelson Mandela was a great example of resilience. He was sent to prison as a young firebrand who believed in taking up violent resistance when the justice system failed him in apartheid South Africa. 27 years later, he walked out of Robben Island prison advocating peace and reconciliation. During his long confinement, Mandela mastered what he later called self-leadership. He took great inspiration in the poem "Invictus," written by

William Ernest Henley, which ends with the lines "I am the master of my fate. I am the captain of my soul."

THE GRATITUDE OF LEADERS

You could say they are two of the most magical words: Thank You.

People want to know that their work is appreciated, says leadership guru Marshall Goldsmith. Showing gratitude to your people is the easiest, fastest, most inexpensive way to boost performance. In *Leading with Gratitude*, Adrian Gostick shows that gratitude boosts employee engagement, reduces turnover, and leads team members to express more gratitude to one another, strengthening the bonds within teams. He also shows that gratitude has benefits for those expressing it, and is one of the most powerful factors in predicting a person's overall well-being, more important than money, health, and optimism.

Despite these benefits, few executives effectively utilise this simple tool. Gostick says that "people are less likely to express gratitude at work than anyplace else". This, he suggests, is because of a series of myths which are almost the opposite of seeking gratitude – some think that fear is the best motivator, that people get enough praise already, that they know it anyway, that there's not time, that it sounds too paternalistic, that it's better to save praise for when people really deserve it, and it can sound fake.

The best leaders look out for how people contribute and seek reasons to express their gratitude. This requires leaders to look for the good things, not just the problems, to pay attention when things are going well, not be consumed by problems. Gratitude is also about recognising effort and intent, even if it doesn't succeed, and small things that might seem trivial but are vital. It's also about being timely, saying thank you in the moment, not at some later review point. And the leader's role modelling encourages others to be grateful to each other too.

We all take gratitude for granted. But it can go a long way, and transform attitudes and performance. I will never forget the boss who gave me his company car for a week to drive. Or the colleague who collected an award and immediately gave it to the youngest team member, rather than putting on their own desk. Or the leader ordering her team new smartphones with special team screensavers for a job well done. Gratitude doesn't need to be about money, it could be a personal gift, a small act of kindness, or two simple words.

Gratitude is also not just at work, but in life. A business leader isn't anything without family and friends. They are the hidden support team who give encouragement, motivation and sacrifice to help leaders achieve more. And it is also yourself. We recognise that we need to challenge ourselves, push ourselves, lead ourselves. Maybe also, just occasionally, indulge yourself too, with a Thank You.

CODE 48: CREATE A BETTER LEGACY
What will you be remembered for? How will you create progress in your business and society, and leave your world a better place for those who follow you?

There is a huge clock ticking deep inside a Texas mountain. It is hundreds of feet tall, and designed to tick for 10 000 years.

Every once in a while the bells chime, each time playing a melody that has never been played before, the melodies are programmed not to repeat themselves over the 10 millennia. It is powered by the energy created through temperature fluctuations between day and night.

The clock is real, an art installation deep underground in western Texas, funded by Amazon founder Jeff Bezos, and managed by the Long Now Foundation, a non-profit organisation.

Bezos contributed $42 million to the project and hopes the clock will be the first of many millennial clocks to be built around the world over the coming years. A second location has already been purchased at the top of a mountain in the middle of a Nevada forest.

Ten thousand years is about the age of civilisation, so the 10 000 Year Clock represents a future of civilisation equal to its past. For Jeff Bezos it is symbolic of our need to protect and nourish our planet for the long term. He calls it his legacy, and sits alongside his $10 billion Earth Fund, which he launched in 2020, as his contribution to the future.

WHAT WILL YOU GIVE TO THE FUTURE?

Legacy is one of the most motivating topics for business leaders. What will you leave behind? What is your contribution to others that follow you?

We are so wrapped up in our current world. Trying to deliver performance, trying to accelerate growth, trying to transform our business to take it to a better place, that we spare few moments to ask what would we leave behind.

Not just a memory. Not just a reputation. But a contribution to the future.

One of the most memorable books I've ever read is Randy Komisar's *The Monk and the Riddle*.

In 2003, having just taken on the role of CEO of a mid-size organisation, I wanted to give my 250 managers some food for thought. Yes, we could develop new strategies and organisation change, but firstly I wanted them to think bigger, about the future and what we could be, and what they themselves could be. I gave each of them a copy of the book.

It starts with a monk on a motorbike driving off into the desert, and then returning back to where he began. Asked where he has been, he answers that he has been on a journey. Sounding like a zen-like philosophy, many would give up at this point, but given that it was published by Harvard Business School, I persisted.

Komisar is a Silicon Valley technology legend and now a partner at Kleiner Perkins Caufield & Byers. He thinks you should look for more in your business career.

He reflects on the number of colleagues and friends he has known in tech start-ups who have pursued their ideas, working relentlessly, and all they think about is the exit strategy. He suggests this is not fulfilment. Yes, they might end up wealthier, but have they really achieved what they want in their lives?

"Passion and drive are not the same at all. Passion pulls you toward something you cannot resist. Drive pushes you toward something you feel compelled or obligated to do. If you know nothing about yourself, you can't tell the difference. Once you gain a modicum of self-knowledge, you can express your passion. It's not about jumping through someone else's hoops. That's drive," says Komisar.

Most people have a dream, and most often the dream is not to simply makes lots of money, but to achieve something. Achieving something is usually quantified by making a difference to the world. This might be achieved through a business route, leveraging the power of brands and consumption, finance and resources, to make a difference to the world. Or it might be in less commercial ways. However, most leaders, according Komisar, defer this for a later act, to do once they've delivered on their initial business, once they've retired maybe. He calls it "the deferred life plan". We have dreams, but we defer them for a later day.

The real passion we have for life, for achieving our life plan, shouldn't be something we defer for another time, when we might not even be fit enough to achieve it, but be part of now. Embracing it within what we do, our job today. Leading our business to achieve both business and personal aspirations.

There is an echo of this in *The Second Mountain* by David Brook.

Brook says that every so often, we meet people who radiate energy and joy, who seem to "glow with an inner light". Life, for these people, has often followed what we might think of as a two-mountain shape. They leave school, start a career, and they begin climbing the career mountain they thought they were meant to climb.

Their goals on this first mountain are the ones our culture endorses – to seek business success, to make your mark. But when they get to the top of that mountain, something happens. They look around and find the view unsatisfying. They realise that this wasn't their mountain after all, and that there's another, bigger mountain out there that really is their mountain.

And so they embark on a new journey, on their second mountain, and their life moves from self-centred to others-centred. They want the things that are truly worth wanting, not the things other people tell them to want. They embrace interdependence, not independence. The difficulty, however, is that most people only find their second mountain when they retire, and then it is often too late.

Your legacy is not what you have done, it's what you give to the future.

HOW WILL YOU CREATE A BETTER WORLD?

At the start of this book we explored the shifts in business, from today to tomorrow, from profit to purpose, with more meaning and impact. This is legacy. Legacy is not creating a legend, its creating a contribution to the future.

I truly believe that business can be a platform for change in our world, but also a platform for good. And that you can achieve more in business, by doing good at the same time.

The best opportunities often arise out of seemingly unsur-mountable challenges, you might call them paradoxes which seem unable to resolve contradictory goals. Apparent para-doxes, at least through our existing lens, offer business leaders new spaces to explore, new ways in which business can make a difference, by combining its huge resources for more positive impact.

Figure 7.3: Here are 15 big questions for business, and the world, which can inspire a better legacy.

- **Climate:** *How can economies grow, whilst also addressing climate change?* The last two decades have been the warmest

FIGURE 7.3 15 big challenges for a better world.

on record. Whilst growth in CO_2 emissions has slowed due to efficiencies and renewables, the earth is still warming. The Paris Agreement seeks a 1.5°C cap above pre-industrial levels.

- **Resources:** *How can population growth and resources be brought into balance?* Global population will grow to 9.8 billion by 2050. If all are to be fed, then food production will have to increase by over 50%, while urban residential areas are expected to triple in size by 2030.

- **Technology:** *How can new technologies, like AI and robotics, work for everyone?* 51% of the world is now connected to the internet. About two-thirds of the people in the world have a mobile phone. The continued development and proliferation of smartphone apps are AI systems in the palm of many hands around the world.

- **Women:** *How can the changing status of women help improve society?* Empowerment of women has been a key driver of social change over the past century. Gender equity is guaranteed by the constitution of 84% of the world's nations, while "the international women's bill of rights" is agreed by almost all.

- **Disease:** *How can the threat and impact of new diseases, like Covid-19, be reduced?* Global health continues to improve, life expectancy at birth increased globally from 46 years in 1950 to 67 years in 2010 and 71.5 years in 2015. Total deaths from infectious disease fell from 25% in 1998 to 16% in 2015.

- **Energy:** *How can our growing energy demands be met efficiently and responsibly?* In China is the biggest producer of solar energy, and its investing huge amounts in other water and wind power too. Meanwhile, a billion people (15% of the world) do not have access to electricity.

- **Water:** *How can everyone on the planet have sufficient clean water?* Over 90% of the world now has access to improved drinking water, up from 76% in 1990. That is an improvement for 2.3 billion people in less than 20 years. However, that still leaves almost a billion people without access.

- **Conflict:** *How can shared values and security reduce conflicts and terrorism?* The vast majority of the world is living in peace; however, the nature of warfare and security has morphed today into transnational and local terrorism, international intervention into civil wars, cyber and information warfare.

- **Crime:** *How can organised crime be stopped from becoming more powerful?* Organised crime accounts for over $3 trillion per year, which is twice all military annual budgets combined. It is estimated the value of black market trade in 50 categories from 91 countries is $1.8 trillion.

- **Democracy:** *How can genuine democracy emerge from authoritarian regimes?* 105 countries are experiencing a net decline in freedom, according to Freedom House think tank, while 61 are improving in net freedom, 67 countries declined in political rights and civil liberties, whilst 36 registered gains.

- **Inequality:** *How can economies reduce the gap between rich and poor?* Extreme poverty fell from 51% in 1981 to 13% in

2012 and less than 10% today, mostly due to income growth in China and India. However, the wealth gap is increasing, 1% have more than 99%, 8 billionaires have more than 3.6 billion people.

- **Education:** *How can we better educate humanity to address global challenges?* Alphabet and others seek everyone on the planet connected to the internet. The price of laptops and smartphones continues to fall, and IoT with data analytics gives realtime precision intelligence. However, successfully applying all these resources to develop wisdom, not just more information, is a huge challenge.

- **Progress:** *How can tech breakthroughs accelerate to address our big challenges?* IBM's Watson already diagnoses cancer better than doctors, Organova can 3D-print human organs including new hearts, robots learn to walk faster than toddlers, and AlphaGo outsmarts the smartest humans. In 2020, China had 40% of all robots in the world, up from 27% in 2015.

- **Ethics:** *How can ethical considerations be incorporated into global decisions?* Decisions are increasingly made by AI, whose ethics are shaped by algorithms without conscience or control. Ethics are also influenced by manipulated information, by "fake news" and political exaggeration, that can distort perceptions, leading us to wonder what is the truth, and who can we trust.

- **Foresight:** *How can we make better future decisions with so much uncertainty?* Although the most significant of the world's challenges and solutions are global in nature, global foresight and decision-making systems are rarely employed, leaving the world's best brains disconnected. Global governance systems are not keeping up with growing global interdependence.

These are not questions just for the United Nations, or governments, or intellectual think tanks. These are questions for you, business leaders who have the power and platforms to make a real difference. So what could you do?

LETTER TO THE FUTURE

What would you write in a letter to your grandchildren?

Talking to Richard Branson about his life seemed like an endless tail of intrepid adventures. We talked about his successes in music and airlines, and his passions for hot air ballooning and kitesurfing. He said he was much more interested in the future than the past. He became particularly animated when we got onto space, the potential for anyone to become an astronaut within his own lifetime. And the future potential of technologies to allow us to do amazing things that are also better for humanity.

He told me that he wanted to write a letter to his grandchildren, Artie, Etta, and Eva-Deia, about his hopes for them and their future. He recently published his letter on his blog, from which here is an extract:

> You are at the very start of life, it is an incredible gift and it is there for the taking. It will deliver highs and lows, trials and tribulations, failures and triumphs. But by living it to the full, by always trying to do the right thing and by never losing that sense of adventure which you now possess with such abundance, it will indeed be wonderful.

> My golden rule in life is to have fun. Life is not a dress rehearsal, so don't waste your precious time doing things that don't light your fire. Do what you enjoy, and enjoy what you do. Trust me; great things will follow.

> Don't let your head always rule your heart. Life's more fun when you say yes – so dream big and say yes to your heart's desires. Dreaming is one of our greatest gifts – so look at the world with wide-eyed enthusiasm, and believe you are more powerful than the problems that confront you.

> Never betray your dreams for the sake of fitting in. Instead be passionate about them. Passion will help you stay the course, and inspire others to believe in you and your dreams too.

Remember to treat others like you would like to be treated. Always be nice, always be caring. Give people the benefit of the doubt. And don't hesitate to give out second chances. It's incredible how much people lift and rise to the challenge when you believe in them and trust them.

Be open with everyone around you, especially your parents. They will always be there for you, willing to share in your adventures, support your decisions and love you unreservedly.

Above all, love and know that you are loved. Love always, Your grand-dude.

CODE 49: BE EXTRAORDINARY

What is it to be extraordinary? As Eliud Kipchoge starts to feel pain, pushes though barriers, and nears the limits of humanity, a huge smile comes across his face.

The future is created by ordinary people, doing extraordinary things.

What does it take to be an extraordinary leader? He or she (in fact, increasingly she) is most likely to be a competent "ordinary" person who has the passion and courage to be more, to be "extra" ordinary. In fact, when you look at most of today's successful leaders, many are incredibly ordinary, but with a burning flame inside.

As we look around us, at a world of incredible diversity and opportunity, perhaps four concepts will inspire you to go beyond ordinary:

- **The beauty of *ikigai*** is the Japanese principle of aligning yourself with the future you want to achieve.
- **The engagement of *goya*** comes from Urdu and means to believe in the power of the path you take.
- **The power of *guanxi*** is the Chinese approach to work with partners to achieve more together.
- **The courage of *sisu*** is the Finnish concept of endurance to overcome adversity and find success.

We can look back at history and see people who were extraordinary in the worlds of religion or politics, science or arts, sports or doing good. Many of them stand out for being extremely genuine, authentic and generous rather than for their power, privilege and fame. They are typically incredibly focused people, able to make new connections, and willing to be imperfect in order to explore newness. And they are positive, optimistic and happy too.

THE PEOPLE WE ADMIRE MOST

Many of the great people that we have encountered in this book are no different from anyone of us. In many cases their backgrounds were far less favourable, their opportunities seemingly far more limited. Yet they each overcame those adversities to be more, and do more, than they ever imagined:

Devi Shetty, the young doctor who was inspired whilst caring for Mother Teresa. Ali Parsa, the refugee who trekked through the Iranian mountains to reinvent healthcare. Emily Weiss, the young blogger at Vogue who transformed beauty. Jos de Blok, the Dutch nurse who knew things could be better. Mikkel Bjergso, the Danish school teacher who loved craft beers. Zhang Xin, working in a Hong Kong factory to join me at college in England.

I recently asked a group of business leaders who they admired most. The response was fascinating. Many people talked about their parents, who had nurtured them and encouraged them to be more, or spouses, who had supported them and were the real heroes in their own careers.

Others mentioned popular names. Bill Gates, not just because of what he did at Microsoft, but what he is now doing for global healthcare. Angelina Jolie, not because of her movie stardom, but because of her humanitarian work. Barack Obama, not because he was the most powerful man in the world, but because he fought for what he believed to be right. Elon Musk, not because of his Tesla cars, but because he dares to dream.

Psychologist David Sack says "being extraordinary isn't reserved for the rich, the famous, the powerful, or the privileged. Extraordinary people exist within even the most seemingly ordinary lives. They are the ones with the knack for living *genuinely* and who inspire us to attempt the same."

We admire people who think bigger, because they have the courage to go beyond their current world and articulate what doesn't yet exist. They seek goals beyond themselves; they don't know if they are possible, but by defining their vision, are more likely to find a way to achieve them. When we dare to follow our dreams, they inspire us.

We admire people with humility and integrity, because they are the honest behaviours of all human beings. They take ownership for what is right, and are prepared to challenge what is not, to do things in the right way. They care about people and the world in which we all live, and fight for them, and for us. They do not have pretensions, and don't pretend to be perfect, but they have passion. When we look at ourselves, we can be the same.

We admire people who have resilience, who are like bamboo in a hurricane, they bend but don't break. They take on difficult challenges and keep going through the toughest times. They start what they finish, undaunted by the many obstacles and opposition that might encounter. They are the ones with gratitude, and don't forget others who support them. When we look to work with others, they are the people who we follow.

HOW WILL YOU FIND YOUR "EXTRA" ORDINARY?

I recently worked with many of the leaders within the United Nations. They represented different agencies – from the International Monetary Fund to the World Food Program, the High Commission for Refugees to the World Health Organisation.

Most of the leaders of these organisations are nominated by the 193 member countries. They come from all parts of the world, and all walks of life. They come with different skills and languages, perspectives and beliefs. Yet they come together to work on some of the most important challenges. What I found so inspiring was how they stepped up to the challenge. They typically let go of their local priorities, and national loyalties, to work as an incredibly diverse group of colleagues, seeking to do better for all of us.

They come from Addis Ababa and Buenos Aires, Casablanca and Denpasar, to UN centres in Geneva, Vienna and New York, to seek more progress together.

Of course they each have their own ambitions, their different strengths to contribute, and obstacles to overcome. At home they still have families to feed, and countries they are proud of. But when they come together, they really do seek to rise above themselves and where they come from. They have the opportunity to take us all forwards.

In the same way, now is the time for business leaders to step up.

Leaders are rarely selected to maintain the status quo, to keep things ticking over. That would be to stagnate as the world moves forwards.

Leaders are there to make progress. To move their organisations forwards. To find new opportunities for profitable growth, where they can add more value to new customers, secure a future for employees, deliver returns to investors, and contribute more to society.

However the enlightened leader finds new ways to achieve that progress.

This takes courage. They need to dare to go beyond what others have done, and dare to operate in ways others have not. There is no perfect moment, there is no perfect approach, it's about stepping up.

As Brené Brown says, "When we spend our lives waiting until we're perfect or bulletproof before we walk into the arena, we sacrifice opportunities that may not be recoverable, we squander our precious time, and we turn our backs on our gifts, those unique contributions that only we can make."

A GOOD TIME TO BE EXTRAORDINARY

I wrote this book at an extraordinary moment. Having brought together what I have learnt and been inspired by over 30 years in business, adding fascinating insights from some of the great business leaders of today, I suddenly find myself at home.

The world is "locked down" by a global pandemic that has left most businesses frozen in the headlights of an oncoming juggernaut. Across the world, the Covid-19 virus has spread like no disease before, accelerated by our connected world of work and travel. Shops and cafés are boarded up, schools and factories are closed down, people work in isolation from home, scientists search for new vaccines, and medics risk their lives to save others.

A crisis, by definition, is dramatic and unexpected. Risk analyst and philosopher, Nassim Nicholas Taleb, calls such shocks "black swan" events, a metaphor that describes an event that comes as a surprise, with huge and unpredictable consequences, often due to a previous lack of awareness of the fragility of a current system, and subsequent unravelling of its logic.

Today's world is incredibly complex. This creates ever more speed and uncertainty, but also stress on our old systems, and as a result, fragility.

Perhaps in crisis we will open our eyes to the change around us. The disruptive impact of technology, the shifting nature of markets, the lack of agility of our organisations, the distrust felt in society, the fragility of our environment, the limitations of our current approaches. Perhaps now, we will ask some of the most difficult questions, and search for better solutions.

However, I am also reminded of the Chinese word for crisis, wei-ji, which is actually two words, which when translated mean danger and opportunity.

Change drives new attitudes and behaviours, new ideas and solutions. If we look through history, we see a pattern of economic upturns and downturns. If we look at the pattern of innovation, it is a mirror image, with most innovations in the tough economic times.

Winston Churchill said "there is nothing like a good crisis", meaning it is the moment to seize the opportunities of change, to shake up rather than be shaken up, and to create the future in your own vision. Or as Andy Grove, former CEO of Intel, once said "Bad companies are destroyed by crisis, good companies survive them, great companies are improved by them."

Now is the time for leaders to step up, to be the change they want to see in the world.

Eliud Kipchoge is also sitting at home, on his farm in Kenya, unable to train like he normally does, and with his swansong Olympics postponed. He is undeterred, enjoying spending time with his young family, and reading books, including the latest from Malcolm Gladwell. He encourages his colleagues and rivals to stay positive and optimistic.

Indeed, he knows how to get through tough times. When he reaches the most painful moments in a marathon, usually over the last few miles, you will see a smile spread across his face. He says that it is positive psychology, knowing that in those toughest moments, he can make the biggest difference to achieving success.

Time to step up. And smile.

SUMMARY: HOW WILL YOU RECODE YOUR LEADERSHIP?

5 questions to reflect on:

- Have more courage ... Are you ready to step up to lead the future?
- Lead in style ... Which leadership style works best for you, and your people?
- Find your strengths ... What are your strengths that you can make more of?
- Create legacy ... How will you work to contribute towards a better future?
- Be extraordinary ... What will you do that is, in some way, "extra" ordinary?

5 leaders to inspire you (more at businessrecoded.com):

- Jim Hagemann Snabe, Siemens ... leading the future with "dreams and details"
- Daniel Ek, Spotify ... the Swedish music entrepreneur, with zero charisma
- Hamdi Ulukaya, Chobani ... the "anti-CEO" of Greek yogurt, giving it all away
- Zhang Zin, Soho China ... how the economist created the Beijing skyline
- Ilkka Paananen, Supercell ... "the world's least powerful CEO" from Finland

5 books to go deeper:

- *The Leadership Code* by Dave Ulrich and others
- *Dare to Lead* by Brene Brown
- *The Future Leader* by Jacob Morgan
- *Endure* by Alex Hutchinson
- *Dreams and Details* by Jim Snabe and Mikael Trolle

5 places to explore further

- Real Leaders
- The Conference Board
- Harvard Leadership
- Center for Creative Leadership
- Positive Psychology

DOING MORE

You can read all stories of many of the world's most inspiring leaders today on Peter's website, including the 45 specific leaders who he researched in developing this book. From Satya Nadella and Emily Weiss to Daniel Ek and Zhang Ruimin, you can find all the case studies at www.businessrecoded.com

Peter also has a wide range of additional resources to build on the insights and ideas in this book, to help you share and apply them in your organisations.

- **Keynote speaking.** Peter brings the themes to life, customising them to your specific industry. Food Recoded, Banking Recoded, Healthcare Recoded, and more. Events can include bulk orders of the book for all participants.
- **Practical workshops.** Peter works with you and your leadership team to develop new approaches for your business – new

strategies, new innovations, new approaches. Workshops are fast and practical, stretching and inspiring.

- **Leadership development.** Peter leads a range of executive programmes for business leaders, based at IE Business School. These include the Global Advanced Management Programme, and short programmes on leadership, strategy and innovation.

ONLINE RESOURCES

You can explore much more at his website, which is packed with articles, daily blog posts, case studies, videos and toolkits, helping to inspire and enable you to go further.

- **Leadership resources**: Peter has a wide range of tools, diagnostics, templates and other resources that can support implementation of new strategies, new innovation projects, and new leadership approaches in your business.
- **Book orders**: Large orders of *Business Recoded* and most of Peter's other books can be made and delivered directly. This can also include co-branding, and customised content if required.
- **Monthly newsletter:** You can also sign up for Peter's free monthly newsletter called *Fast Leader*. This is a fantastic way to keep up to speed with all the latest ideas and insights from the world of business, and the leaders shaping the future.

Simply visit www.peterfisk.com or email peterfisk@peterfisk.com.

ACKNOWLEDGEMENTS

Firstly, an immense thank you to my amazing wife, Alison, who is always there, supporting and encouraging me. And also to my two daughters. Anna, currently studying psychology at university, was a great help in researching this book and developing new ideas for the leadership approaches, whilst Clara stepped up with frequent cups of tea.

Thank you to my good friend and agent, Cosimo Turroturro, who is constantly searching for new ways to support and inspire the world's business leaders, and is a huge support to me. Thanks to my colleagues in Madrid, at IE Business School, in particular Teresa Martin-Retortillo for her leadership and Stephen Adamson for making so many new ideas happen.

The European Business Forum would never have been possible without Bjarke Wolmar in Denmark, and also great collaborations in other countries, such as Henrik Lauridsen in Germany, Tanyer Sonmezer in Turkey, Eithne Jones in the Netherlands, and Renee Strom in USA. And for the Future Book Forum, thanks to Joerg Engelstaedter and Mark Allin.

Thinkers50, founded by my colleagues Stuart Crainer and Des Dearlove, has enabled me to work with and learn from so many great business thinkers, including Michael Porter, Alex Osterwalder, Erin Meyer, Scott Anthony, Whitney Johnson, Howard Yu, Rita McGrath, Roger Martin and Amy Edmondson. It has been a special privilege to design and host the European Business Forum each year, with so many great business and thought leaders. Around the world I have also been inspired when collaborating with people like Ryan Holiday, Martin Lindstrom, Tom Goodwin, Dave Ulrich, Antonio Nieto Rodriguez, Mark Esposito, and many more.

And also thank you to the many organisations, large and small, which have provided practical insights: Aster transforming fashion in Turkey, Atos Medical taking healthcare direct in USA, Canon reimagining publishing in Germany, Coesia creating smart factories in Italy, CMS reinventing education in South Korea, Fundgrube transforming retail in the Canary Islands, KEBA exploring technology futures in Austria, Greiner making plastics better, Gulf Bank transforming banking in

Kuwait, Valio making better food in Finland, Vifor creating smart services in Switzerland, Yildiz rethinking the world of snacks in Turkey, and Zacco reimagining the future in Sweden.

Thank you, finally, to the great team at Wiley, for making this book happen.

ABOUT THE AUTHOR

Peter Fisk lives in Teddington, England, and is married with two daughters. When he's not working or travelling around the world, he can usually be found running around the nearby Bushy Park, or Richmond Park, and along the River Thames.

He is a leading business thinker, bestselling author and inspiring speaker, whose career was forged in a superconductivity lab, accelerated by managing supersonic travel brands, shaped in corporate development, evolved in a digital start-up, and formalised as CEO of the world's largest marketing network.

He now leads GeniusWorks, a strategic innovation accelerator based in London. He is a professor of leadership, strategy and innovation at IE Business School in Madrid, where he leads their flagship executive programmes. He is also Thinkers50 Global Director and founder of the European Business Forum.

He has 30 years of practical business experience, working with business leaders in over 300 companies and 55 countries, from Adidas to American Express, Bosch and BNP Paribas, Cartier to Coca Cola, McKinsey and Microsoft, P&G to Pfizer, Virgin and Visa. His distinctive approach is future back and outside in, fusing insights with inspiration, creativity and structure.

His insights come from a rich diversity of projects: creating flatbeds for aircraft, sustainable strategies for fashion, transforming energy companies to renewables, reinventing cheese from Persia and sportswear with technology, creating AI-driven solutions for business, reimagining stock exchanges, new business models for lawyers, developing railways to Asia, direct channels for retail, new services for healthcare, and better leaders.

His eight books in 35 languages – including *Gamechangers, Creative Genius, People, Planet Profit, Customer Genius* and *Marketing Genius* – fuse the brains of Einstein and Picasso, explore the creativity of Leonardo da Vinci, reframe sustainability for innovation and growth, connect leadership and strategy to create more future-focused organisations, and are inspired by the ideas of the world's most innovative companies.

INDEX

Please note that page references to Figures will be followed by the letter 'f', to Tables by the letter 't'